THE SERMON ON THE MOUNT

THE SERMON ON THE MOUNT

Inspiring the Moral Imagination

DALE C. ALLISON, JR.

A Herder & Herder Book
The Crossroad Publishing Company
New York

The Crossroad Publishing Company
www.CrossroadPublishing.com

Printed in the United States of America

Library of Congress Cataloging-in-Publication Data

Allison, Dale C.
    The Sermon on the mount : inspiring the moral imagination / Dale
  C. Allison, Jr.
        p.   cm.
    "A Herder & Herder book."
    Includes bibliographical references.
    ISBN 0-8245-1791-1 (pbk.)
    1. Sermon on the mount—Criticism, interpretation, etc.
  2. Christian ethics—Biblical teaching.   I. Title.
  BT380.2.A64   1999
  226.9'06—dc21   99-11108
                                                             CIP

For

Chris

Warren and Kathleen

and

Jim and Judy

The old gang, much missed

Contents

Preface to the Series

THE COMPANIONS TO THE NEW TESTAMENT SERIES aims to unite New Testament study with theological concerns in a clear and concise manner. Each volume:

- engages the New Testament text directly.
- focuses on the religious (theological/ethical) content of the New Testament.
- is written out of respect for the integrity of the religious tradition being studied. This means that the New Testament is studied in terms of its own time and place. It is allowed to speak in its own terms, out of its own assumptions, espousing its own values.
- involves cutting-edge research, bringing the results of scholarly discussions to the general reader.
- provides resources for the reader who wishes to enter more deeply into the scholarly discussion.

The contributors to the series are established scholars who have studied and taught the New Testament for many years and who can now reap a wide-ranging harvest from the fruits of their labors. Multiple theological perspectives and denominational identities are represented. Each author is free to address the issues from his or her own social and religious location, within the parameters set for the series.

It is our hope that these small volumes will make some contribution to the recovery of the vision of the New Testament world for our time.

Charles H. Talbert
Baylor University

Preface

SOME PEOPLE WOULD SAY THAT THE Sermon on the Mount is the quintessence of Christianity. I am not among them. The erroneous conviction comes from the unfortunate habit of viewing the Sermon in isolation. Readers, especially modern readers, have again and again interpreted Matthew 5–7 as though the chapters were complete unto themselves, as though they constituted a book rather than a portion of a book. Symptomatic is the occasional reprinting of the Sermon in anthologies of literature. But the three chapters that constitute the Sermon on the Mount, chapters surrounded on either side by twenty-five additional chapters, neither summarize the rest of Matthew nor sum up adequately the faith of Jesus, much less the religion of our evangelist. How could anything that fails to refer explicitly to the crucifixion and resurrection be the quintessence of Matthew's Christian faith? Here context is everything. Any credible interpretation of Matthew 5–7 must constantly keep an eye on Matthew 1–4 and Matthew 9–28. For the part (the Sermon) loses its meaning apart from the whole (Matthew's Gospel). The Sermon on the Mount is in the middle of a story, and it is the first goal of this little commentary to interpret the discourse accordingly.

There is a second way in which this commentary seeks to place the Sermon in context. All too often in the past—the strategy goes all the way back to Tertullian and Augustine—the Sermon has been read against Judaism. That is, the superiority of Jesus and the church over against Judaism has been promoted by arguing that this word of Jesus or that expression of Matthew brings us, within the world of first-century Judaism, something startlingly new, or even impossible. Most such claims, however, do not stand up under scrutiny. What we rather have in the Sermon is the product of a messianic Judaism; and, as we know from the writings of G. Friedlander (1911), I. Abrahams (1917, 1924), and C. G. Montefiore (1927, 1930), most of the sentiments found in the Sermon already appear, at least here or there, in old Jewish sources. It is primarily the relationship of those sentiments to one another and, above all, their relationship to the person of Jesus and his story that gives them their unique meaning for Christians. Responsible exegesis, therefore, will seek to highlight the continuity between the Sermon and Jewish teaching, whether within the Hebrew Bible or without, and moreover the immense debt of the former to the latter. The time of polemic against Judaism is over. So too is the time when Christians could pretend, in the words of Adolf Harnack, to find in the Sermon on the Mount teaching "freed from all external and particularistic features" (*What Is Christianity?* 74).

I have yet a third goal herein, and that is to avoid isolating the Sermon from the history of its interpretation. Too many modern commentators seem to have read only other modern commentators. But the text has been pondered for almost two thousand years, and it is terribly unfortunate that the treasures of the past are so often neglected, and precisely by those who should know themselves to be the heirs of such wealth. Perhaps the explanation is sloth—Do we not have enough contemporary literature to read without the burden of the past? Or maybe it is ignorance—Can anything said so long ago still be interesting or relevant? Or perhaps some arrogance is involved—Does not exegesis progress like the hard sciences, so that today's work makes yesterday's obsolete? In any event the present commentary continually engages patristic sources, medieval theologians, the Protestant reformers, as well as more recent works, critical and otherwise.

One result of my attention to older interpreters is that I have much more to say about traditional exegetical options than about important contemporary issues. I have, for instance, been unable to consider how modern ethical debates in philosophy impinge upon our understanding of the Sermon. I do, however, take some comfort in the fact that the series in which this book appears requires that I focus first upon the text in itself, not issues of the moment or contemporary application. Beyond that, no interpretation can be comprehensive. I indeed wholly agree with Daniel Patte, who in his recent work on the Sermon argues that competing interpretations can be legitimate: there is no one right way to construe the text. This is hardly a postmodern insight. Rabbinic literature regularly offers multiple interpretations of a text without establishing one and only one as correct ("These and these are both the words of the living God"). Similarly, Aquinas, in his commentary on the Lord's Prayer, sometimes records various interpretations and refrains from selecting one over the others, finding rather truth in each. It is not false modesty that moves me, then, like Augustine at one point in his *Retractions,* happily to acknowledge that my discussion ought not to suffice, and that readers should—as my bibliographies imply—consult other accounts that deal with the Sermon in different and perhaps better ways.

Dale C. Allison, Jr.

1

Interpreting the
Sermon on the Mount

IN FYODOR DOSTOYEVSKY'S NOVEL *The Brothers Karamazov* the
Grand Inquisitor at one point declares that Jesus "judged humanity
too highly," for "it was created weaker and lower than Christ
thought." More recently the Jewish scholar Joseph Klausner has
declared that the Sermon on the Mount presents an "extremist morality," one that "has not proved possible in practice," one that contains
"too high an ideal for ordinary mankind, and even too high for the man
of more than average moral calibre" (*Jesus*, 395, 397). The complaint is
a very old one. It can already be found in Justin Martyr's *Dialogue with
Trypho*, in the middle of the second century. In this, Justin's Jewish
interlocutor confesses, "I am aware that your precepts in the so-called
Gospel are so wonderful and so great, that I suspect no one can keep
them; for I have carefully read them" (*Dial.* 10.2). This is precisely the
great problem of the Sermon and its "ultrapiety" (Derrett). The words
may please, but who can live them? Is it realistic to ask people to love
their enemies? Would not obedience to this imperative be a recipe for
the prosperity of evil? Would it not be more prudent to have thieves
arrested rather than to give them one's cloak if they have taken one's
coat? How can good people stand by while evil people do what they
will? What is the harm in taking an oath in the courtroom? Should one
stay married to an abusive husband just because he is not known to
have committed adultery? Can Jesus really have been so obtuse as to
imagine that he could banish the sexual impulse with an imperative?

   Toward the end of his life Leo Tolstoy, who believed that the Russian Orthodox Church of his age had eviscerated the force of Christ's

1

commandments, urged a literal or, perhaps it is fairer to say, an absolutist approach to the Sermon—and he fully recognized how radical
this made him. (His posthumous and incomplete novel *The Light
Shines in Darkness* shows us a Tolstoy-like character whose attempt
to implement a radical program based on the Sermon is met with resistance all around.) Tolstoy argued that Jesus' prohibition of oaths is
absolute; that is, Christians should never take an oath. If one objects
that a legal system cannot survive without demanding oaths from
witnesses in court, then one has seen the truth. Matt. 5:33–37 is an
implicit abolition of the legal system. Tolstoy was additionally per-
suaded that love of enemy means that war is never justified, and that
one should not serve in any army or join a police force, even though
this might well jeopardize the well-being of innocent people. He likewise said that the command not to store up treasure on the earth
requires the giving away of all possessions. He thus opposed private
property (and Tolstoy did, if only near the end of his life, abandon family and estate). All this—whose context we should not forget was the
crimes of czarist Russia—has been called Christian anarchism, and it
does seem a good recipe for anarchy.

Although portions of the Anabaptist tradition offer much that is
close to Tolstoy, most Christian groups, following what they have
thought of as common sense, have not wanted to abolish courts or mil-
itaries or police forces. Every attempt has accordingly been made to
avoid the sort of social prescriptions Tolstoy found implied in the Sermon on the Mount. One venerable way of surmounting the difficulties, found importantly in the *Opus imperfectum in Matthaeum* (an
anonymous commentary of perhaps the sixth century) and later in
Rupert of Deutz (ca. 1075–1130), had some currency in medieval and
later Catholicism (Bonaventure and Maldonatus being prominent proponents). It is known as the monastic interpretation. The point of
departure was 5:48, where Jesus enjoins perfection. This was interpreted in the light of 19:21, where Jesus says to a rich man, "If you wish
to be perfect, go, sell your possessions, and give the money to the poor,
and you will have treasure in heaven; then come, follow me." Here
Jesus, so it was thought, spoke of two sorts of believers, the perfect (to
be equated with the religious, that is, monks, nuns, ascetics) on the
one hand and, on the other, the run-of-the-mill Christian. On this reading, the imperatives of the Sermon were made out to be not commandments requisite for salvation but instead evangelical counsels,
some of which (for instance, the demand not to store up treasure on the

earth) can only be kept by those with a special religious calling (see Aquinas, *Summa* 2.1, q. 108, art. 4). There is then a sort of double standard. The *Didache*, an early Christian writing which perhaps appeared shortly after Matthew, already appears to be moving in this direction. At one place it says, "If you are able to bear the whole yoke of the Lord, you will be perfect; but if you are unable, do what you are able to do" (6.2). The same sort of distinction between religious grades of people, one better or more advanced than the other, was known to the Manichees and Bogomils and appears in the Syriac *Book of Steps* (fourth or fifth century). And long before that the Jewish sect known as the Essenes (authors presumably of the Dead Sea Scrolls) divided themselves into two groups—those at the Qumran settlement near the Dead Sea and those scattered in the camps—and many have thought that certain rules adopted by the former were not incumbent upon the latter. So it is possible that something like the Roman Catholic distinction between the religious and the nonreligious could have had a home in ancient Judaism and early Christianity.

Protestants, with their emphasis on the priesthood of all believers, have traditionally dismissed this interpretation (which was, one should note, never so prominent as their polemic has implied) rather curtly. But Erasmus and Juan de Valdés, both Roman Catholics, also had problems with it; and in our own time most Catholics have come to view it with dissatisfaction, perhaps in part under modern ideas of democracy and equality. However that may be, the interpretation does not appear in the earliest fathers, including Chrysostom and Augustine, and there are weighty objections to it. Although it is true that the historical Jesus must have made demands on his closest followers that he did not make on the populace at large, neither the Sermon itself nor its larger context does anything to make us think in terms of two sorts of believers. Matt. 5:48 by itself certainly does not suggest such; and when in 28:16–20 the risen Lord commands that disciples be made of all peoples, he speaks of them observing "all that I have commanded you." Where is the hint that some people may do just some things? Is it not implied rather that all should do all? Beyond this, the Sermon functions in its larger literary context as a general summary of Jesus' moral demand to all Israel, while 7:28–29 makes it plain that even the crowds hear Jesus' words. So the evangelist has done nothing to indicate that the Sermon on the Mount is aimed at a special group of people.

If some Catholic theologians once reduced the offense of the Sermon with their monastic interpretation, Protestants have attempted to gain the same end by other means. Lutheranism, for example, is often associated with the theory of the impossible ideal. According to this, no one can truly fulfill the Sermon on the Mount. The reality of sin is such that Jesus' words cannot be lived. What then was his purpose in speaking them? Why did he ask people to do what they could not do? The point was to teach the necessity of grace. When one sincerely undertakes to obey the commandments, one inevitably fails. But this can only be a boon, for it leads one to confess inadequacy, which in turn should throw one back upon God's grace. In other words, Jesus wanted to teach his hearers that they could not, in their own strength, fulfill the will of God. The Sermon on the Mount is preparation for the gospel: through its impossible impositions it leads to the proclamation of the good news, which is not about what we can do but about what God in Christ has done and will do. Paul's epistles immediately come to mind.

This influential interpretation is clearly correct in maintaining that the Sermon should, as we shall see in the next chapter, be firmly associated with a doctrine of grace. It makes this association, however, in an artificial way. The Sermon itself nowhere hints that believers are not really expected to live it. Quite the contrary. "Fulfillment is the natural and normal response" (so Hans Windisch, whose book on the Sermon contains an extended and largely persuasive attack on opinions to the contrary). "Not everyone who says to me, 'Lord, Lord,' will enter the kingdom of heaven, but only the one who does the will of my Father in heaven." "And everyone who hears these words of mine and does not act on them will be like a fool who built a house on sand . . . and great was its fall!" It is inevitable that the Sermon impinges directly upon the faithful reader. This is in fact its major thrust. Again, one cannot easily avoid the force of 28:20: "teaching them to observe everything that I have commanded you." How can this not include the Sermon? The Sermon on the Mount is a call for decision and action, not a theological lesson. As Origen, sounding a bit like Pelagius but nonetheless on target for that, wrote,

> When the savior says, "I say to you, do not resist an evildoer," and "Whoever is angry with a brother you will be liable to the judgment," and "Everyone who looks at a woman with lust has already committed adultery with her in his heart," and in any other commandment he gives, he tells us that it lies in our power to observe the injunctions and that we shall with good reason be "liable to judgment" if we transgress them. (*On First Principles* 3.1.6)

The theory of the impossible ideal, then, must in the end be dismissed as an attempt to read Luther's view of Paul into the Sermon: it goes against the chief intention of the text.

Also associated particularly with Lutheranism is what is known as the "doctrine of the two kingdoms." This distinguishes between the spiritual order and the civil order, between the private realm and the public realm. The Sermon pertains primarily to the former, not the latter. It is addressed to the Christian, not to the government. The Sermon, that is, enjoins an individual morality; it does not prescribe public policy. Further, because Christians may find themselves servants or employees of the state, one must differentiate between a person and the office that person holds. A Christian might, in his or her capacity as secular officeholder, do something he or she would never do as a private, Christian citizen. The victim of a crime, for instance, may well forgo all personal revenge and indeed proffer forgiveness to the perpetrator and yet support the state in its attempt to exact a just penalty.

From an exegetical point of view, the two kingdoms approach is not without merit, and much of the exegesis in the present commentary harmonizes with it. Neither Jesus nor Matthew was interested in addressing secular authorities or in laying down legislation for them. There is also the seeming coherence with the command to give both Caesar and God their due (Matt. 22:15–22).

One must nevertheless ask: When does responsibility to the state end and responsibility to God begin? When does giving to Caesar become taking away from God? Martin Buber sought to answer the perennial question in this way:

> It is true that we are not able to live in perfect justice, and in order to preserve the community of man, we are often compelled to accept wrongness in decisions concerning the community. . . . [But] what matters is that in every hour of decision we are aware of our responsibility and summon our conscience to weigh exactly how much is necessary to preserve the community, and accept just so much and no more. (*Israel*, 246)

This may well be all that can be said, and perhaps Matthew would have heartily concurred, knowing that the eschatological "not yet" requires that the will of God cannot be perfectly done on earth as it is in heaven. Still, there will always be disagreement over "exactly how much" is required of those who are citizens of both what Augustine called the city of God and the city of man. Further, many would say that the Sermon on the Mount, with its prohibition of oaths and

demand for love of enemy, implies only a minimal contribution to
Caesar. Most important of all, the two kingdoms approach can encourage a schizophrenic worldview that stifles our capacity to stand over
against the world and to criticize the powers that be, including the law,
when such is necessary. The situation of the German Lutheran
churches in the 1930s and 1940s supplies only the most obvious modern illustration; there are countless others. I recall the following anec-
dote, which illustrates on a very small scale the sort of dichotomy
between Caesar and conscience that should give us all pause:

> I ran across the case of a boy who had been sentenced to prison, a poor,
> scared little brat, who had intended something no worse than mischief,
> and it turned out to be a crime. The judge said he disliked to sentence the
> lad; it seemed the wrong thing to do; but the law left him no option. . . .
> The judge, then, was doing something as an official that he would not
> dream of doing as a man; he could do it without any sense of responsi-
> bility, or discomfort, simply because he was acting as an official and not
> as a man. On this principle of action, it seemed to me that one could
> commit almost any kind of crime without getting into trouble with one's
> conscience. (Nock, *On Doing the Right Thing*, 134)

There obviously are times when the state is wrong, when commitment
to its laws and patriotism are specious; and here the powerful biblical
tradition—so important for contemporary liberation theologians—of
the prophet speaking against institutional evils must be given its due.
Nothing in the Sermon undermines that tradition. So we still have our
questions.

Yet another attempt to come to terms with the Sermon's seemingly
impossible demands has come from some modern scholars (e.g., Wilhelm Hermann and E. F. Scott), who have proposed that the Sermon
contains an ethic of intention. Echoing the teaching of Abelard, their
point is that the Sermon does not consist of laws for the church or the
world but speaks instead to the individual about attitudes and internal
dispositions. It is, to put it baldly, not about what we should do but
about what we should be; it is about thinking, willing, and feeling, that
is, about a new way of being spiritual. "You desire truth in the inward
parts" (Ps. 51:6). Martin Dibelius put it this way: the Sermon "does not
demand of us that we *do something* but that we *be something*" (*Sermon on the Mount*, 137).

On the surface much also commends this interpretation. The Sermon declares that it is not enough to avoid murder or to refrain from
committing adultery: one must hold no anger at all, and there must be

no lust in the heart. Certainly 6:1–18, with its demand for right intention in almsgiving, prayer, and fasting, is largely about inward dispositions; and surely the beatitudes "require us not to do such and such things, but to be such and such people" (Gore, *Sermon,* 15). The interpretation in terms of attitude, however, cannot accommodate the ruling on divorce in 5:31–32. Here a concrete action is the subject. Intention has nothing to do with observing the prohibition of divorce and remarriage. More damaging, because 5:31–32 is the exception to the rule that the Sermon is not legislation, is the crucial fact that the Sermon winds up with exhortations about doing. Can the ethic of intention really do justice to this stress upon action? The crux of the problem is this: the Sermon does not separate the inward from the outward, being from doing, intention from performance. It commends now this action, now that attitude; that is, it addresses beings who are psychosomatic wholes. In short, while the Sermon is much concerned about intention, it is concerned with much else besides.

*   *   *   *   *

The various approaches to the Sermon on the Mount just outlined all err by, among other things, being one-sided and by unduly simplifying. The Sermon does so many things at once that its goals cannot be succinctly summarized: it has no one end, no one *telos.* Having said this, however, several generalizations may serve us as exegetical guidelines in what follows.

1. During the last two centuries scholars have examined the Sermon with the tools of modern historical criticism. Their labors have been directed to, among other things, the problem of pre-Gospel sources, the possible detection of anti-Pauline polemic, the question of what really goes back to Jesus, the issue of what should be attributed to Matthew's editorial hand, and the matter of gathering parallels to the Sermon's teaching. Concerning this last, throughout modern commentaries on the Sermon, attention is frequently called to history-of-religion parallels, mostly Jewish parallels, less frequently Greco-Roman parallels. Occasionally one may even see Egyptian or Buddhist sources cited. The scholar's ability to collect such parallels means that any interpretation of the Sermon that sees it as altogether a bolt from the blue, as something fundamentally unprecedented, is mistaken. This is not to say that there are no novel or unusual elements. There are, and it is appropriate when the audience reacts as it does: "the crowds were astounded at his

teaching" (7:28). Matthew, however, must have known as well as we do that, for example, the golden rule did not originate with Jesus.

The point is extremely important. An inordinate desire to emphasize Jesus' alleged uniqueness will lead to misinterpretation. But the truth of Jesus' teaching cannot in any way depend on its novelty. The Sermon contains much that, if not exactly universal, is at least attested here and there in religious and philosophical texts from other times and places, its links to the Hebrew Bible and Jewish tradition being, as documented herein, especially close and numerous. So far from this being an embarrassment, as though a brand new morality, an ethics *de novo*, would be desirable, this is perhaps one answer to those who would accuse the Matthean Jesus of being an erratic boulder on humanity's moral landscape—and one reason for doubting that the Sermon is nothing more than an impossible ideal. Does his wisdom not stand in significant continuity with much else that has been said and taught by others, especially in the Jewish tradition? Does not the Sermon in myriad ways direct us to "the ancient paths, where the good way is" (Jer. 6:16)? Samuel Johnson was right when he wrote that we are "more often required to be reminded than informed"—and this is what the Sermon does. Jesus came not to abolish the moral awareness of humanity as a whole but to fulfill it. Hence the ease with which one finds Hellenistic and other parallels.

2. To do justice to Matthew, the reader must take seriously 5:17–20, verses which plainly say that the Law and the Prophets are still in force. This declaration stands as the preface to the imperatives in 5:21–48, about which there has been so much debate and confusion. We have here not a vestigial sentiment of an obsolete Jewish Christianity but a hermeneutical key—and one that proves fatal for the absolutist approach of Tolstoy and like-minded others. For their interpretation of 5:21–48 lands one in fundamental, irreconcilable conflict with the Hebrew Bible, which accepts armies, courts, and oaths as necessary; and it would seem to follow, on that interpretation, that "Jesus Christ had retracted what had earlier been established by God his Father" (Calvin, *Brieve instruction . . . Anabaptistes* 4). But for Matthew old and new hang together. Jesus did not recklessly contradict or abandon Moses and his laws. "I came not to abolish the law and the prophets." As 9:17 has it, old and new are to be preserved together. What follows? If the absolutist position be maintained, then Matt. 5:17–20, understood in its natural sense, must be reckoned misleading and indeed false, for the main purpose of the passage is to deny any gen-

uine contradiction between Jesus and the Torah. In view of this, however much one may admire the courage it takes to try to live the Sermon literally, and however true it may be that the Sermon demands radical obedience, a literal-minded and legalistic observance cannot be, at least over the whole range of life, in accord with the Matthean intention. Tolstoy himself recognized that his interpretation of the Sermon contradicts the Jewish scriptures, which is why he was so insistent that the new revelation replaces the old. He criticized the church for harmonizing the Sermon with the revelation that was given before it. But here Eastern Orthodox, Roman Catholic, and Protestant have rightly been closer to the letter and spirit of Matthew's Gospel.

3. The Sermon on the Mount belongs to a book apart from which it was never intended to be read. This matters because so often interpretation has gone astray by ignoring the Sermon's context. For example, within Matthew as a whole, chapters 5–7 function as an elaboration of Jesus' call for Israel to repent (4:17). This, along with 7:28–29, which informs us that Jesus was speaking not just to the disciples (5:1–2) but also to the crowds, means that any interpretation that thinks of the Sermon as addressed to a *corps d'élite,* as it were, must be mistaken. Again, the reader of all of Matthew knows that Jesus is not just a moral authority but additionally a gracious religious presence whose demand is accompanied by a helping presence (18:20; 28:20). So the informed reader of the Sermon will not make any dichotomy between task and gift, law and grace, demand and benefit.

Perhaps the way in which the context of the Sermon matters above all is this: most of the topics covered in the Sermon come up again elsewhere in Matthew, where they are often treated at further length, so that what is dark in the Sermon is often illumined by other verses. The demonstration of this will be constant throughout this commentary. But here, to make the point, is a list of ten rather obvious illustrations:

- "Blessed are the meek" (5:5). Jesus himself embodies meekness (11:29; 21:5). So our understanding of this virtue must be consistent with the character of Jesus, who turns over tables in the temple and harshly rebukes scribes and Pharisees.

- "Blessed are those who are persecuted for righteousness' sake" (5:10). The sorts of persecution here envisaged and their occasions are elaborated in the missionary discourse (chapter 10) and the eschatological discourse (chapter 24).

- "Do not think that I have come to abolish the law and the prophets" (5:17). This pronouncement is illustrated and confirmed by 8:4, by Jesus' frequent quotations of the Hebrew Bible, and by the editorial treatment of Mark 7:1–23 in Matt. 15:1–20.

- "Everyone who divorces his wife . . . causes her to commit adultery" (5:32). The reason for Jesus' prohibition of divorce is given not in the Sermon but in 19:3–9.

- "Except on the ground of *porneia*" (5:32). The story of Joseph, "a righteous man," who seeks to divorce Mary because of suspected adultery (1:18–25), helps us fix the content of *porneia*: it must include adultery (Joseph's suspicion) and does not (against some commentators) refer to incest.

- "Do not swear at all" (5:34). The teaching of 23:16–22 seems to tell us that 5:33–37 is not a blanket prohibition of all oaths.

- "Be perfect" (5:48). The call to perfection also appears in 19:21, which obviously has implications for interpreting 5:48 (e.g., 19:21 cannot refer to sinlessness).

- "When you fast . . ." (6:16–18). The justification for Christian fasting is given in 9:14–17.

- The radical teaching on what to do with wealth in 6:19–24 is illustrated by 4:18–22 and 10:9–11 and is explicated by 19:16–26, the story of a man who could not give up his wealth.

- "Beware of false prophets" (7:15). Additional characteristics are given to the false prophets in 24:24–27, which aids us in understanding better who those prophets might be.

Because any valid interpretation of Jesus' words in Matthew 5–7 must apply equally to the rest of Jesus' words, the exegete of the Sermon should equally be an exegete of Matthew. Even though the Sermon has a narrative beginning and conclusion, it should not be partitioned off and given a special interpretation. What is said of 5:29–30 (on cutting off limbs) must be also said of its twin in 18:8–9, and one's view of 5:17–20 must be informed by the remainder of the Gospel. The broader context must always be kept in mind. Likening the First Gospel to a sentence, the Sermon is only one word: and who could determine the meaning of a word while ignoring the sentence in which it occurs?

4. One must reckon seriously with the fact that the Sermon on the Mount is partly a poetic text. By this is meant that it is, unlike codes of law, dramatic and pictorial. The reader sees a man offering a sacrifice in Jerusalem (5:23), someone in prison (5:25–26), a body without eye and hand (5:29–30), someone being slapped (5:39), the sun rising (5:45), the rain falling (5:45), someone praying in a closet (6:6), lilies in a field (6:28), a log in an eye (7:4), wolves in sheeps' clothing (7:15). These images and the comments upon them hardly add up to anything that can be called legislation. The Sermon does not offer a set of rules—the ruling on divorce is the exception—but rather seeks to instill a moral vision. Literal (mis)interpretation accordingly leads to absurdities. The text, which implies that God demands a radical obedience that cannot be casuistically formulated, functions more like a story or myth than a legal code: these precepts are proverbs. In this connection one recalls the distinction Cardinal Newman drew between principles and rules of conduct. The latter "are adapted for immediate purpose; they aim at utility. . . ." The former, which is what we find for the most part in the Sermon, are, on the other hand, "great truths or laws which embody in them the character of a system, enable us to estimate it, and indirectly guide us in practice. . . . It is a characteristic of such statements of principles to be short, pointed, strong, and often somewhat paradoxical in appearance. . . . They mean nothing, or something wide of the truth, taken as literal directions" (*Lectures*, 333–34).

J. Duncan M. Derrett would, then, seem to have things exactly backwards when he urges that "the blacks and whites of the [Sermon on the Mount] encourage an archaic single-minded and simple-hearted impatience with reflection" (*Ascetic Discourse*, 21). Rather, as James Denney put it, "they are not meant to save us the trouble of thinking, but to kindle in us the most intense and vivid thought" (in Dods, Denney, and Moffatt, *Literal Interpretation*, 31). Dibelius suggestively called the Sermon a collection of "signs"—signs of what he called "the pure will of God"—rather than of programs. The Sermon's primary purpose is to instill principles and qualities through a vivid inspiration of the moral imagination. What one comes away with is not a grossly incomplete set of statutes but an unjaded impression of a challenging moral ideal.

In line with this, we must be wary of missing the Sermon's use of hyperbole. It was a Semitic habit to make hyperbolic declarations in hortative material; and, as we shall see, when Jesus, in Matt. 7:13–14, says that "many" are headed for destruction and "few" for life, we would be ill-advised to find here a numerical estimate of how many will be saved, how many damned. The meaning is rather: act as if only a very few will enter through the gates of paradise. In like manner, it is unlikely that 5:23 really assumes the possibility of people interrupting the sacrificial ritual in the temple. Here is rather a parabolic—and therefore more memorable—way of saying that the efficacy of religious activity is conditioned by the spiritual and moral state of the one making sacrifice. It is also unlikely that Jesus, in telling followers to give away cloak as well as coat (5:40), is saying that nudity is just fine; and the command, "Let your word be 'Yes,Yes' or 'No, No'" (5:37), must be some sort of rhetorical flourish. Certainly Jesus, when asked to swear before Caiaphas the high priest, says more than that. Martin Bucer observed that "Do not let your left hand know what your right hand is doing" (6:3) is "hyperbole with metaphor" and belongs to a discourse full of "figures of speech" (*Enarrationes perpetuae in Sacra quatuor Evangelia* fol. 62r.41). So we must hope that there is a difference between taking a text literally and taking it seriously, that one can do the latter without doing the former.

5. One cannot understand the Sermon without grasping its eschatological orientation. What does this mean? Many, following Johannes Weiss and Albert Schweitzer, have supposed the truth to be this: Jesus' demands were so radical because he believed the kingdom, understood as a divinely wrought utopia, to be so close. His injunctions were issued in the conviction that normal, ordinary, day-to-day existence was soon to be a thing of the past. Why not be rid of wealth, if shortly it will have no value? This interpretation, particularly popular with Jewish scholars wrestling with Jesus' radicalism but also enshrined in the influential studies of Martin Dibelius and Hans Windisch, is in the first place a thesis about the historical Jesus, not the Sermon on the Mount. And whatever its merits with regard to Jesus—I for one think they are considerable—it does not much illuminate the text of Matthew as it stands. The author of our Gospel probably did, like so many other early Christians, hope, indeed believe, that the end would come sooner rather than later, but nowhere does the Sermon clearly ground its imperatives in near eschatological expectation.

How then does the eschatological future impinge upon Jesus' words? The Sermon may address ordinary circumstances, but it sees all through the eyes of eternity. It does not so much look forward, from the present to the consummation, as it looks backwards, from the consummation to the present. The Sermon presents the perfect, unadulterated will of God, the will of God in its nakedness, because it proclaims the will of God as it should be lived in the kingdom, when God's will is done on earth as in heaven. This explains why it is seemingly heedless of all earthly contingencies, why it is so radical, why it always blasts complacency and shallow moralism, disturbs every good conscience and instills terror in those who take it seriously. The Sermon is not primarily concerned with what is practical or possible in the here and now but with the unobstructed, perfect will of God. Here the words of Albert Schweitzer are worth pondering:

> that which is eternal in the words of Jesus is due to the very fact that they are based on an eschatological worldview and contain the expression of a mind for which the contemporary world with its historical and social circumstances no longer had any existence. They are appropriate, therefore, to any world, for in every world they raise the man who dares to meet their challenge, and does not turn and twist them into meaninglessness, above his world, making him inwardly free, so that he is fitted to be, in his own world, and in his own time, a simple channel of the power of Jesus. (*Quest*, 402)

6. A command to add a cubit to one's height would be senseless, for it asks the impossible (6:27). Similarly, one may think the charge to be perfect in love (5:48) senseless, for it too asks for what cannot be given. But there is a difference. While one can do nothing at all about one's height, one can do something about one's capacity to love. It is not a question of all or nothing. Like the kingdom, love may be pursued or sought (6:33). Love can always be increased, deepened, its circumference enlarged. This explains why John Climacus (ca. 570–649) could speak of love as "the progress of eternity" (*Ladder of Divine Ascent* 30). It can never come to completion. It is no different from many of the other qualities called for by the Sermon. These by their very nature cannot in any straightforward sense be fully possessed or mastered, exhausted, perfected, either by the community or by the individual. "There is no boundary to virtue" (*Ladder* 26).

In this connection one is reminded of Gregory of Nyssa's innovative doctrine of perpetual progress. In his *Life of Moses* and elsewhere he rejects the Platonic notion that change is a defect and affirms that "the one definition of perfection is its not having any limit. . . . Why? Because every good is by its very nature unlimited" (*Life of Moses* 1.5). Again:

One should not be distressed when one considers this tendency [toward mutability] in our [human] nature; rather let us change in such a way that we may constantly evolve toward what is better, being transformed from glory to glory, and thus always improving and ever becoming perfect by daily growth, and never arriving at any limit of perfection. For that perfection consists in our never stopping in our growth in good, never circumscribing our perfection by any limitation. (*De perfectione et qualem oporteat esse Christianum,* in Migne, *PG* 46:285C–D)

From this point of view one may interpret the Sermon as a ladder to be climbed, rung by rung, or as a challenge which, its call being constant, can become ever more effective over the course of time. This accords not only with the nature of the qualities prescribed by the Sermon (who would say of such: So much, and no more?) but also with 7:13–14, where the words of Jesus are set forth as a *way.* The approach likewise harmonizes with Paul's discussion in Philippians 3, where he calls himself "perfect" and yet declares that he has not yet obtained perfection, for that consists precisely in pressing ever onward: "Not that I have already obtained this or have already reached the goal . . . but this one thing I do; forgetting what lies behind and straining forward to what lies ahead, I press on toward the goal for the prize of the heavenly call of God in Christ Jesus. Let those of us then who are mature be of the same mind." As Jan Van Ruysbroeck, the Flemish mystic (1293–1381), would later write, the perfect Christian "will constantly grow and increase in grace, in all the virtues, and in knowledge of the truth before God and all upright people" (*The Sparkling Stone,* preface). It should really be no surprise that the Matthean Jesus demands everything, up to and including the impossible, because anything less than that, anything less than the eschatological will of God, would put a limit on goodness.

There is another, related point to make. People do not search for the end of the rainbow, for it cannot be found. The perfection of the moral life, however, is not analogous. For while moral perfection cannot be achieved, nevertheless one's character is built up as one earnestly struggles, with no relaxation, to reach the unreachable. The ever-receding and unconquerable ideal recreates those who fix their gaze upon it, steer their course by it, and move themselves toward it. Gustavo Gutiérrez aptly speaks of "the utopia that sets history in motion for Christians" (*God of Life,* 120).

Continuing this line of thought, can it not be urged that "realistic" moral instruction is self-defeating? Unlike good civil laws, which, in order to be enforced, must be concrete and capable of being kept, should not the call for moral virtues and qualities always involve injunctions to do what has not yet been done? To settle instead for the readily obtainable—would that not be to exchange "ought" for "is"? Would it not be to acquiesce to the ordinary condition of humanity, which so obviously tends toward sin, sloth, and mediocrity? Is not pragmatism concession? The one thing needful is to be inspired and so empowered—hence the traditional wisdom of listening to the legends of the saints, who do so many impossible things. Where is the father or mother who refrains from telling his or her children to be unselfish simply because their being selfish is inevitable? We know from experience that the standard must be upheld even when failure to live up to it is certain. The ideal is necessary because, while it may not raise humanity to the heights, it can lift us from the depths. The behest to be perfect and complete will not be answered by perfection, but may it not effect much more than would a call for something less? Here the words of the Jew Pinchas Lapide are apposite:

> to aspire to the unattainable is perhaps what is most human in our species. It is certainly the quintessence of Judaism. . . . To Jews a pseudo-realism that accepts the status quo as final and unchangeable seems false. Genuine realism, in contrast, is the restlessness of those thirsting for salvation, the impatience roaring through the Sermon on the Mount; it is the sister of the "Jewish haste" that steadfastly refuses to call today good or to sanctify any status quo. (*Sermon*, 7)

7. All too often in the modern world the Sermon on the Mount has been divorced not only from its larger literary context but from the person of its speaker, as though it contains an ethic that can be separated from christology. The Sermon, however, is not a book of proverbs with an anonymous and faceless author. Rather, the discourse presupposes and teaches important things about its speaker, whose identity is crucial for interpretation. This appears from several facts that require treatment at some length.

Jesus as Isaiah's eschatological prophet. Several beatitudes draw upon, or rather allude to, Isaiah 61, which opens thus:

> The spirit of the Lord God is upon me,
>   because the Lord has anointed me;
> he has sent me to bring good news to the poor,
>   to bind up the brokenhearted,
> to proclaim liberty to the captives,
>   and release to the prisoners;

> to proclaim the year of the Lord's favor,
> > and the day of vengeance of our God;
> to comfort all who mourn.

"Blessed are those who mourn, for they will be comforted" borrows from Isa. 61:2. "Blessed are the poor in spirit, for theirs is the kingdom of God" is inspired by Isa. 61:1. And "Rejoice and be glad" recalls Isa. 61:10 ("I will greatly rejoice in the Lord, and my whole being shall exult in my God").

The implicit meaning of these allusions is unfolded explicitly in Matthew 11. Here John the Baptist, from his prison, sends to Jesus and asks him, "Are you the one who is to come, or are we to wait for another?" Jesus answers with a series of phrases that come from Isaiah:

> the blind see (Isa. 61:1)
> the lame walk (Isa. 35:6)
> the deaf hear (Isa. 35:5)
> the dead are raised (Isa. 26:19)
> the poor have good news preached to them (Isa. 61:1)

The opening and closing lines refer to Isaiah 61. So it is plain that Jesus is the anointed herald of that passage (as also in Luke 4:18–19 and Acts 4:27). The Spirit of the Lord is upon him (3:16), and he has been anointed to bring good tidings to the poor, to bind up the broken-hearted, to proclaim liberty to the captives, to comfort those who mourn.

The Dead Sea Scrolls use Isa. 61:1–3 to portray the eschatological liberation of Israel's captives, and an eschatological interpretation of these verses also appears in the targum on Isaiah. It seemingly follows that Matthew's readers would have understood Jesus to be the eschatological fulfillment of prophetic expectation. But what does this mean for the interpretation of the Sermon on the Mount? It means above all that the authority who speaks the Sermon belongs to a history. Jesus is not an isolated novum on humanity's religious landscape. He is rather the goal of a story, the history told in the Jewish Bible. To say that Jesus is the anointed one prophesied by Isaiah 61 is to say that he has been sent by the same God who spoke to Abraham, Moses, David, and the prophets; it is to imply that there is continuity between the new and the old and that ultimately the one who speaks here through his anointed prophet is the one whose words and deeds constitute the religious story of Israel.

That this is indeed the case is confirmed by 5:17–20. Sometimes religions begin when a charismatic figure overthrows the traditions of the past. Buddha, for instance, appeared and rejected the Hinduism of his time and place. But Jesus does not reject his religious tradition; he is rather a reformer of it. He comes not to abolish the law and the prophets, whose imperatives remain in force. The God who spoke then speaks again now, in the Sermon. And he does not contradict himself.

Jesus as the new Moses. It is common to view the mountain of 5:1 as a counterpart to Sinai. In the words of Matthew Henry, "Christ preached this sermon, which is an exposition of the law, upon a mountain, because upon a mountain the law was given" (*Commentary*, 1628). Not only does Matthew's Greek (*anebē eis to oros*) recall pentateuchal passages having to do with Moses (e.g., Exod. 19:3, 12, 13), but Jewish tradition spoke of Moses *sitting* on Sinai (so already the *Exagōgē* of Ezekiel; cf. Babylonian Talmud *Megillah* 21a). Furthermore, other Moses typologies from antiquity have their Mosaic heroes sit on a mountain (e.g. 4 Ezra 14) while *Mekhilta* on Exod. 19:11 and 29:18 and other sources claim that Israel was healed at the foot of Sinai (cf. Matt. 4:23); and 8:1, the conclusion of the Sermon, is identical to Exod. 34:29 LXX A, which recounts Moses' descent from Sinai. All of this means that the Jesus of the Sermon is supposed to remind us of Moses.

This is confirmed by what has come earlier in the Gospel. Indeed, an extensive Moses typology runs throughout Matthew's first few chapters (see especially Allison, *Moses*). The story of Joseph's contemplation of what to do about Mary, suspected of adultery, and of the angel who bids him not to fear and then prophesies his son's future greatness (see Matthew 1) parallels the story of Amram, Moses' father, as told by Josephus, in *Antiquities* 2.210–16: Amram, ill at ease over what to do about his wife's pregnancy, has a dream in which God exhorts him not to despair and prophesies his son's future greatness. Matthew's "You are to name him Jesus, for he will save his people from their sins" (1:21) reminds one, moreover, of Moses' status as "savior" of his people (Josephus, *Antiquities* 2.228; Babylonian Talmud *Soṭa* 12b).

In chapter 2 Herod's order to do away with the male infants of Bethlehem (2:16–18) is like Pharaoh's order to do away with every male Hebrew child (Exodus 1). And if Herod orders the slaughter of Hebrew infants because he has learned of the birth of Israel's liberator (2:2–18), in Jewish tradition Pharaoh slaughters the Hebrew children because he has learned of the very same thing (Josephus, *Antiquities* 2.205–9; *Targum Ps.-Jonathan* on Exod. 1:15). Further, whereas Herod hears of the coming liberator from chief priests, scribes, and magi (2:1–12), Josephus (*Antiquities* 2.205 and 234) has Pharaoh learn of Israel's deliverer from scribes, while the *Jerusalem Targum* on Exod. 1:15 says that Pharaoh's chief magicians (Jannes and Jambres, the sons of Balaam) were the sources of his information. The quotation of Hos. 11:1 in Matt. 2:15 further evokes thought of the exodus, for in its original context "Out of Egypt I have called my son" concerns Israel. And then there is 2:19–22, which borrows the language of Exod. 4:19–20: just as Moses, after being told to go back to Egypt because all those seeking his life have died, takes his wife and children and returns to the land of his birth, so too with Jesus: Joseph, after being told to go back to Israel because all those seeking the life of his son have died, takes his wife and child and returns to the land of his son's birth.

In chapter 3 Jesus is baptized by John the Baptist. We know from 1 Cor. 10:1–5 that baptism could be likened to passing through the Red Sea. In chapter 4, commentators have long associated Jesus' forty days of fasting with Moses' forty days of fasting, as well as with Israel's forty years of wandering and being tempted in the wilderness. In line with this, when the devil takes Jesus to a very high mountain to show him all the kingdoms of the world (4:8), one may think of Moses on the top of Pisgah, for, among other things, not only does Matt. 4:8 use the language of Deut. 34:1, 4 LXX, but Jewish tradition expands Moses' vision so that it is of all the world.

Austin Farrer long ago observed that the apparent allusions to Moses and the exodus in Matthew 1–5 appear in their biblical sequence:

Exodus—	slaughter of infants	return of hero	passage through water	temptation—	mountain of lawgiving

Matthew—	slaughter of infants	return of hero	passage through water	temptation—	mountain of lawgiving

This is not the upshot of chance.

Given his status as one like Moses, it is no surprise at all that Jesus, when he goes up on a mountain, exhorts his hearers about murder, adultery, divorce, oaths, revenge, and love. These are all topics that Moses addresses in Deuteronomy, and Jesus in fact more than once quotes Moses himself regarding them. So Jesus is like the lawgiver in this regard too.

It is quite common for Christian interpreters to turn Matthew's

Moses typology into a statement that Jesus is greater than Moses. But this is not where the weight of Matthew's narrative lies. It is not on the differences but on the parallels. In Matthew's world, "Moses said" was the equivalent of "God said." So to make Jesus one like Moses was a way of saying that, in similar fashion, Jesus' word is God's word. That is, the parallels with Moses are intended to exalt the authority of Jesus, to make him a dispenser of divine revelation. The Moses typology functions very much like the closing words of the discourse, where we are told that Jesus taught "as one having authority" (7:29).

The stress on Jesus' authority is necessary if the discourse is to be taken seriously. For the Sermon is not a compilation of common sense. Much of it is counterintuitive and radical. Moreover, its imperatives make no promise that obedience to them will create a better world. Jesus does not say that those who turn the other cheek will be well treated. Nor does he promise that love of enemies will turn them into friends. Quite the contrary, the picture that the Sermon offers of the saints is that they are persecuted (5:11–12) and financially insecure (6:19–34). So why should one do what the Sermon says?

The answer can only lie in the authority of the speaker. To be sure, the speaker makes eschatological promises—the saints will be comforted, receive mercy, have treasure in heaven. But those realities belong to the unseen future; they cannot be confirmed in the present. If one is to believe them, it must be on the authority of the one who makes the promises. Thus it is that Jesus is like Moses. He has authority and is trustworthy, and he speaks for God.

Jesus as moral exemplar. E. Thurneysen, a close associate of Karl Barth, argued that the Sermon is a way of preaching Christ—this because it is a self-portrait. Jesus brought the kingdom and accomplished the law; he alone lived his own words. Hence, he is "the true content of his sayings." The "life of the new man has been lived once and only once, in Jesus Christ." "The single content of the Sermon is Jesus and confrontation with him" (*Sermon,* 39).

Much is to be said for Thurneysen's approach, which in this particular is akin to that of Segundo Galilea's liberationist commentary on the beatitudes. Not only does 5:3–12 imply that Jesus is the eschatological herald of Isaiah 61, but in 5:17 there is a loaded "I came" saying that interprets the Law and the Prophets in terms of Jesus' appearance. Further, the Sermon is indeed a sort of summary of the deeds of Jesus. As Barth says somewhere, "The Commander . . . embodies the command."

That this is the truth appears first in the beatitudes. Jesus blesses the so-called meek. Commentators always discuss the meaning of this word, which in common usage today is hardly a desired virtue. But they sometimes miss the fact that the word occurs elsewhere in Matthew, and that both times it characterizes Jesus. In 11:29 Jesus says that he himself is "meek and lowly in heart." The implication is that, whatever this virtue may be, Jesus embodies it. This being the case, "meek" cannot mean submissiveness or lack of spirit. For Matthew's Jesus enters into arguments, speaks harshly about opponents, and overturns the tables of the money changers in the temple. The word "meek" also is used in 21:5 to depict Jesus' entry into Jerusalem: he does not enter as a warrior on a war-horse but as a peaceful king seated on a donkey.

Jesus also illustrates other beatitudes. He is, for instance, an obvious example of one who is persecuted for righteousness' sake, of one who is reviled and spoken against (5:10–12). And if he congratulates the merciful in the fifth beatitude (5:7), he himself is merciful. Throughout the Gospel people ask him to show mercy, to have compassion, and he complies (see 9:27; 15:22; 20:30).

In 5:17–20 Jesus says that he has not come to undo Moses, and the rest of the Gospel shows him being faithful to the Torah. In 8:4 he tells a healed leper to go show himself to a priest. In 9:20 and 14:36 people touch the *kraspedon* of his garment—a probable reference to the "tassel" which, according to Num. 15:38–39 and Deut. 22:12, the pious Jew was to wear on the outer garment. In 12:1–8 Jesus defends the disciples' act of plucking grain on the Sabbath by, among other things, referring to Moses: "Have you not read in the law that on the Sabbath the priests in the temple break the Sabbath and yet are guiltless?" In 15:1–20 Jesus disputes the traditions of the Pharisees but upholds the law. And in 23:23–24 he castigates the scribes and Pharisees for tithing mint, dill, and cumin while rejecting justice, mercy, and faith and then goes on to say they ought to have practiced these last "without neglecting the others." So Jesus may debate with the experts the application of the law, but he does not debate the validity of the law.

In 5:33–37 Jesus declares that oaths are not needed (cf. Jas. 5:12). The presupposition behind the oath is that there are two types of statements, one of which demands commitment (the oath), one of which does not (the statement without an oath). But Jesus enjoins invariable commitment to every statement so that the oath becomes superfluous. It is no surprise, then, that, when the high priest at the trial tries to put Jesus under an oath, Jesus does not use an oath formula. He rather responds with the laconic "You have said so" and then goes on to make his own point (26:63–64).

In 5:38–42 Jesus says, "Do not resist an evildoer. But if anyone strikes you on the right cheek, turn the other also; and if anyone wants to sue you and take your coat, give your cloak as well; and if anyone forces you to go one mile, go also the second mile." These words, which vividly represent the demand for an unselfish temperament, for naked humility and a will to suffer the loss of one's personal rights, borrow from Isa. 50:4–9 LXX. There are also thematic parallels—both Matt. 5:38–42 and Isa. 50:4–11 depict the unjust treatment of an innocent individual and use the terminology of the law court. Clearly at this point the Sermon alludes to the third servant song. The allusion does more than inject a vague scriptural aura. Rather do we see the truth when we observe that Isa. 50:4–9 is again alluded to in the passion narrative, in 26:67 (cf. 27:30): the scriptural text associated with turning the other cheek is also associated with the passion of Jesus. Furthermore, of the seven words shared by Matt. 5:38–42 and Isa. 50:4–9, two appear again in the passion narrative—"strike" (*rhapizō*, 26:67) and "cloak/clothes" (27:31, 35). Indeed, "strike" appears only twice in the First Gospel, in 5:39 and 26:67; and in both places an innocent person is struck—just as in 5:40 and 27:31 and 35 an innocent person's clothes are taken. So the allusions to Isa. 50:4–9 are in effect allusions to the passion of Jesus. Put otherwise, 5:38–42 superimposes three images: the suffering Christian, the suffering Christ, and the suffering servant. Again, then, Jesus' own story offers an illustration of his imperative. If he speaks of eschewing violence and not resisting evil, of being slapped, of having one's clothes taken, and of being compelled to serve the Romans, the conclusion to his own life makes his words concrete: he eschews violence (26:51–54); he does not resist evil (26:36–56; 27:12–14); he is struck (26:67); he has his garments taken (27:28, 35); and his cross is carried by one requisitioned by Roman order (27:32).

The imperatives of Matthew 6 also find illustrations outside the Sermon on the Mount. In 6:5–6 Jesus says, "whenever you pray, go into your room and shut the door and pray to your Father who is in secret. . . ." How does Jesus himself pray? Matt. 14:23 tells us that, after feeding the five thousand, Jesus "dismissed the crowds" and "went up the mountain by himself to pray." Again, before he prays in Gethsemane (chapter 26), he orders his disciples: "sit here while I go over there and pray." He does take Peter and James and John with him, but then Matthew tells us that he went "a little farther" away to pray. Before Jesus can speak to the special group of three he has to "come" to them.

The story in Gethsemane further illustrates Jesus' teaching on prayer. Matt. 6:9–13 contains the Lord's Prayer, which includes the address "Our Father" and the petitions "Your will be done" (6:10) and "Do not bring us to the time of trial" (6:13). It is striking that these phrases reappear on Jesus' lips during his time of crisis. Jesus addresses God as "My Father" (26:39, 42) and then resignedly says, "if this cannot pass unless I drink it, your will be done" (26:42). Moreover, he asks his disciples, "So, could you not stay awake with me one hour?" and then orders them to "Stay awake and pray that you may not come into the time of trial" (26:40–41).

In 6:19–34 Jesus addresses the problem of what to do with wealth. The message is that one must not store up treasure on earth but serve God instead of mammon. Because doing this will inevitably create hardship, Jesus goes on to offer words of encouragement: "Do not be anxious" (6:25, 31, 34). Jesus lives according to his words. Not only does 8:20 declare that "the Son of man [= Jesus] has nowhere to lay his head," but Jesus obviously trusts God, even though that takes him to a cross.

In the light of the various correlations between the Sermon and the rest of Matthew, it is plain that the Sermon is indeed partly a summary of its speaker's deeds. The First Gospel is about a figure who imaginatively and convincingly incarnates his own moral imperatives. Jesus embodies his speech; he lives as he speaks and speaks as he lives. It is not going too far to say that Matthew 5–7 proclaims likeness to the God of Israel (5:48) through the virtues of Jesus Christ.

Implicit then in the Sermon is the motif of the imitation of Christ. If Jesus demands the perfect imitation of God (5:48), he himself is the perfect instance of such imitation. The early church father Ignatius put it this way: "Be imitators of Jesus Christ, as he was of his Father" (*Letter to the Philadelphians* 7.2). On the moral level at least our Gospel encourages its readers to identify closely with the main character, whom the evangelist clearly regarded as, to use the words of another first-century Christian, "the pioneer and perfecter of our faith" (Heb. 12:2).

All this has often been insufficiently appreciated, in part because there has been, since Luther, a necessary reaction against an unimaginative and literalistic *imitatio Christi* (such as that exhibited by Francis of Assisi), and in part because the notion of the imitation of the canonical Jesus has been condemned as a purely human effort which, in the event, cannot be achieved. (But this objection could not be brought against Matthew's concept of the imitation of Jesus; for in the First Gospel Jesus is an ever-abiding, helpful presence; in other words, the believer is never thought of as standing alone, in isolation from the divine activity, so the problem of a purely human effort does not arise [cf. 18:20; 28:20].) Matthew would surely have contended as strongly as did Kierkegaard that his conception of imitation was not at odds with grace. There is also the fact that many have been anxious to preserve Jesus' unique status as a savior whose salvific accomplishments cannot be emulated: the Christian gospel is not—surely Matthew himself would have agreed—moral imitation of a human hero or fine example. But Matthew, in whose Gospel there is no trace of docetism, wrote long before Nicaea, at a time when it was still possible to think of Jesus as a real human being—if also much more—and therefore as a real ethical model; and our evangelist, like Paul (if not in Phil. 2:5–11, then at least in Rom. 15:1–7), Origen (see, e.g., *On First Principles* 4.4.4; cf. *Exhortation to Martyrdom* 41–42), and other early Christians (John 13:15, 34; 15:12; 17:16; Heb. 12:1–4; 13:12–13; 1 Pet. 2:21; 3:17–18; 1 John 2:6; Ignatius, *Letter to the Philadelphians* 7:2; Irenaeus, *Against Heresies* 2.22.4; Clement of Alexandria, *Teacher* 1.1) thought of Jesus as a model to be emulated.

All this is reinforced by Matthew's use of the word "righteousness" (*dikaiosynē*). Probably everywhere in his Gospel the word indicates either God's norm for human conduct or behavior in accord with that norm. Moreover, Jesus not only demands "righteousness," as in 5:20 ("unless your righteousness exceeds that of the scribes and Pharisees"); he also lives it. Thus he is recognized in 27:19 as being a "righteous" (*dikaios*) person. And according to 3:15, in submitting to baptism by John, he fulfilled "all righteousness." The meaning of this last phrase has been much contested. But "fulfilled" should probably be given an eschatological sense (cf. 5:17), so that the meaning is that Jesus is the eschatological fulfillment of the will of God, which in turn implies that his behavior, his courageous self-command, which became humble obedience to God and left nothing good undone, is for Matthew programmatic and exemplary: the Son of God first does what he later asks others to do. Jesus is, throughout our Gospel, a consistent "example," to quote Irenaeus, "of piety, righteousness, and submission" (*Against Heresies* 2.22.4). If Aristotle regarded the "good man" as the "canon" in ethics (*Nicomachean Ethics* 3.4), in Matthew Jesus is the "canon" of Christian morality.

Explicit statements. Thirteen times the speaker of the Sermon uses the phrase, "I say to you" (*legō hymin*; 5:18, 20, 22, 28, 32, 34, 39, 43; 6:2, 5, 16, 25, 29). This expression raises acutely the issue of his authority. Who is it that can speak to us like this? And why should we obey his imperatives?

This speaker also blesses those who suffer "on my account"—not those who suffer in general (5:11). He further says that those who hear and do his words may be likened to those who build a house on rock that will endure storms, whereas those who do not hear his words to do them are like those who foolishly build a house on sand, a house that will fall to the storms that beat upon it. Obviously the speaker makes himself out to be somebody.

The speaker's most lofty claims for himself appear in 7:21–23. Here we read of people who, on the last day of judgment, will say to Jesus, "Lord, Lord." They will tell of their many deeds in his name—of prophesying in his name, or casting out demons in his name, or doing mighty miracles in his name. But he will tell them to depart, because "I never knew you." His last word to them will be a damning sentence, "Go away from me, you evildoers." Here the speaker of the Sermon appears to be the judge of the great eschatological judgment, or at least one of its major players.

What do we make of all this? It is crystal clear that the Sermon does not just make moral demands upon us; it also presses religious questions. The careful reader cannot but see that to take the Sermon seriously must involve evaluation of the status of the speaker, about whom it makes truly stupendous claims. We have here something very different from a list of moral rules or good advice that would hold apart from the identity of their presenter. One may heed the *Analects* of Confucius without paying much heed to the person of Confucius, for most of the sayings commend themselves on their own grounds. It is not so clear one can do this sort of thing with the Sermon. Although Hans Dieter Betz has sought to show that the Sermon offers arguments (often only implicit) for the positions it takes, he is not always convincing about this. Tolstoy was also not convincing when he affirmed that the Sermon contains "clear and intelligible moral precepts, which commend themselves to everyone" (*What I Believe*, 84). The truth seems rather to be that the authority of the speaker adds to its plausibility and is indeed, so to speak, part of its argument.

Certainly the Sermon does not obviously appeal to our common sense. Those of us who have grown up in the Christian West may perhaps be so used to it that we fail to see how counterintuitive and extreme it is. Is "Love your enemies" truly good advice? Socrates wanted Athenian citizens to love Athenian citizens; but he did not want them to love slaves and barbarians. One understands why. Loving outsiders, especially enemies, would appear, on the face of it, to be disaster. Gandhi's infamous letter to the Jews of Hitler's Germany, in which he told them in effect to love their enemies, has not been thought very practical; many have found it an offense. More recently some feminists have wondered about Jesus' teaching on nonresistance and its possible deleterious effects upon women in situations of domestic violence. Whether their complaints are valid is something that need not be decided here. The point is simply that one can dispute much of the Sermon on ostensibly plausible grounds. A famous Jewish scholar once told me that he found Jesus' teaching on lust in 5:27–30 to be utter nonsense: it is a futile polemic against hormones, a vain arguing with biological facts. How, he said, can men not desire women?

The Sermon on the Mount does not directly answer these and other like objections that can be raised against it. But it does perhaps indirectly deal with them—by confronting us with the authority of the speaker. The Sermon presents Jesus as an eschatological prophet and one like Moses who has the integrity to embody his speech and will even play a role in the eschatological assize. And the remainder of Matthew reveals that Jesus is God's revealer. "All things have been handed over to me by my Father; and no one knows the Son except the Father, and no one knows the Father except the Son and anyone to whom the Son chooses to reveal him" (11:27). This declaration, which is part of the wider context of the Sermon, means that Jesus is a channel, indeed the supreme channel, of divine revelation. To take such a claim seriously requires that one wrestle with the Sermon, even if there are things within it that puzzle or do not appeal to common sense.

FOR FURTHER READING

Allison, Dale C., Jr. *The New Moses: A Matthean Typology.* Philadelphia: Fortress, 1993.

Davies, W. D. *The Setting of the Sermon on the Mount.* Cambridge: Cambridge University Press, 1964.

Dibelius, Martin. *The Sermon on the Mount.* New York: Charles Scribner's Sons, 1940.

Dods, Marcus, James Denney, and James Moffatt. *The Literal Interpretation of the Sermon on the Mount.* London: Hodder & Stoughton, 1904.

Luz, Ulrich. *Matthew 1–7.* Minneapolis: Fortress, 1989.

Müller, Johannes. *Die Bergpredigt verdeutscht und vergegenwärtigt.* Munich: Oskar Beck, 1906.

Thurneysen, E. *The Sermon on the Mount.* Richmond: John Knox, 1964.

Tolstoy, Leo. *What I Believe.* London: Elliot Stock, 1885.

Windisch, Hans. *The Meaning of the Sermon on the Mount: A Contribution to the Historical Understanding of the Gospels and to the Problem of Their True Exegesis.* Philadelphia: Westminster, 1950.

2

The Structure of the Sermon on the Mount and Its Meaning

APART FROM THE WOES (Luke 6:24–26) and two short proverbs (Luke 6:39–40), all of the units in Luke's Sermon on the Plain have parallels in Matthew's Sermon on the Mount, and even the two proverbs appear elsewhere in Matthew (10:24–25; 15:14). Indeed, all of the materials common to the two sermons, with the sole exception of the golden rule, are in the same order:

Luke 6:20a	cf. Matt. 5:1–2
Luke 6:20b–23	cf. Matt. 5:3–12
Luke 6:24–26	——
Luke 6:27–36	cf. Matt. 5:38–48; 7:12
Luke 6:37–38	cf. Matt. 7:1
Luke 6:39	(cf. Matt. 15:14)
Luke 6:40	(cf. Matt. 10:24–25)
Luke 6:41–42	cf. Matt. 7:3–5
Luke 6:43–45	cf. Matt. 7:16–18
Luke 6:46	cf. Matt. 7:21
Luke 6:47–49	cf. Matt. 7:24–27
Luke 7:1	cf. Matt. 7:28–8:1

Luke 6:20–49 is usually regarded as a speech that Luke only lightly retouched: it brings us very close to part of an old source (conventionally called "Q") that both Matthew and Luke used in constructing their sermons. The Sermon on the Mount, on the other hand, is most commonly attributed to the author of the rest of the Gospel. Drawing upon Mark, Q, and distinctive traditions, our evangelist forged a new

discourse in accord with his own interests. On this account the Sermon is not the transcript of one of Jesus' sermons but, in Calvin's words, "a brief summary of the doctrine of Christ . . . collected out of his many and various discourses" (*Commentary*, 259). Modern scholars would only add that one must investigate the history of each saying to determine whether it goes back to Jesus. But however interesting such investigation is, our focus herein will be on the Sermon as it stands.

BEGINNING AND END

The Sermon on the Mount opens with a short narrative introduction (4:23–5:2) and ends with a brief narrative conclusion (7:28–8:1). The two units clearly correspond to each other, for the latter takes up the vocabulary of the former:

4:23-5:2	7:28-8:1
"great crowds followed him"	"great crowds followed him"
"the mountain"	"the mountain"
"going up"	"going down"
"teaching"	"teaching"

Moreover, when 7:28 tells us that Jesus "finished these words," this is the closing counterpart of 5:2, "opening his mouth."

Two results—one literary, the other theological—follow from the observation that 4:23–5:2 and 7:28–8:1 mirror one another. First, it is evident that the two corresponding units mark off 5:3–7:27 as a distinct literary unit. This in turn means that the simplest outline of the Sermon is this triad: Introduction (4:23–5:2), Discourse (5:3–7:27), Conclusion (7:28–8:1).

The second result is that if indeed 4:23–5:2 is the introduction to the Sermon, then it can help us with interpretation. Often expression has been given to the conviction that the Sermon on the Mount is unremitting in its requirements, that it does nothing more than make demands. But this overlooks, among other things, the role of 4:23–5:2. For this last tells us that the Sermon was addressed not only to the disciples but also to "the crowds," and that among these crowds were people who had been healed by Jesus: he went throughout Galilee "curing every disease and every sickness among the people . . . and they brought to him all the sick, those who were afflicted with various diseases and pains, demoniacs, epileptics, and paralytics, and he cured them." So before Jesus makes any demands, he shows his compassion by healing the sick among the crowds. The act is pure grace, for the crowds have done nothing. The implicit lesson is that grace comes before task, succor before demand. Jesus' first act is not the imposition of difficult imperatives but the selfless service of others. Today's command presupposes yesterday's gift.

BLESSINGS AND WARNINGS

Following the narrative introduction, Jesus' first words are the beatitudes, the nine sentences that open with "Blessed are . . . ." Whether there is any significance to the number nine is unclear. Further, although attempts have been made, no one has yet succeeded in discovering the key to the arrangement of the nine sentences. The one sure fact is that the last beatitude (5:11–12) is much the longest and in other respects different from the rest. Whereas the first eight all have "Blessed are the . . . for theirs/they," 5:11–12 has "Blessed are *you* when" plus a command ("rejoice and be glad"). We have here a rhetorical convention, for there are other ancient texts—including collections of beatitudes—which add emphasis to the concluding member of a series by making it long and irregular (see 4Q525; *1 Enoch* 99:10–15; Matt. 1:2–16; 23:13–36; Luke 6:24–26, 37–38; *1 Clement* 13.2; Polycarp, *Letter* 2.3; *Didache* 1.3–5; *Acts of Paul and Thecla* 5–6; *2 Enoch* 42:6–14 J).

In one respect the beatitudes function similarly to 4:23–5:2. For they too speak the language of grace. Matt. 5:3–12 does not, as we shall see, so much list the entrance requirements for the kingdom as it offers comfort to the saints, to the poor in spirit, to those hungering and thirsting after righteousness. The first half of each beatitude depicts the community's present; the second half foretells the community's future; and the juxtaposition of the two radically different situations permits the trials of everyday life to be muted by contemplation of the world to come. This hardly excludes the implicit moral demand: one is certainly called to become what the beatitudes praise. But Matthew's beatitudes are not formally imperatives. Like the eschatological blessings in 13:16 as well as Rev. 19:9 and 22:14, they offer hope and indeed function as a practical theodicy. Although there is no explanation of evil, the imagination, through contemplation of God's future, discovers hope and so finds the present tolerable. In other words, before readers face Jesus' hard imperatives they are built up, encouraged, consoled.

One cannot fail to see that the promises paint a very happy picture indeed of the disciples' future in the kingdom of heaven. The congregation of the righteous will inherit the earth (5:5), see God (5:8), and receive a grand and glorious reward (5:12). One also cannot fail to see that none of these things could be obtained by purely human effort. If they are to be gained at all it is only because they will have been given. The beatitudes proclaim that someday God will give human beings what they cannot obtain for themselves on their own. Again the lesson is grace.

If Jesus' commands come after beatitudes, they are in turn followed by stern warnings. Matt. 7:13–14 (on the two ways), 7:15–23 (on false prophets), and 7:24–27 (on hearers and doers of the word) confront readers with strong exhortations that underscore the importance of doing the will of the Father in heaven as this is set forth in 5:13–7:12. "Enter through the narrow gate" means one must follow the way set forth in the Sermon. "Beware of false prophets" means that one must pay heed to the truth as revealed by Jesus and not be deceived by those whose teachings contradict it. Lastly, one must be like the wise who built upon rock, that is, one must hear Jesus' words and do them. There is a path to perdition. There are heretical teachers. And there are fools whose destiny is destruction. Obviously the grace of the Sermon does not mean one can take it easy. Grace is rather the strength to do the difficult.

Salt and Light

Between the introductory eschatological blessings (5:3–12) and the concluding eschatological warnings (7:13–27) are three major sections, each one primarily a compilation of imperatives: Jesus and the Torah (5:17–48), Jesus and the cult (6:1–18), Jesus and social issues (6:19–7:12; the first and third of these sections, incidentally, are almost exactly the same length and may balance each other as part of a chiastic scheme;

see below). But preceding these segments are the prefatory parables about salt, light, and lamp (5:13–16). It is not the Torah or the temple or Jerusalem or Israel that is said to be the salt or light of the world (as in Isa. 60:1–3; Bar. 4:2; and Babylonian Talmud *Berakhot* 28b) but Jesus' followers. As the second-century *Epistle of Diognetus* has it, "What the soul is in a body, this the Christians are in the world."

But Matthew's words do not tell us how to become salt or light or lamp, nor exactly what those things mean. This is because the sayings together constitute a transitional passage that functions as a general heading for 5:17–7:12, where those issues are addressed. Matt. 5:13–16 moves readers from the life of the blessed future (depicted in 5:3–12) to the demands of the present, and so the theme switches from gift to task.

JESUS AND THE MOSAIC TORAH (5:17–48)

The next major section of the Sermon concerns Jesus and the Mosaic Torah (5:17–48). Its structure is manifest: six paragraphs are prefaced by a general introduction (5:17–20). The introduction has two functions, one positive, one negative. Negatively, 5:17–20 looks forward and anticipates an incorrect interpretation of 5:21–48, namely, that Jesus' words contradict Moses. That is, 5:17–20 introduces 5:21–48 and declares that the paragraphs that have so often been labeled "antitheses" are not antitheses but, in Pinchas Lapide's words, "supertheses." They "deepen, intensify, and radicalize the biblical commandments" (*Sermon*, 46). Matthew's Jesus does not overturn Moses or set believers free from the law. Alternative interpretations of 5:17–20 are often motivated by a desire to bring Matthew closer to Paul and Mark and our own theological sentiments. But the New Testament appears to have more than one judgment on the status of the Torah, and we should read Matthew on its own terms.

Positively, 5:20 announces what 5:21–48 is really all about—the greater righteousness, a righteousness that goes beyond that of the scribes and Pharisees. This is indeed the clue to right interpretation. Matt. 5:20, in announcing that the righteousness of disciples must exceed that of the Jewish leaders, anticipates that Jesus' words in the subsequent paragraphs will require even more than the Torah itself and Jewish tradition require. At the same time, 5:17–18 means that the tension between Jesus' teaching and the Mosaic law is not that those who accept the former will transgress the latter; rather it is that they will achieve far more than they would if the Torah were their only guide.

Regarding 5:21–48, the section falls into two triads: 5:21–26 + 27–30 + 31–32 make up one subsection, 5:33–37 + 38–42 + 43–48 another. One can see this at a glance:

First triadic set:
   "You have heard that it was said to those of ancient times"
      Citation of Scripture (Exod. 20:13; Deut. 5:17)
         "But I say to you that"
   "You have heard that it was said" (*abbreviated formula*)
      Citation of Scripture (Exod. 20:14; Deut. 5:18)
         "But I say to you that"
   "It was also said" (*abbreviated formula*)
      Citation of Scripture (Deut. 24:1–4)
         "But I say to you that"

Second triadic set:
   "Again,
   you have heard that it was said to those of ancient times"
      Citation of Scripture (Lev. 19:2)
         "But I say to you" + imperative
   "You have heard that it was said" (*abbreviated formula*)
      Citation of Scripture (Exod. 21:24; Lev. 24:20; Deut. 19:21)
         "But I say to you" + imperative
   "You have heard that it was said" (*abbreviated formula*)
      Citation of Scripture (Lev. 19:18)
         "But I say to you" + imperative

These six paragraphs have generated many conflicting interpretations, but four propositions seem more probable than not. First, 5:21–48 does not set Jesus' words over against Jewish *interpretations* of the Mosaic law. Rather there is contrast with the Bible itself. "You have heard that it was said to those of ancient times" refers to Sinai. This is why, in each instance, Scripture is cited.

Second, although Jesus' words are contrasted with the Torah, the two are not contradictory—unless one wishes to overlook the plain sense of 5:17–20. As confirmation it may be observed that if one were to obey 5:21–48 one would not find oneself breaking any law of Moses. Thus, one who does not divorce or take an oath hardly does anything against pentateuchal law.

Third, 5:21–48 is not exactly Jesus' interpretation of the Torah. The declaration that remarriage is adultery, for example, is set forth as a new teaching grounded not in exegesis but in Jesus' authority. The same is true of the imperative not to swear at all.

Finally, the main point of 5:21–48 seems to be that the six paragraphs illustrate, through concrete examples, what sort of attitude and behavior Jesus requires and how his demands surpass those of the Torah without contradicting the Torah. For example, in 5:21–26 we are reminded that Moses prescribed punishment for murder. Obviously Jesus does not approve of murder. But the hyperbolic equation of murder with anger (also found in Jewish tradition) shifts attention from the outward act to the inward state and makes anger and harsh words grievous sins to be exorcised at all costs. Here Jesus is asking for more than the Decalogue without overthrowing the Decalogue. It is similar in 5:27–30. Jesus' prohibition of lust and its equation with adultery do not contradict the biblical injunction against adultery (Exod. 20:14; Deut. 5:18), for Jesus himself speaks against this sin (5:32; 15:19; 19:9). Rather does he pass beyond the Decalogue to require more: 5:27–30 at once upholds and supplements the law. While the verses assume that the external act is evil, no less evil is the intention that brings it forth, and "it is each one's intention that is examined" (*Pseudo-Phocylides* 52).

ALMSGIVING, PRAYER, AND FASTING (6:1–18)

While the subject of 5:21–48 is Jesus and the Torah, in 6:1–18 the cult becomes the subject. The former has mostly to do with actions, the latter with intentions. That is, 6:1–18 is a sort of commentary on 5:21–48. Having been told what to do, one now learns how to do it.

The little "cult-didache" (Betz) opens with a general statement of principle (cf. the introductory function of 5:17–20). Righteousness is not to be done in order to be seen by others (cf. Rom. 2:28–29); right deeds must come from right intention, which involves humility and self-forgetfulness (6:1). The idea is elaborated upon in the three subsequent paragraphs. The first is on almsgiving, the second on prayer, the third on fasting. Each opens with a declaration of subject (6:2a, 5a, 16a), follows with a prohibition of wrong practice (6:2b, 5b, 16b), and ends with instruction on proper practice (6:3–4, 6, 17–18).

The structure of the Sermon on the Mount's second major section

(6:1–18) is remarkably like the first major section (5:17–48). Both have a general introduction with the key word "righteousness." In both this is followed by specific examples (5:21–48; 6:2–18). Further, the examples in both, which consistently begin in similar fashion ("[You have heard that] it was said" for 5:21–48; "Whenever you" + verb for 6:1–18), are formulated with contrasts between traditional teachings and Jesus' instruction. And while the positive statements in 5:21–48 commence with "But I say to you," those in 6:2–18 are introduced by "Amen I say to you." The only major structural difference between 5:17–48 and 6:1–18 is that whereas the former has six (3 + 3) examples, the latter has only three:

> The Christian cult
>   i. General principle (6:1)
>   ii. A triad of specific instruction (6:2–18)
>   a. Almsgiving (6:2–4)
>   b. Prayer (6:5–15)
>   c. Fasting (6:16–18)

SOCIAL ISSUES

The four paragraphs that follow 6:1–18 have to do with earthly treasure—vv. 19–21 with not storing it up, vv. 22–23 with being generous, v. 24 with serving God instead of mammon, and vv. 25–34 with not being anxious about food and clothing.

Matt. 6:19–24 contains three antitheses—earth/heaven (6:19–21), darkness/light (6:22–23), mammon (= wealth)/God (6:24). The focus of the first antithesis is the heart ("where your treasure is, there your heart will be also"), the second the eye ("the eye is the lamp of the body"), the third service ("you cannot service God and wealth"). The determination of the heart to store up treasure in heaven or on earth creates either inner light or darkness, while the resultant state of one's "eye" (= intent) moves one to serve either God or mammon. So one's treasure tells the tale of one's heart.

Matt. 6:24–34 follows 6:19–23 as encouragement follows demand. The command to serve God instead of mammon, especially when interpreted in the light of the rest of the Gospel (e.g., 5:39–42; 19:16–30), is excruciatingly difficult, and its observance will bring insecurity. So 6:24–34 is the pastor's addendum: it is respite from the storm that is the Sermon on the Mount. Those who undertake the hard demands of the Gospel have a Father in heaven who gives good gifts to his children.

In 7:1–12 we now turn from one social issue, what to do with and about mammon (6:19–34), to another, how to treat one's neighbor. The new subject opens with the imperative not to judge or condemn. This is not a prohibition of simple ethical judgments but rather a way of calling for mercy, humility, and tolerance. The verses about the "speck" (not "mote") and the "log" (7:3–5) continue the theme of vv. 1–2 but focus on hypocrisy. But v. 6, which tells us not to give what is holy to dogs, is notoriously difficult. Some have even thought it without meaning in its present context. The point, however, is probably that if there must not be too much severity (vv. 1–5), there must at the same time not be too much laxity (v. 6)—even if we cannot determine what or even whether "your pearls" stands for any particular thing.

Matt. 7:7–11 follows. It is the twin of 6:24–34. Both follow an exhortation (6:19–21; 7:1–2), a parable on the eye (6:22–23; 7:3–5), and a second parable (6:24; 7:6), and both refer to the heavenly Father's care for his own. Both also argue from the lesser to the greater and offer encouragement for those bombarded by the hard instruction in the rest of the Sermon (cf. the rhetoric of 10:16–23 and its function within the missionary discourse). Given all this and the other triads of the Sermon, one is sorely tempted to see in the section on social issues two parallel sections reminiscent of the two parallel sections in 5:21–48:

Three Imperatives

exhortation, 6:19–21	7:1–2, exhortation
parable on the eye, 6:22–23	7:3–5, parable on the eye
second parable, 6:24	7:6, second parable

Encouragement

the Father's care, 6:25–33	7:7–11, the Father's care

On this analysis, the breaking of the triads reminds one of the broken sevens in Revelation.

However that may be, the so-called golden rule brings to a climax the central section of the Sermon on the Mount (5:17–7:12). Mention of "the law and the prophets" creates an inclusion within which Matthew has treated the law, the cult, and social issues. Matt. 7:12 is then, in good rabbinic fashion, a general rule that is the quintessence not only of the Law and the Prophets but also of the Sermon on the Mount. Interpreted within the Gospel as a whole, it is certainly not an expression of "naive egoism" (Rudolf Bultmann); nor is it even an expression of "common sense" or "natural law" (Theophylact). Rather, the golden rule means living the commandments of Jesus on behalf of all other people.

The preceding discussion leads to an outline of the Sermon very much like that proposed by Ulrich Luz in his commentary on Matthew. See the chart on the next page. Perhaps we do not go wrong to see a chiastic arrangement running through the whole (see Dumais, *Le Sermon*, 88–89):

Introduction (5:1–2)
    Blessings (5:3–12)
        Law and Prophets (5:17–20)
            Jesus and Torah (two triads) (5:21–48)
                Almsgiving, Prayer, Fasting (6:1–4)
            Social issues (two triads) (6:19–7:11)
        Law and Prophets (7:12)
    Warnings (7:13–27)
Conclusion (7:28–8:1)

On this analysis, the Lord's Prayer, which is at the center of the section on prayer, is at the very center of the Sermon on the Mount as a whole. One wonders whether Matthew did not design it to be so.

THE TRIADS OF THE SERMON ON THE MOUNT

Perhaps the most striking fact about the arrangement of the Sermon is the author's use of triads. As we have seen, the Sermon addresses three major topics—Jesus and the Torah, Jesus and the cult, and Jesus and social issues. Matt. 5:21–48 contains two series of triads. The section on the cult treats three issues—almsgiving, prayer, and fasting. Matt. 6:19–24 and 7:1–6 contain three sets of related imperatives. Even Matthew's version of the Lord's Prayer (unlike Luke's version) contains three "your" petitions ("hallowed be your name, your kingdom come, your will be done") and three "us" petitions ("give us this day our daily bread, and forgive us our debts . . . . do not bring us to the time of trial but rescue us from the evil one"). See the chart on p. 38.

```
┌──────────────────────────────────────────────────────────────┐
│  5:1–2              Framework              7:28–8:1            │
│  Situation                          Reaction of the hearers   │
│  ┌──────────────────────────────────────────────────────┐   │
│  │  5:3–12                                 7:13–27         │   │
│  │  Blessings                              Warnings        │   │
│  │  ┌────────────────────────────────────────────────┐  │   │
│  │  │              5:13–16                              │  │   │
│  │  │  Heading for Body of Sermon on the Mount:         │  │   │
│  │  │    general description of discipleship            │  │   │
│  │  │                                                   │  │   │
│  │  │              Main section                         │  │   │
│  │  │  5:17–20                              7:12         │  │   │
│  │  │  Introduction                      Conclusion     │  │   │
│  │  │  ┌──────────────────────────────────────────┐   │  │   │
│  │  │  │       The Law and the Prophets             │   │  │   │
│  │  │  │  5:21–48                 6:19–7:11          │   │  │   │
│  │  │  │  Jesus and Torah       Social issues        │   │  │   │
│  │  │  │  ┌────────────────────────────────────┐  │   │  │   │
│  │  │  │  │       The Christian cult             │  │   │  │   │
│  │  │  │  │  6:1–6           6:16–18             │  │   │  │   │
│  │  │  │  │  Almsgiving     Fasting              │  │   │  │   │
│  │  │  │  │                                      │  │   │  │   │
│  │  │  │  │       6:7–15                          │  │   │  │   │
│  │  │  │  │     Prayer and                        │  │   │  │   │
│  │  │  │  │   the Lord's Prayer                   │  │   │  │   │
│  │  │  │  └────────────────────────────────────┘  │   │  │   │
│  │  │  └──────────────────────────────────────────┘   │  │   │
│  │  └────────────────────────────────────────────────┘  │   │
│  └──────────────────────────────────────────────────────┘   │
└──────────────────────────────────────────────────────────────┘
```

These triads are plainly the product of a compositional habit of Matthew, for elsewhere in the First Gospel he arranges things in threes. The Gospel opens, for instance, with a genealogy that is explicitly divided into three parts (1:17). The miracle stories in chapters 8–9 are artificially arranged into three clusters of three: (i) 8:1–4, 5–13, 14–15; (ii) 8:23–27, 28–34; 9:1–8; (iii) 9:18–26, 27–31, 32–34. In chapter 13 the three parables of the tares, mustard seed, and leaven are given a common introductory formula, and the three parables of the treasure, pearl, and net are prefaced by a different introductory formula which unites them into a second set of three parables.

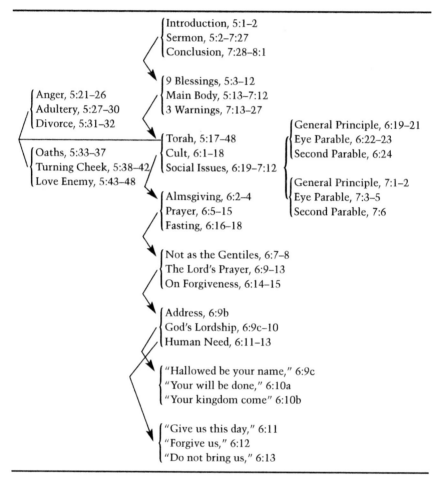

Matthew's proclivity for the triad is nothing unusual. Tripartite structures appear throughout the Bible and world literature. The plagues of Exodus group themselves into three sets of three plus a climactic tenth. Triads are the key to the arrangement of Leviticus 1–7. Paul used triads in constructing 1 Corinthians 13 and in compiling the list of the "fruits of the Spirit" in Gal. 5:22–23. Col. 3:18–4:1 contains six matching instructions in three parts (wives and husbands, children and fathers, slaves and master). And Thomas Fielding's *History of Tom Jones* contains three large sections of six chapters each. Triads help us to order our thoughts. Freud found it convenient to divide the mind into the id, ego, and superego.

In Matthew's world the triad may have been particularly popular due to its common use to structure oral materials. There is no denying that arranging things in threes helps the memory and enables one to repeat something learned. This is why fairy tales are so often full of threes. Jack goes up the beanstalk three times. The three little pigs have three sorts of houses. And Goldilocks meets three bears—who have three bowls of porridge, three chairs, and three beds. In Matthew's case, it seems likely enough that he used triads as a way of mentally composing his book before he wrote it out. He probably worked as did Plotinus, according to Porphyry: "He used to work out his design mentally from first to last. When he came to set down his ideas he wrote out at once all he had stored in his mind as though he were copying from a book" (Porphyry, *Life of Plotinus* 8).

But there may be more than this to the Sermon's triads. Matthew's Gospel shows some significant points of contact with early rabbinic Judaism, and this matters because our sources for that Judaism show us that great rabbis from days gone by were often remembered as having said three things. The first chapter of tractate *ʾAbot* in the Mishnah contains, for example, the following traditions:

> Jose b. Johanan of Jerusalem said:
>> Let your house be open wide
>>> and let the needy be members of your household
>>> and talk not much with women.

> Shammai said:
>> Make your study of the Torah a fixed habit;
>>> say little and do much,
>>> and receive all men with a cheerful countenance.

> Rabban Gamaliel said:
>> Get yourself a teacher
>>> and remove yourself from doubt
>>> and do not tithe overmuch by guesswork.

Of all the general maxims preserved in *ʾAbot* 1, perhaps the most famous is that attributed to Simeon the Just, a rabbi of the Maccabean period. He is purported to have said this:

> Upon three things the world stands:
>> upon Torah,
>>> upon temple service,
>>> and upon deeds of loving kindness.

According to this, three things matter most: the Torah, the cult, and pious social acts of a benevolent character. W. D. Davies was evidently the first to observe that this triad outlines the major sections of the Sermon on the Mount. Matthew 5–7 addresses the same three fundamental issues—the law, the cult, and social behavior—and it addresses them in precisely the same order. Is the Sermon then a Christian interpretation of the three traditional pillars?

This seems to be a good guess, although certainty is beyond us. During the period when Matthew was written, namely, the last quarter of the first century A.D., Simeon's three famous pillars were, if we may trust the rabbinic sources, seemingly being discussed and reinterpreted. The reason was that the temple lay in ruins. This made the central member of Simeon's triad problematic. How could Judaism rest upon the Torah, the temple cult, and deeds of loving kindness if the temple had been demolished by the Roman army? The obvious question generated reinterpretation. Thus, Johanan ben Zakkai, citing Hos. 6:6 ("I desire steadfast love and not sacrifice"), is reported to have said that the temple cult with its sacrifices had been replaced by deeds of loving-kindness.

Now because Matthew comes from the same time as Johanan, and because his Gospel otherwise seems to show knowledge of and involvement with emergent rabbinic Judaism, it might be unwise to regard the correlation between the structure of the Sermon on the Mount and Simeon's foundational statement as coincidence. The Sermon may rather have been constructed as a Christian version of Simeon's three pillars, that is, a Christian version of what matters most. On this reading, Jesus' teaching on Torah, his words about almsgiving, and his commandments concerning social behavior constitute the things upon which the world stands.

FOR FURTHER READING

Allison, Dale C., Jr. "The Structure of the Sermon on the Mount." *Journal of Biblical Literature* 106 (1987): 423–45.

Davies, W. D. *The Setting of the Sermon on the Mount.* Cambridge: Cambridge University Press, 1964.

Luz, Ulrich. *Matthew 1–7.* Minneapolis: Fortress, 1989. Pp. 210–13.

Scott, Bernard Brandon, and Margaret E. Dean. "A Sound Map of the Sermon on the Mount." In *Society of Biblical Literature 1993 Seminar Papers,* edited by Eugene H. Lovering, Jr., 672–725. Atlanta: Scholars Press, 1993.

Syreeni, Kari. *The Making of the Sermon on the Mount: A Procedural Analysis of Matthew's Redactional Activity, Part I, Methodology and Compositional Analysis.* Helsinki: Suomalainen Tiedeakatemia, 1987.

3

Blessings

LTHOUGH MATT. 5:3–12 IS OFTEN thought of as containing "the beatitudes," ancient Jewish and Christian writings contain numerous "beatitudes" or blessings. Not only does Luke, in his Sermon on the Plain, have four blessings with close parallels in Matt. 5:3–12, but there are beatitudes elsewhere in Matthew (11:6; 13:16; 16:17; 24:46), and the Jewish Scriptures and the New Testament are otherwise full of them.

Biblical beatitudes generally fall into two types. There are, first of all, those that bless God. The most obvious examples are the standard Jewish prayers that begin with "Blessed art Thou, O Lord our God . . . ." The other type blesses not God but human beings. Gen. 30:13 ("And Leah said, 'Happy am I! For the women will call me happy'") and Ps. 1:1–2 ("Happy are those who do not follow the advice of the wicked . . .") are illustrations.

The beatitudes that have human beings as their object can in turn be divided into two classes. One class speaks of people who are blessed because of their present circumstances. Prov. 3:13 ("Happy are those who find wisdom, and those who get understanding") and Ps. 32:1 ("Happy are those whose transgressions are forgiven, whose sin is covered") supply examples of the first sort. The second sort blesses individuals because of what lies in store for them in the future. Tob. 13:14 ("Blessed are those who grieved over all your [Jerusalem's] afflictions; for they will rejoice for you upon seeing all your glory, and they will be made glad for ever") and *1 Enoch* 58:2–3 ("Blessed are you, righteous and elect ones, for glorious is your portion") are instances of this second class.

The beatitudes in Matthew belong to this last category—a fact crucial for interpretation. In 5:3–12 Jesus blesses believers because of what lies in store for them. This explains the future tenses—"will be comforted," "will inherit the earth," "will be filled," "will receive mercy." We have here not commonsense wisdom born of experience but eschatological promise which foresees the unprecedented: the evils of the present will be undone and the righteous will be confirmed with reward. The first part of each blessing describes the believers' present, whereas the second half represents "anticipated eschatological verdicts" (Betz):

Present condition	*Future condition*
poor in spirit	possess kingdom
mourn	obtain comfort
meek	inherit the earth
desire righteousness	obtain satisfaction
merciful	obtain mercy
pure in heart	see God
peacemakers	sons of God
persecuted	possess kingdom
oppressed	great reward

The right-hand column in its entirety is a picture of the blessed future, which can be summarily characterized as experiencing in its fullness "the kingdom of heaven."

It is true that we find a present tense in both the first and eighth beatitudes ("for theirs *is* [*estin*] the kingdom of heaven"). The emphasis, however, obviously lies upon things to come. So we should probably explain the two present tenses as expressions of certainty: the surety of the saints' possession of the kingdom is underlined by use of a proleptic present. Greek can use a present tense to indicate a circumstance which, although it has not yet occurred, is regarded as so certain that it is spoken as having already happened—as in Matt. 26:2: "the Son of man is handed over to be crucified." The very last line in Matthew's beatitudes—"for your reward is great in heaven, for in the same way they persecuted the prophets who were before you"—illustrates the point nicely. Although reward is yet to be bestowed, its secure reality is here conveyed through a present tense. This is probably how we should interpret "theirs is the kingdom of heaven."

If the second half of each beatitude sees a wrong undone or a good rewarded, it often does this through a reversal of ordinary values. Although few in the ancient world would have opposed mercy or peacemaking, it was obviously no good thing to mourn. Nor did "poor" or "meek" or "thirst" or "hunger" always have better connotations then than now, and in no time or place do normal people wish to be persecuted or reviled. So in 5:3–12 Jesus takes up words with negative connotations and associates them with the saints. Chrysostom saw the truth: "What could be newer than these injunctions wherein the very things which all others avoid, these he declares to be desirable? I mean being poor, mourning, persecution, and evil reputation. . . . And hearing things so grievous and galling, so contrary to the accustomed ways of human beings, the multitudes were astonished" (*Commentary on Matthew* 15.7).

We are so used to hearing the beatitudes that usually we miss this dimension. Originally the beatitudes were intended to startle. Simple observation of the world as it is informs us that the rich, not the poor, are blessed; that those who are happy, not those who mourn, are blessed; that those who have power, not the meek, are blessed; that those who are filled, not the hungry and thirsty, are blessed; and that those who are well treated, not those who are persecuted, are blessed. So the beatitudes have things backward. To take them seriously is to call into question our ordinary values.

Popular books on the Sermon on the Mount often spend much time exploring the meaning of the Greek word traditionally translated "blessed" in the standard English Bibles but now rendered "happy" in the New Revised Standard Version (NRSV). There is, however, nothing much mysterious here, no need to hunt for some special signification. "Blessed" is just the opposite of "woe," as in "Woe to you, Capernaum" (11:23). The Greek word (*makarios*) is a way of expressing a good fortune which, because it is known, brings joy. "Fortunate are the poor in spirit" would be as accurate a translation as "Blessed are the poor in spirit" or "Happy are the poor in spirit."

Matthew's beatitudes have often been viewed as imperatives, and there is truth in this, above all for the fifth, sixth, and seventh beatitudes. After hearing the merciful, the peacemakers, and the pure in heart promised reward, one cannot avoid the implicit obligation to be pure in heart and to be a peacemaker. This is all the more true given the correlations between the beatitudes and imperatives elsewhere in the Sermon. For instance, if 5:6 praises those who hunger and thirst after righteousness, 5:20 demands a righteousness greater than that of the scribes and Pharisees. And if 5:7 praises those who show mercy, 6:12 enjoins forgiving our debtors.

But in Matthew's beatitudes the ethical thrust does not eliminate or even overshadow the elements of consolation and promise. This is evident above all in 5:10–12, verses that bless the persecuted. Being persecuted is hardly a virtue in and of itself, nor can it be obtained on one's own, nor is it normally something to be exhorted to. So in 5:10–12 the faithful are not being called to behave any differently than they are now; rather are they being offered consolation in their present trying circumstance.

In this connection our examination of the structure of the Sermon is relevant. The beatitudes come between 4:23–5:2 and 5:13–16. The former serves to put Jesus' harsh demands within a context of grace: before exhorting, Jesus heals. The latter is the general heading for what follows: the disciples are to be salt and light. So structurally the beatitudes come before the detailed commands of the Sermon proper; that is, they are separated from the main body of imperatives. This is because 5:3–12 functions less as demand than as blessing. It is only after hearing the comforting words of 5:3–12, words that tell of rewards that human beings cannot create for themselves but can only receive as gifts from God, that one is confronted by the Messiah's demands. So when Jesus speaks in 5:3–12, the chief result is not the burdening of the faithful with moral imperatives. Rather, 5:3–12 instead brings solace. By exhibiting to the religious imagination the good things of the life to come, it compensates those who are, because of their commitment to Jesus, suffering in this world.

THE INDIVIDUAL BEATITUDES

Discussions of the first beatitude, "Blessed are the poor in spirit, for theirs is the kingdom of heaven" (5:3), usually focus on the meaning of the peculiar phrase "poor in spirit." The words (which seem to appear in no old Greek text except Matthew and literature dependent on Matthew) do not mean "poor-spirited," "fainthearted," or "despondent." Nor do they refer to literal poverty ("poor through one's spirit" or "poor through the Holy Spirit")—although Luke's parallel (which is generally the preferred version of those battling the evils of poverty) has such in mind (6:20). "Poor in spirit" rather refers to those who acknowledge their spiritual need: they are (whatever their socioeconomic situation) beggars before God and have accordingly abandoned human ambition (cf. Hilary, *Commentary on Matthew* 4.2). "Poor in spirit" is close in meaning to "humble" (cf. Augustine, *On the Sermon on the Mount* 1.3). Albert Nolan puts it this way: the word "'poor' can be extended to cover all the oppressed, all those who are dependent upon the mercy of others. And this . . . is why the word can even be extended to all those who rely entirely upon the mercy of God—the poor in spirit (Matt 5:3)" (*Jesus*, 29). Gustavo Gutiérrez says that our beatitude is about "spiritual childhood," by which he means the state of dependence on and openness to the will of God (*God of Life*, 121).

This beatitude is difficult for many today because of the modern focus on what is called "self-esteem." By contrast, throughout exegetical history the idea that God calls people to recognize their spiritual poverty, their inner need for the transcendent, has been enthusiastically promoted. For although monastic texts often take 5:3 to praise the life of literal poverty, most interpreters, including the early fathers and the Reformers, have instead rightly found in our text the acclamation of humility. They have often done so with the observation that the beatitude with "poor in spirit" heads its list and so names the fundamental virtue (cf. Ambrose, *Commentary on Luke* ad loc.). Theophylact is typical: Jesus "lays down humility as a foundation. Since Adam fell through pride, Christ raises us up by humility; for Adam had aspired to become God. The 'poor in spirit' are those whose pride is crushed and who are contrite in soul" (*Commentary on Matthew* ad loc.). This is right interpretation—as is the patristic tendency to observe that Jesus himself is the exemplar in humility. His own declaration, in 11:29, that he is "meek and lowly in heart," makes this evident, and it means that he is included in his own beatitude, "Blessed are the poor in spirit, for theirs is the kingdom of heaven."

Although "the poor" has a "spiritual" meaning in 5:3, it has a more literal sense everywhere else in Matthew, in 11:5; 19:21; 26:9, 11. So while one hesitates to cite 5:3 in support of what we now call a preferential option for the poor, such an option can appeal to other texts in Matthew, where Jesus preaches good news to the poor (11:5) and commends giving to them (19:21). Moreover, when one takes into account that the faithful hearers of the Sermon suffer persecution (5:11–12), missionize and witness to God (5:13–16), pray for daily bread (6:11), do not serve mammon (6:24), and must trust God for basic necessities (6:25–33), so that the image we have of them is of marginal missionaries with few possessions, we are not far from Boff's claim that the poor are not just those "in need . . . but they are also the group with a historical strength, a capacity for change and a potential for evangelization" (*Church*, 10).

What is meant in 5:3 by "kingdom of heaven," a phrase that appears again in the Sermon on the Mount in 5:10, 19, 20; 6:33; 7:21? The words refer above all to the ideal, eschatological state, when, in the words of the Lord's Prayer, God's will "will be done on earth as it is in heaven." (Although some ancients [e.g., Evagrius Ponticus] and moderns [e.g., dispensationalists] have distinguished between "kingdom of God" and "kingdom of heaven," the two are synonymous; see 19:23–24.) Elsewhere in Matthew this kingdom is the center of the public proclamation of John the Baptist (3:2), Jesus himself (4:17), and the disciples (10:7). Matt. 4:17 indicates that it is near; 12:28 indicates that it has, in some manner, already come. What we appear to have in Matthew is the notion of gradual arrival (cf. Isaiah 40 and *Jubilees* 23). Many of the expectations associated with the end were fulfilled in Jesus' ministry; others were fulfilled in his death and resurrection; and others remain to be fulfilled in the future. So God's eschatological activity as ruler has already made itself manifest, and human beings can avail themselves of it. But that eschatological activity has still not conquered the world, which remains full of evil, so the Sermon instructs disciples still to pray, "Your kingdom come."

The second beatitude, "Blessed are those who mourn, for they will be comforted" (5:4), is obviously false as a statement about this life: many sad people die without consolation. But Jesus here uses eschatology to encourage those who mourn: God will indeed bring them comfort (the passive verb has God as its implicit subject). One thinks of Rev. 21:4, where it says that God will wipe away every tear from their eyes: "neither shall there be mourning nor crying nor pain any more, for the former things have passed away."

But what causes the saints to mourn? Although Augustine suggested that it is because of the earthly things they gave up when they became Christians (*Sermon on the Mount* 1.5; cf. Cyril of Alexandria, *Commentary on Luke* 28), the dominant answer in exegetical history is sin. In Theophylact's words, believers mourn "for their sins, not for things of this life. Christ said, 'They that mourn,' that is, they that are mourning incessantly and not just one time; and not only for our own sins, but for those of our neighbor" (*Commentary on Matthew* ad loc.; so too Hilary, *Commentary on Matthew* 4.3).

Here, however, the tradition is likely wrong. The key to mourning is probably to be found in the scriptural allusion. As observed above on p. 16, 5:4 draws upon Isa. 61:2: "to proclaim the year of the Lord's favor, and the day of vengeance of our God: to comfort all who mourn." In the Isaiah passage Israel is oppressed at the hands of its heathen captors; its cities are in ruins; its people know shame and dishonor. So God's own are on the bottom, their enemies on top. Mourning is heard because the righteous suffer, the wicked prosper, and God has not yet righted the situation (cf. Rev. 6:9–11). It is the same in the Sermon on the Mount. The kingdom has not yet fully come. The saints are reviled and persecuted (5:10–12). The meek have not yet inherited the earth (5:5). The righteous still have enemies (5:43–48) who misuse them (5:38–42). In short, God's will is not yet done on earth as it is in heaven (6:10), and that can only mean mourning for God's people. To those who understand the truth about the present age, grief cannot be eliminated.

Gene L. Davenport brings together our beatitude and Matt. 9:15 and offers a christological interpretation: "The wedding guests cannot mourn as long as the bridegroom is with them, can they? The days will come when the bridegroom is taken away from them, and then they will fast" (*Into the Darkness*, 57). This verse interprets the post-Easter period as the time when Jesus is absent, and so mourning, in the form of fasting, is appropriate for the disciples. "By rejecting food and drink, followers of Jesus enact ceremoniously the recognition that the one who is true bread has been taken away, that he is not yet with us in the fullness of glory" (ibid.).

The third beatitude declares, "Blessed are the meek, for they shall inherit the earth" (5:5). This is nearly synonymous with the first beatitude. The "meek" are the "poor in spirit," that is, the humble whose avoidance of hubris corresponds to their powerlessness in the eyes of the world (cf. the situation of Jesus in 11:29 [Jesus is kind] and 21:5 [Jesus enters Jerusalem not on a war horse but on a donkey]). Perhaps, however, we should be wary of seeing here nothing but a passive state. Georg Strecker thinks that "Blessed are the meek" "contains an indirect summons to active deeds that fulfill the new law of Christ: active dedication to the high goal of meekness, friendliness, and gentleness— deeds that are determined not by anger, brutality, or enmity, but entirely by goodness" (*Sermon*, 36).

To "inherit the earth" is to have "the kingdom of heaven," for the ideal future state was often conceived of as possession of the land of Israel or of the entire earth. (In the latter case one might think of the inheritance as recovery of the dominion of what Adam and Eve lost; cf. Gen. 1:26–28). Once again Jesus promises that the future will reverse the present. If now the powerful rule the world, in the future the meek will have charge. This is another rendition of "The last will be first" (19:20) and "All who humble themselves will be exalted" (23:12).

Matthew 5:5 follows 5:3 in several early authorities, and there is a good chance that that was the original sequence. If so, then it is possible that 5:5, which is a quotation from Ps. 37:1 in its Greek version, was added at some point in the tradition as an attempt to clarify 5:3. It in any case offers a roughly synonymous sentence, which offers accurate exposition of 5:3.

Given Matthew's great attention to Moses (see pp. 17–19 above), it is interesting that exegetical history has associated the third beatitude, in both its parts, with Moses. In Judaism Moses was meekness' own self. As it says in Num. 12:3, "Now the man Moses was very meek, more than all men that were on the face of the earth" (cf. Ecclus. 45:4; Philo, *On the Life of Moses* 1.26; Babylonian Talmud *Nedarim* 38a). So some have illustrated the "meek" of Matt. 5:5 by remembering Moses. When Theodoret of Cyrrhus sought to characterize the "simplicity of character, gentleness of behavior, and modesty of spirit" displayed by the monk Romanus, on account of which "he emitted the radiance of divine grace" (cf. Exod. 34:29), the bishop joined Matt. 5:5 and Num. 12:3: "'Blessed are the meek, for they shall inherit the earth.' And this was the distinguishing feature of the achievements of Moses the lawgiver: 'Moses', he says, 'was very meek, more than all men that were on earth'" (*Religious History* 11.2).

Like the first half of 5:5, the second half has also cultivated memories about Moses. Eusebius commented: "Moses . . . promised a holy land and a holy life therein under a blessing to those who kept his laws; while Jesus Christ says likewise: 'Blessed are the meek, for they shall inherit the earth'" (*Demonstration of the Gospel* 3.2). For Eusebius, Matt. 5:5 brought to mind not Moses' meekness but rather Moses' role as the one who promised Israel inheritance of the land, and thus he instanced the text as belonging to the parallels between Messiah and lawgiver: both gave the same promise to their followers (cf. Deut. 4:1).

One is sorely tempted to follow the interpretive lead of Theodoret and Eusebius and set Matt. 5:5 against the Moses traditions. Moses was, in meekness, the exemplar. He promised the Israelites inheritance of the land. *And he himself did not enter the land.* From this last fact, sufficiently unexpected to have engendered much later reflection, one might extract that the third beatitude pledges something Moses never gained. On such an interpretation, the followers of Jesus are more blessed than the great Moses himself: if, in the past, the meek one did not enter the land, in the future "the meek . . . shall inherit the earth."

"Blessed are those who hunger and thirst for righteousness for they will be filled" is Matthew's fourth beatitude (5:6). The big question regarding it is the meaning of "righteousness." Two interpretations have dominated the commentaries. The usual interpretation in the fathers and Roman Catholicism understands "righteousness" to be behavior according to God's will—"the whole of virtue" in Chrysostom's words (*Commentary on Matthew* 15.6). That is, 5:6 blesses those who, like Joseph, are "righteous" (1:19). Protestants, however, have typically found here God's action: the reference is either to justification (cf. Paul's use of "righteousness") or to God's eschatological bringing of justice. In Donald Hagner's words, "the poor, the grieving, and the downtrodden (i.e., those who have experienced injustice) are by definition those who long for God to act" (*Matthew 1–13*, 93).

The Catholic interpretation is probably more in line with Matthew's intention. For if the "righteousness" of 5:6 is equivocal, this is not the case when the word appears in 5:10, 20; and 6:1. In 5:10 persecution "for righteousness' sake" can have nothing to do with God's gift. In 5:20 Jesus, in connection with demanding obedience to the Torah, asks for a "righteousness" greater than that of others, and in 6:1 "righteousness" is not to be done in order to be seen by others. So if we interpret the uncertain (5:6) by way of the certain (5:10, 20; 6:1), the fourth beatitude means that God will satisfy those who earnestly and habitually seek to do the divine will as though it were meat and drink.

Matthew 5:6, it is worth observing, does not congratulate those who are as a matter of fact righteous. Instead it encourages those who are hungering and thirsting for conformity to the will of God. The distinction is a matter of some remark. "Righteousness," it is implied, must be ever sought, must always be a goal that lies ahead. One is reminded of Phil. 3:12–16, where Paul says he has not already obtained his goal but presses on. Those who think themselves to be righteous are not (Luke 18:9–14).

Although I have followed the NRSV in translating the Greek *dikaiosyne* as "righteousness," some recent commentators have objected that this "tends to evoke the narrowly individualistic version of sin and justification that is often the focus of post-Reformation interpreters (both Protestant and Catholic), obscuring the communal concerns with God's justice and the demand for moral rightness and equity, especially economic equity for the poor, that are central to early Judaism and Christianity" (Mary Rose D'Angelo in Eigo, *New Perspectives*, 64). This is true enough, but translating *dikaiosynē* by "justice" might equally distort, for in Matthew justice is the product of individual holiness. As Gutiérrez has it, "righteousness" implies "a relationship with the Lord—namely, holiness; and at the same time a relationship with human beings—namely, recognition of the rights of each person and especially of the despised and the oppressed, or, in other words, social justice" (*God of Life*, 120).

The fifth beatitude promises like for like: "Blessed are the merciful, for they will [at the last judgment] receive mercy" (5:7; cf. 2 Tim. 1:18). Matthew has a great deal to say about the virtue of mercy, which is typically the external manifestation of an internal feeling of compassion for the unfortunate. It is a fundamental demand (9:13; 12:7), on a par in importance with love and faith (23:23). Jesus himself enjoins it (18:21–35), even when the word itself does not appear (25:31–46). And he himself embodies it (9:27–31; 15:21–28; 17:14–18; 20:29–34). In 25:31–46 it appears to be the criterion for salvation at the final judgment, and 18:23–35 teaches that those who do not show mercy cannot receive it from God.

Note that in 5:7 the means of mercy are unspecified. This allowed Chrysostom to write: "Here he seems to me to speak not of those only who show mercy in giving of money, but those likewise who are merciful in their actions. For the way of showing mercy is manifold, and this commandment is broad" (*Commentary on Matthew* 15.6). Chrysostom also helpfully commented that despite the reciprocal formulation in our verse, there is here no "equal recompense," for human mercy and divine mercy are not on the same level: "as wide as is the interval between wickedness and goodness, so far is the one of these removed from the other" (ibid.).

The Hebrew Bible and Jewish tradition also have much to say about mercy and, like Jesus, place it near the center of moral life. But Jesus gives the attribute special emphasis and vividness by making plain that its scope is unrestricted: one should show mercy even to enemies (5:38–48; cf. Rom. 12:14–21). A striking example of this appears in Jesus' own ministry, in 15:21–28, where he rescinds his own demand to focus on Israel (10:5–6; 24) in order to have mercy on the daughter of a Gentile woman.

Matthew 5:8 contains the sixth beatitude, which has perhaps generated more discussion than any of the others: "Blessed are the pure in heart, for they will see God." "Pure in heart" is a biblical expression, as in Ps. 24:4 ("those who have clean hands and pure hearts" ascend the hill of the Lord and stand in his holy place). The heart is the real or true self, the human principle of integration, the psyche at its deepest level (and so is close to "spirit," as in 5:3). Jews spoke of the heart as feeling (e.g., Deut. 28:47; cf. Matt. 5:27–28; 22:37), willing (e.g., Jer. 3:17), and thinking (e.g., Judg. 5:16; cf. Matt. 9:4).

Early church tradition typically understood "purity of heart" to mean a heart purified of evil desires through asceticism. The apocryphal *Acts of Paul* follows our beatitude with this: "Blessed are they who have kept the flesh pure, for they shall become a temple of God. Blessed are the continent, for to them will God speak" (3.5). Byzantine spirituality equated "purity of heart" with *apatheia*, freedom from the passions (see Symeon the New Theologian, *Chap.* 3). But in Matthew "purity of heart" is not likely to have much to do with asceticism or the passions. The meaning rather appears from the rest of the Sermon. Matt. 6:1–18 portrays a piety that is concerned not with outward show but with the private encounter between the individual and God; 6:21 says that one's treasure tells the tale of one's heart; and 7:16–20 observes the correlations between outward actions and inward states. So "purity of heart" presumably has to do with what Augustine called a "simple heart" (*Sermon on the Mount* 1.8), that is, a heart undivided in allegiance and so rightly directed. The "pure in heart" have hearts and minds given over wholly to the will of God. As Kierkegaard famously put it, purity of heart is to will one thing.

The reward for the pure in heart is that they will "see God." This is difficult, in part because the biblical tradition appears to contradict itself on the matter of the vision of God. Some texts put this out of the realm of possibility (e.g., Exod. 33:20; John 1:18; 1 Tim. 6:16). Others make it a blessed goal (e.g., Ps. 11:7; Job 19:26; 1 John 3:2; Rev. 22:4). One wonders how we should resolve this tension. Should we give only metaphorical sense to the texts that speak of seeing God? Or should we think (as I believe the author of 1 John 3:2 thought) of one set as applying to this life, another to the life to come? Or do we have here genuine and ineradicable disagreement? The interested reader may consult Augustine's discussion of this issue in *On the City of God* 22.29.

Seeing God and the so-called beatific vision have been variously understood. How can one ever "see" the incorporeal? One possibility of course is that implicit in our beatitude is the notion that God has a physical body. Augustine discussed (if only to reject) this idea, and it can be found in rabbinic texts as well as in the Christian *Pseudo-Clementine Homilies* 17.7. This last claims that God "has shape, and he has every limb primarily and solely for beauty's sake, and not for use. For he has not eyes that he may see with them, for he sees on every side." The author goes on to state that God "has the most beautiful shape on account of man, that the pure in heart may be able to see him." We are wont to think this a very primitive view of God, something that we entertained as little children and then outgrew (although I did once hear an Eastern Orthodox priest declare his belief in it). This anthropomorphic notion, however, could lie behind the use of "image of God" in Genesis; and the undeniable fact that rabbinic thinkers could speculate about God's body means that a first-century Christian might have been less sophisticated about this matter than we, who are so much more at home with John's declaration that "God is spirit" (John 4:24).

But there are other possibilities. Some, accepting the Christian confession that Jesus is himself God, have urged that believers will someday see Jesus, and that this will be the beatific vision. Col. 1:15 speaks of Jesus as "the visible image of the invisible God," and in John 14:9 Jesus says, "Whoever has seen me has seen the Father." Now the promise that believers will see Jesus when he comes again is all over the New Testament, and it appears in Matthew itself (e.g., 26:64). So if (as Robert Gundry in his recent commentary has argued) Matthew presents Jesus as God, then one could entertain the possibility that Matt. 5:8 will be fulfilled at the *parousia.* On the other hand, the one other verse in Matthew to refer to the beatific vision makes it plain that God the Father is in view. In 18:10 Jesus says, "in heaven their angels continually see the face of my Father in heaven."

One might also think of the vision of God as some sort of special vision that does not encompass God but is nonetheless a manifestation of the divine reality. Scripture is full of such visions. In Exodus 3 Moses meets God in the burning bush. In Isaiah 6 the prophet has a vision of a throne room. In Daniel 7 the seer sees symbolic beasts as well as a court in judgment. Perhaps the Sermon on the Mount should make us think of something akin to Isa. 40:5, where all humanity sees the "glory" of God. Byzantine Hesychasts such as Gregory Palamas believed one could see even now the uncreated light of Christ that was once manifested at the transfiguration.

Origen thought that the sixth beatitude referred not to physical

sight but to spiritual and intellectual apprehension. When we say, "I
see the point," we are usually not talking about dots. "The names of
the organs of sense are often applied to the soul, so that we speak of
seeing with the eyes of the heart, that is, of drawing some intellectual
conclusions by means of the faculty of intelligence." There are "in us
two kinds of senses, the one being mortal, corruptible and human, and
the other immortal and intellectual, which here he [Solomon in
Proverbs] calls 'divine.' By this divine sense, therefore, not of the eyes
but of a pure heart, that is, the mind, God can be seen by those who are
worthy" (*On First Principles* 1.1.9). A similar interpretation was
offered in the seventeenth century in Jeremiah Burroughs's mammoth
commentary on the beatitudes, *The Saints' Happiness:* because God is
an invisible spirit that cannot be seen with bodily eyes, the saints
"shall know God by the eye of their understanding." Friedrich
Schleiermacher thought the same thing: the vision of God is the
"unimpeded knowledge of God in all and along with all" (*Christian
Faith*, §163).

Augustine took a different path. He contended that in the new
world the perfected saints will be able to perceive God directly through
a perfected creation. The thought seems to be that we can sometimes
perceive things through their effects. Although we only see what the
wind does to things and never see the wind itself, we sometimes say,
"Look at the wind!" Maybe God will someday similarly be plainly perceived through God's effects.

One of the more novel interpretations of "to see God" was for-
warded by Gregory of Nyssa. In his commentary on the beatitudes and
elsewhere he suggested that we will, in the world to come, see God in
ourselves and in our neighbor. In the eschatological paradise the likeness to God originally given to Adam and Eve but then obscured
through sin will be perfectly regained, which will enable us see God in
our neighbor. And the same thing happens, so Gregory argues, in the
here and now, when the saints gain purity of heart. Just as we cannot
look directly at the sun but can see it only indirectly, in a mirror, so
too is it with God: our perception can never encompass more than a
reflection. Perhaps we may compare 25:31–46, where in some sense
people serve Jesus when they serve the unfortunate. Here at least Jesus
is somehow encountered in or with others.

A final suggestion is perhaps the simplest of all. Sometimes the
idiom "to see" (as in "I hope to see that day") can mean "to experience." This at least appears to be the likely meaning in those psalms

in which people go up to the Jerusalem temple to "see God" (see Pss. 27:4; 42:3; 63:3). One might think it significant that Matt. 5:7 has often been thought to allude to Ps. 23:4 (quoted in part above), and that this has to do with going up to the temple. One could make this a reason for connecting our verse with the meaning of "to see God" in the Psalms. On this reading, Martyrius might be right to equate the vision of God with an interior spiritual experience (*Book of Perfection* 47). On the other hand, the use of "to see" to mean "to experience" does not seem to be otherwise attested in Matthew, and the reference to seeing God in 18:10 is unlikely to be metaphorical.

In the end one must confess that Matthew's Gospel only raises the question of the content of the beatific vision; it does not answer it. But whatever one does with that issue, it should be noted that 5:8 speaks only about the eschatological future. The possibility of attaining the beatific vision in the present life—something taken for granted by medieval theologians and Christian mystics of every stripe—is neither implied nor denied. Elsewhere, however, as already observed, we read that even now some angels see the face of the Father in heaven (18:10). So one can, if so inclined, bring this strange text into connection with 5:8: the saints will enjoy in the future what the angels experience even now. Such an interpretation at least has the virtue of being congruent with 22:23–33, where Jesus affirms that, in the life to come, the saints will be "like the angels in heaven."

Matthew's seventh beatitude is "Blessed are the peacemakers, for they will be called children of God" (5:9). Exegetical history provides a slew of possibilities for what it means to be a peacemaker. Pacifists have thought it refers to the healing and prevention of political and military conflicts (and it has occasionally been suggested that our beatitude may have been composed not by Jesus but by someone during or immediately after the Jewish War of A.D. 66–70). Others—including the majority of critical exegetes today—have thought more in terms of personal relationships: one should make strenuous efforts to be reconciled to others both within and without the community (so, e.g., Luz). Still others have thought in terms of making peace with God (cf. Col. 1:20), and especially of missionaries, who bring others to faith (Theophylact, *Commentary on Matthew* ad loc.). The strangest suggestion came from Origen (*Philocalia* 6.1), who thought of exegetes reconciling conflicting texts.

Given Matthew's keen interest in the subject of reconciliation (18:21–35), especially within the Sermon itself (5:21–26; 6:14–15), one suspects that the interpretation that emphasizes interpersonal relationships (cf. Prov. 10:10; Mark 9:50) comes closest to the authorial intention. Yet it would perhaps be unwise to restrict the application to this. For there is after all no qualification after "peacemakers," and one can find ancient texts that juxtapose social and interpersonal peace (e.g., *Mekhilta* on Exod. 20:25). Perhaps Pinchas Lapide is justified in suggesting that "directed within," peace "is purity of heart (Lam. 3:17); directed above, it is being at one with God (Judg. 6:24); and directed to all sides it is human unity (1 Kings 5:4)" (*Sermon*, 34).

The precise connection between peacemaking and "they will be called children [Greek: sons] of God" is unclear. The Mishnah associates the making of peace with benefit in the world to come (*Peah* 1:1). 1 Chr. 22:9–10 promises David that Solomon, in whose days Israel will have peace, will be God's "son." The best guess is that Jewish liturgical language is in the background. The Palestinian recension of the prayer of the Eighteen Benedictions ends with: "Blessed art Thou, O Lord, the maker of peace." Matt. 5:9 may well assume, against the background of a well-known liturgical line, that God makes peace, from which it follows that others who make peace are like God and so God's children. However that may be, our text is illuminated by 5:44–45, where God's children are like God in being good to all, even enemies.

The unstated subject of "they will be called children of God" is presumably God, and it is assumed that to be called something by God is to be that something. Here the tense is future, and the eschatological goal of history is in view, when intimacy with and likeness to God will be perfected (cf. *Jub.* 1:24; Rev. 21:7). But elsewhere in the Sermon believers are even now the children of God (5:45), whom they address as "Father" (6:9, etc.).

The eighth beatitude raises the subject of persecution: "Blessed are those who are persecuted for righteousness' sake, for theirs is the kingdom of heaven" (5:10; cf. 1 Pet. 3:14). The line looks as though it has been pieced together from the other beatitudes. "Persecuted" anticipates the "persecute you" in the following verse. "Righteousness" is the object of hunger and thirst in 5:6. And "for theirs is the kingdom of heaven" is also the conclusion of the very first beatitude (5:3).

The verb translated "persecuted" may refer to physical violence or verbal abuse or both. What is envisioned is all hostility brought on because of "righteousness," that is, because of faithful obedience to God's will. God's ways are not our ways, which means they are not always pleasant ways, so those who demand obedience to them will always meet opposition. Matthew's story of John the Baptist illustrates this fact. But the preeminent illustration is Jesus (who in this resembles the Socrates of Greek tradition): the one who proclaims the truth and makes hard moral demands ends up hanging on a cross.

"For theirs is the kingdom of heaven" repeats, as already observed, 5:3. The effect is to create an *inclusio*. The inclusion marks the beginning and end of the formally similar beatitudes (the ninth is very different). It also serves to tell us that the promises in the second half of the second through seventh beatitudes are all different ways of explicating the kingdom of heaven.

The final beatitude is much the longest: "Blessed are you when people revile you and utter all kinds of evil against you falsely on my account. Rejoice and be glad, for your reward is great in heaven, for in the same way they persecuted the prophets who were before you." The lengthy, irregular form (note the shift from third person to second person) is one instance of a literary convention we find elsewhere, the convention of making the final line in a series different from and longer than its predecessors (see p. 29). The effect is twofold—to signal that the end of the series is near and to put emphasis on that which is given extra attention. Matt. 1:2–16; 10:40–42; 23:13–36; and Luke 6:37–38 offer examples of sequences that follow this pattern.

It has been said that the display of joy in hardship is "distinctive of Christianity and of its saints and apostles and martyrs. And doubtless many thousands of humble sufferers have risen superior to their troubles and afflictions through the memory and influence of the beatitudes" (Montefiore, *Synoptic*, 485). But this display of joy is not characteristic of Matthew. Indeed, whereas Luke has much to say about joy and rejoicing, Matthew rarely mentions them (although see 2:10 and 13:44). One imagines that this reflects both his solemn character and his combative circumstances: our Gospel was written by a man making urgent argument in a polemical environment.

One should take special note that, in Matthew, it is above all Jesus who is reviled and spoken evil of. People say that he blasphemes (9:2; 26:65) and acts unlawfully on the Sabbath (12:1–14). The Pharisees accuse him of consorting with sinners (9:11) and of casting out demons by the power of Satan (9:34; 12:24). Crowds laugh at him (9:24) and mock him (27:30, 38–44). Others call him Beelzebul (10:25) and accuse him of being a glutton and drunkard (11:19).

FINAL REMARKS ON THE BEATITUDES

The beatitudes promise that the kingdom of God will bring eschatological comfort, a permanent inheritance, true satisfaction, the vision of God, and unprecedented intimacy with God. Clearly the coming of the kingdom will mean human experience of the fullness of God's presence, and it is rightly considered the *summum bonum* of both the Sermon on the Mount and Matthew as a whole. No other subject, then, could more fittingly lead off the Sermon, Matthew's first and most important discourse.

Insofar as the promises connected with the kingdom bring consolation and comfort, they function as a practical theodicy. The beatitudes hardly explain evil or human suffering. They do, however, lessen pain and anguish by putting into perspective the difficulties of the present. This happens through an exercise of the imagination. Eschatological promises for those on the bottom reveal that all is not what it seems to be. That is, the truth, like the kingdom, is hidden. Only the future, with its rewards and punishments, will bring to light the true condition of the world and those in it (cf. 25:31–46). Those who use the eye of the mind in order to foresee and live for the future promised by the beatitudes will, with their faith, possess a secret vision and hope that makes powerlessness and suffering bearable.

FOR FURTHER READING

Barclay, William. *The Beatitudes and the Lord's Prayer for Everyman.* New York: Harper & Row, 1968.

Eigo, Francis A. *New Perspectives on the Beatitudes.* Villanova, Penn.: Villanova University Press, 1995.

Galilea, Segundo. *The Beatitudes: To Evangelize As Jesus Did.* Maryknoll, N.Y.: Orbis Books, 1984.

Guelich, Robert. "The Matthean Beatitudes: 'Entrance-Requirements' or 'Eschatological Blessing'?" *Journal of Biblical Literature* 95 (1976): 415–34.

McEleney, Neil J. "The Beatitudes of the Sermon on the Mount/Plain." *Catholic Biblical Quarterly* 43 (1981): 1–13.

Powell, Mark Allan. "Matthew's Beatitudes: Reversals and Rewards of the Kingdom." *Catholic Biblical Quarterly* 58 (1996): 460–79.

4

Anger, Lust, Divorce
(5:17–32)

JESUS AND THE TORAH (5:17–20)

THE SIX PARAGRAPHS HAVING TO DO with Jesus and the Torah (5:21–48) are prefaced by 5:17–20. As already observed in chapter 2, the latter has two main functions: it anticipates and precludes an incorrect interpretation of 5:21–48 (Jesus abolished Moses) and then offers the correct interpretation: 5:21–48 illustrates the righteousness that goes beyond that of the scribes and Pharisees.

In 5:17 Jesus rebuts a real misunderstanding: somebody—maybe like the heretic Marcion in the second century—thinks that Jesus came to abolish, that is, annul and replace, the Law and the Prophets (= the Jewish Scriptures, the Christian Old Testament; Tolstoy's attempt to find here "not the written law of Moses but the eternal law of God" is wholly unfounded). If we seek to go behind our text and set it in a real-life context, we could think of Jesus defending himself against opponents who made him out to be an antinomian, or perhaps of law-observant Jewish Christians attacking lax Gentile Christians or followers of Paul, or we might envisage Christians replying to the slander of Jewish opponents that Jesus was an enemy of the law of God. But if we stick with the function of 5:17 within its literary context, its purpose must be to help us with reading the paragraphs that follow. For the issue of Jesus and the law is raised only by the subsequent paragraphs, not by anything that comes before. Obviously Matthew was aware that 5:21–48 could be misinterpreted.

Jesus says that he has come "not to abolish but to fulfill." What is the meaning of the Greek word translated "fulfill"? Here, because the proposals are so many, perusal of the commentaries can lead to increasing confusion. But perhaps most of the suggestions can be fairly placed somewhere among the following: (1) "Fulfill" really means "add." Jesus' imperatives go beyond and so add to those in the Hebrew Bible. (2) The meaning is "do" or "execute" or even "obey": Jesus follows and performs the law perfectly. (3) Jesus fulfills the law by bringing it to perfection with a new law of his own. (4) Jesus enables others to keep the Torah. (5) Jesus reduces everything to love, which is the fulfilling of the law. (6) The fulfillment is, as Eusebius thought (*Demonstration of the Gospel* 8.2), eschatological: Jesus does not abolish the Torah but, on the contrary, fulfills its prophecies.

In a case such as this, certainty cannot be obtained. Wisdom should, moreover, recognize that some of these meanings do not exclude others, so that some combination of them could be correct. My own judgment, in fact, is that there is some truth in each of the proposals. In the end, however, the sense of (6) seems strongest. This is because Matthew usually uses the verb in question ("fulfill") with reference to prophetic fulfillment (1:22; 4:14; 12:17; etc.) and because our sentence refers not just to the Law but also to the Prophets. So Jesus' new teaching brings to realization that which the Torah prophesied. And that realization does not set the Law and Prophets aside. Fulfillment rather confirms the Torah's truth.

One should recall in this connection that our Gospel understands Jesus to be the eschatological prophet like Moses, the prophet foretold in Deut. 18:15–20: "the Lord your God will raise up for you a prophet like me [Moses] from among your own people." This oracle foretells that God will speak anew: "I will put my words in the mouth of the prophet, who shall speak . . . everything that I command." For early Christians the Pentateuch was a prophetic book which foretold the coming of Jesus (cf. Acts 3:22). So Jesus can prophetically "fulfill" not only the prophets but also the Torah.

Matthew 5:18 opens with the solemn and authoritative "Amen I say to you" (which was probably a characteristic feature of Jesus' speech). This is followed by the strong assertion that not even the smallest part of the law will pass away until heaven and earth are gone. The purpose is to reinforce and clarify 5:17: that Jesus, instead of abolishing the Law and Prophets, fulfills them, is consistent with their lasting until the new creation comes. One may have difficulty reconciling this view of things with Paul. (Did Matthew believe that Jewish Christians but not Gentile Christians should observe the Mosaic commandments?) But

Matthew's view of things seems manifest. Nothing outside the Sermon on the Mount calls the law into question. On the contrary,
Matthew's Jesus tells the Pharisees that they should practice justice
and mercy and faith without neglecting the minor matters of the law
(23:23–24). The Jewish scholar Pinchas Lapide has even gone so far as
to say, "in all rabbinic literature I know of no more unequivocal, fiery
acknowledgement of Israel's holy scripture than this opening to the
Instruction on the Mount. Jesus is here more radical even than Rabbi
Hiyya bar Abba and Rabbi Johanan, both of whom were prepared to
renounce a letter—that is, a written character of the Torah if doing so
would publicly sanctify the name of God (see Yeb 79a)" (*Sermon*, 14).

Matthew 5:19 elaborates on 5:18 in a way reminiscent of how the
latter elaborates on 5:17: if all of the law remains in force, then all of
the law must be obeyed. (Matt. 5:19 is not, despite many, a statement
about Jesus' commands.) So whoever relaxes even one of the least of
the Mosaic commandments and teaches others to do so will "be called
least in the kingdom of heaven," whereas those who do and teach
them will be called great. Whether "be called least" means exclusion
from heaven or a low rank therein is unclear.

Matthew 5:20 is a transitional verse. It takes up the theme of being
in the kingdom, implies that one must do at least what the scribes and
Pharisees do, namely, keep the law of Moses, and explicitly states that
one must do even more, namely, obey the demands of Jesus, which are
to follow. One implication is that "if we reduce them [Jesus' com-
mandments] to a meaning in which we lose the sense of the extraordi-
nary, we have missed the mark" (Denney, in Dods, Denney, and
Moffatt, *Literal Interpretation*, 27). Another, perhaps, is that righteousness "is not limited to obeying precepts [cf. Matthew's caricature
of the scribes and Pharisees] but draws its inspiration from an ever new
and imaginative love" (Gutiérrez, *God of Life*, 119).

What does all this mean for the interpretation of 5:21–48, the most
difficult section of the Sermon on the Mount? It contains six paragraphs that treat six different topics—anger, lust, divorce, oaths,
revenge, love. In each case Jesus quotes traditional teaching found in
the Jewish Scriptures and then goes on to add his own: "You have heard
that it was said to those of old . . . . But I say to you . . . ." Many have
construed Jesus' words to be the undoing of Moses. As Calvin clearly
saw, however, this interpretation cannot correspond to the intention
of the text. For 5:17–20 plainly anticipates it and refutes it. Matthew,

as we have seen, has Jesus affirm quite unambiguously: "Do not think that I have come to abolish the law. . . ."

In what follows, then, we shall attempt to understand 5:21–48 as something other than a collection of instances in which Jesus abolishes the Law and the Prophets. This does not, one should hasten to add, mean that there can be no tension between Moses and Jesus. Jewish texts sometimes teach that the Torah will be better understood in the future than in the present, and others even reveal an awareness that certain details might one day (e.g., in the messianic kingdom) have to be altered. Further, whoever wrote the Dead Sea Scroll known as 11QTemple could offer legislation that seems at some points out of harmony with the Pentateuch, and the great rabbi Hillel introduced legislation that does not accord with Scripture: but certainly neither Jew took himself to be abolishing Moses. In like manner, if Matthew sensed any tension between Jesus and the Pentateuch he could only, as 5:17 indicates, have thought not in terms of contradiction but in terms of fulfillment.

In this connection 19:3–9 is quite instructive. Here Jesus prohibits divorce. He concedes that Moses allowed it (Deut. 24:1–14), and so one might claim that here the Messiah abolishes the law. But Jesus goes on to say that from the beginning divorce was not God's intention, for in Genesis 1–2 marriage is an indissoluble union. The tension discerned here within Scripture is exploited and then resolved in favor of Genesis, which refers to how things were with Adam and Eve in paradise. Jesus appears to assume, in accordance with Jewish tradition, that the end will be like the beginning (where strict monogamy was the rule), and that, in the kingdom, at the end, God will no longer need to make concessions to sin (which is assumed to be the root cause of divorce). It follows not that Jesus contradicts Scripture but that he rightly interprets it according to his eschatological outlook. A similar line of thinking may lie behind some of the following paragraphs, which make so little concession to sin or human frailty.

MURDER AND ANGER (5:21–26)

Murder is prohibited in the Ten Commandments (Exod. 20:13; Deut. 5:17), and the Pentateuch elsewhere declares that the one who commits murder will be put to death (e.g., Exod. 21:12; Lev. 24:17). Jesus, however, after summarizing the traditional teaching (which he explicitly affirms in 19:18), adds to it by saying that those who direct anger toward another and speak insulting words should or will suffer punishment. The point is that it is insufficient to refrain from the act of murder, for the latter is simply the symptom of something else. The source of murder must be uprooted; anger must be eradicated. As Gregory of Nyssa put it, "One can divide wickedness under two headings, one concerned with works, the other with thoughts. The former, the iniquity which shows itself in works, he [God] has punished through the old law. Now, however, he has given the law regarding the other forms of sin, which punishes not so much the evil deed itself, as guards against even the beginning of it" (*Homily 6 on the Beatitudes*).

Jesus' hyperbolic identification of murder with anger is something that also appears in 1 John 3:15 ("All who hate a brother or sister are murderers") and Jewish tradition, as in the late *Derekh Ereṣ Rabbah* 57b ("He who hates his neighbor is among the shedders of blood"). The striking equation shifts attention from the outward act to the inward state (cf. 5:27–30) and makes anger and harsh words grievous sins to be exorcised at all costs. Anger is not just perilous because "anger leads to murder" (*Did.* 3.2) (the point made by Gregory): anger—the companion of hate, which is the opposite of love—is in and of itself dangerous and deserving of condemnation.

The illustrations in 5:23–24 ("when you are offering your gift at the altar . . ."—because Christians no longer make literal sacrifices in a literal temple, our passage has usually been applied to prayer, e.g., Aphraates, *Demonstrations* 4.13) and 25–26 ("Come to terms quickly with your accuser while you are on the way to court . . .") offer few difficulties. The first teaches that reconciliation with others is paramount and even more important than important religious ritual. The second depicts the evil consequences that can follow the failure to make peace with others. (St. Isaiah the Solitary's equation of "your accuser" with one's conscience is bad exegesis but has much homiletical potential; see the *Philocalia,* St. Isaiah the Solitary 3. One should also note that "you will never get out until you have paid the last penny" was one of the classical proof texts for the doctrine of purgatory. This is also bad exegesis, as the Reformers had little difficulty showing: Calvin, *Institutes* 3.5.7; Zwingli, *True and False Religion* 25).

Our passage in all likelihood alludes to the story of Cain (which is also alluded to in Matt. 18:22 and mentioned in 23:35). To readers steeped in Jewish tradition, the mention of murder in conjunction with hating one's brother could readily have called to mind Genesis 4, particularly as the enmity between Cain and Abel grew out of God's rejection of Cain's sacrificial gift, and the offering of a gift is the situation described in 5:23–24. Certainly it was traditional to use the story of Genesis 4 to illustrate how anger can lead to murder. Wisd. 10:3 tells the story of Cain this way: "But when an unrighteous man departed from her [Wisdom] in anger, he perished because in rage he slew his brother." 1 John 3:15, after referring to Cain, "who was from the evil one and murdered his brother," goes on to say that "all who hate a brother or sister are murderers." Cyprian offered these comments on our passage: "One who comes to the Sacrifice with a quarrel he [Jesus] calls back from the altar and commands him first to be reconciled with his brother and then, when he is at peace, to return and offer his gift to God. For neither had God respect for Cain's offering, for he could not have God at peace with him, who through envy and discord was not at peace with his brother" (*The Unity of the Church* 13).

The chief question with regard to 5:21–26 concerns the prohibition of anger in 5:22. Christian tradition is divided on how we should take this. Jesus does not say that we should not be angry for the wrong reason. Nor does he imply that there might be some good reason for being angry with another. He seemingly prohibits the emotion altogether: "if you are angry with a brother or sister, you will be liable to the council" (5:22). While it is unclear exactly what "liable to the council" means—does it mean "should be liable to judgment"?—the sense of the whole seems clear enough: anger is wrong. The prohibition is absolute. But this is problematic. Where is the allowance for justified anger? Nothing is said about moderation, or striking a balance. This has seemed to many very strange. Is not 5:21–26 one of the reasons we should judge the Sermon on the Mount to be impractical and unreasonable?

One way of countering this objection is to argue that the prohibition (perhaps hyperbole?) was never intended to cover all circumstances, to prohibit anger for every reason. And there are, in fact, some seemingly good reasons for thinking this to be the case. Matt. 5:17–20 says that Jesus came not to abolish the Law and the Prophets, but does not the Hebrew Bible make room for justified anger? Ps. 4:4 says, "When you are angry, do not sin," and there are scriptural examples of heroes becoming angry for a righteous cause—Moses (Exod. 32:19) and Jeremiah (Jer. 6:11), for instance. Indeed, God is very often said to be angry or full of wrath (Exod. 4:14, etc.). Ecclus. 1:22 seems rightly to catch

the spirit of much of the Jewish Scriptures when it says that "unrighteous anger cannot be justified"—a sentiment which implies that a
righteous anger can be justified. This, however, is precisely what is
missing from the Sermon on the Mount. Does it not follow that Matt.
5:22, if taken literally, is a genuine contradiction of the Hebrew Bible
and so of 5:17–20?

A second reason for seeking to mitigate the apparent force of Matt.
5:21–26 is that early Christian tradition reveals that an injunction
against all anger may not have been well known. Eph. 4:26 counsels,
"Be angry, but do not sin; do not let the sun go down on your anger."
Even more impressive are the texts in the Gospels where Jesus himself
is said to have been caught in anger. Some extant witnesses, and perhaps the original text of Mark 1:41, tell us that Jesus, when dealing with
a leper, "was moved with anger." And in Mark 3:5 Jesus is said to have
looked around at the people of a synagogue "with anger" (here the text
is firm). Also relevant is Matt. 21:12–17, the story of Jesus driving out
those who were buying and selling in the temple and then overturning
the tables of the money changers and those selling doves. One has difficulty envisaging this as an act unaccompanied by some sort of anger.

For the most part later Christian tradition followed Eph. 4:26 and
did not demand the elimination of all anger—only anger misdirected.
Chrysostom, in commenting on the Sermon on the Mount, wrote that
anger "is even useful, if we know how to use it at the suitable time."
Augustine, also commenting on the Sermon, excused Paul's anger
against the Galatians and his calling them "fools" (Gal. 3:1)—an apparently blatant contradiction of Matt. 5:22—by urging that the apostle
had just cause for doing so (*Sermon on the Mount* 1.9.25). Evagrius
Ponticus thought anger appropriate when aimed at evil thoughts
(*Skemmata* 8), and John Climacus spoke for many when he said that
demons are fitting objects of righteous anger (*Ladder of Divine Ascent*
26). Thomas Aquinas, in the *Summa*, said that if "someone becomes
angry for a good reason, then it is praiseworthy to become angry." In
the nineteenth century A. Tholuck thought that Jesus must have been
speaking not about anger in general but only about "a blind and irra-
tional anger," the sort that grows into the hatred from whence murder
comes.

All this seems common sense. We understand why Aristotle said
that those who are angry at the right things and with the right people
at the right time for the right length of time are to be praised (*Nicomachean Ethics* 5.4). Perhaps some will even understand Martin

Luther's comment that he could write, pray, and preach better when he was angry (*Table Talk* H319).

There is also an exegetical argument that one might urge against a literal reading of Matt. 5:22 and so bring the verse into harmony with the dominant Christian tradition. Jesus speaks about being angry with a "brother" (5:22), about insulting a "brother" (5:22), and about remembering a "brother" with "something against you" (5:33). Throughout Matthew "brother" regularly means "Christian brother" (as in 18:15–20). Perhaps, then, 5:21–26 is not about anger in general but about being angry with a fellow Christian in particular. Maybe outsiders and heretics and opponents—those who might be thought the appropriate objects of what theologians have called "holy hate"—are excluded.

Despite the force of these several observations, some commentators have held, on the contrary, that, according to Matthew's text, one should utterly control the emotion of anger to the point of eliminating it altogether. Such is the view of Ulrich Luz in his great commentary on Matthew: he "take[s] v. 22 literally as a serious demand which is valid for all." But Luz is far from being the first so to read the text. Above all in the monastic tradition we find the unqualified obligation to forsake all anger. Abba Agathon, according to the *Apophthegmata Patrum*, said, "A man who is angry, even if he were to raise the dead, is not acceptable to God." The same source has John the Dwarf imploring that "when you are despised do not get angry," Isidore the Priest declaring that he has never consented to anger nor allowed it "to reach my lips," a certain Nilus asserting that "prayer is the seed of gentleness and the absence of anger," and Abba Nisterus the Great saying that getting angry should be "alien to monks." Macarius the Great, according to Zosimus, warned that "it is completely foreign to a monk to grow angry, and if one should grow angry, unless he is swiftly protected by humiliating himself, in a short time, troubled as he is, and troubling others, he comes under the power of the devil."

One of the more compelling expositions of Matt. 5:21–26 appears in the *Institutes* of John Cassian, which set forth the rules for monastic life. In 8.1–22 Cassian discusses the spirit of anger. He knows there are people who use the scriptural references to the wrath of God to justify "being angry with the brethren who are wrong." But he contends that we cannot think of God's wrath any more literally than we think literally of God's hands or fingers: we have here nothing more than a human way of speaking, upon which it would be foolish to build anything. Cassian then goes on to quote Eph. 4:31 and interprets "Put away all bitterness and wrath and anger" to admit of no exceptions. Nothing is said here about "necessary or useful" anger. The only conceivable profitable use of anger Cassian admits is that which is directed to the sins within us; it is never to be directed toward another human being.

One cannot successfully argue against Cassian and the monastic position by appealing to the rest of the Christian tradition, for that tradition was led astray by a textual variant in Matt. 5:22. The King James Version (KJV) has this: "whosoever is angry with his brother without a cause shall be in danger of the judgment." The phrase "without a cause" translates a little Greek word (*eikē*) that was added to the text by at least the end of the second century. It was added precisely because our text does not seem to allow for justified anger.

Cassian himself already knew this. He knew not only of those who used the scriptural references to the wrath of God to justify "being angry with the brethren who are wrong," but he also knew of copies of Matthew that read, "If you are angry with a brother or sister without cause . . . ." He argued, however, that the words, "without cause," are "superfluous." "They were added by those who did not think that anger for just causes was to be banished. For certainly no one, however unreasonably disturbed, would think his or her anger without cause." (Augustine, incidentally, also knew the variant reading, but he thought it unimportant because his view of the passage was that Christians can be angry with a brother or sister's sin but not with a brother or sister [*Retractions* 1.18].)

It is also telling that early Christian tradition does, apart from Matt. 5:21–26, contain blanket prohibitions of anger. If Eph. 4:26 ("Be angry, but do not sin") is a concession to anger, Col. 3:8 condemns the passion without qualification: "you must get rid of all such things—anger, wrath, malice, slander, and abusive language from your mouth." This imperative, which reads like a summary of Matthew's text, says nothing about a justified anger or wrath. Even Ephesians itself at one point demands this: "put away from you all bitterness and wrath and anger and wrangling and slander, together with all malice" (4:31). There is here no qualification. Similarly, the author of 1 Tim. 2:8 writes of his desire "that in every place the men should pray, lifting up holy hands without anger or argument . . . ." Jas. 1:20 declares that "your anger does not produce God's righteousness." Ignatius, in his letter to the Philadelphians, says that "where there is division and anger, there God does not abide." In line with all this, if in the Hebrew Bible it is Moses and Jeremiah, two great worthies, who become enraged, in the New Testament it is Herod the Great (Matt. 2:16), Jesus' adversaries (Luke 4:28; John 7:23), Paul's opponents (Acts 19:28), ungodly nations (Rev. 11:18), and the devil (Rev. 12:12) who express anger.

One is still left, it is true, with Mark 3:5 (where Jesus looks around "with anger") and perhaps 1:41 (where the original text may have had Jesus "moved with anger"). But whatever one makes of these two texts, it is crucial to observe that Matthew, who copied extensively from Mark, does not have them. In other words, on the assumption of Markan priority, he rewrote his source so that his Gospel no longer tells us that Jesus was angry. It appears, then, that Matthew thought anger an inappropriate passion for Jesus, and this is a reason for suspecting that Matt. 5:22 speaks against all anger, not just anger without good cause.

One cannot, moreover, get around the literal meaning of our passage by restricting the prohibitions against anger and insults to Christian brothers and sisters. Not only would this fail to explain Matthew's omission of Mark's one or two reference to Jesus' being angry (there Christians are not the objects of anger), but the spirit of 5:38–48 seems to demand that the Christian be reconciled with believer and unbeliever alike.

What finally of the apparent contradiction with the Jewish Scriptures? Here two things must be said. One is that there is certainly no commandment in the law to be angry, which means that one who refrains from being angry will in no way break any divine law. The other is that the Hebrew Bible itself—like the New Testament—may speak with two minds on this issue. Although, as we have seen, anger is often associated with God and sometimes with heroes, the Hebrew Bible at the same time also counsels against anger. Eccl. 7:9 says, "Do not be quick to anger, for anger lodges in the bosom of fools." Ps. 37:8 tells us, "Refrain from anger, and forsake wrath. Do not fret—it leads only to evil." Genesis 4 recounts the story of Cain's anger and how it led to the murder of his brother Abel (cf. Wisd. 10:3), while Gen. 49:7 curses the anger of "Simeon and Levi" because it is "fierce, and their wrath . . . is cruel." Jonah 4 offers the ridiculous spectacle of Jonah's self-pitying anger, which accomplishes nothing. If one wishes, one can harmonize these texts with those in which anger serves a good cause by thinking of a righteous anger and an unrighteous anger. But the fact remains that the Hebrew Bible itself has texts that discourage the cultivation of anger. So if Matthew's Jesus does the same thing, this can hardly be said to be an intentional contradiction of Moses and the prophets.

What then, in the end, are we to think? Maybe Luz and Cassian have the better of the argument. Maybe our text does imply that "even if there be a cause for being angry, there ought to be no anger" (Bengel, *Gnomon*, ad loc.). In other words, anger is in and of itself against the will of God. But as soon as one comes to this tentative conclusion, there is another problem. What is the point of an unrealistic injunction? In addition to the obstacles thrown up by ordinary experience—How many of us know anyone who never gets angry?—we now know that anger is a biological fact. Not only can scientists describe its physiological basis in the limbic system and analyze its chemical correlates, but the sociobiologists offer us speculations about the positive roles anger has played in the evolution of our species. In the light of such knowledge and speculation it might seem more foolish than ever to condemn anger utterly, or to follow Plato in thinking it an "ungracious element" of our nature. This is all the more so as the world of modern psychology, through its popular expressions in self-help books, often tells us to be creative with our anger, to express it. As justification we are sometimes even told that unexpressed anger may lead to psychosomatic illnesses. Is not anger just unexpressed energy that has to come out one way or the other? Why should we fight it? How can we feel guilty about a normal human emotion?

Perhaps one point to make in wrestling with these questions is that the Sermon on the Mount is at least not alone in its seemingly unconditional condemning of anger. The Stoic philosophers, contrary to the Peripatetics, sought to rid themselves altogether of this emotion, and so did some Jews, if the Jewish Apocrypha and Pseudepigrapha are any indication. According to Ecclus. 27:30, "anger and wrath, these are also abominations, and the sinful person will possess them." *Sibylline Oracles* 3.377 prophesies that the future will see many evils, including anger, flee from humanity. In the *Letter of Aristeas* one finds the question, "How can one avoid anger?" answered this way: "If all are obedient and there is no opposition, what will be the point of getting angry? You must know that God governs the whole universe with kindliness and without any anger, and you, O King, must follow him." Rabbinic sources also speak against anger. As it says in Babylonian Talmud *Nedarim* 22b, angry students forget what they learn and become more and more stupid, and the sins of angry people outweigh their merits.

The few times Moses fell into error it was because he gave way to anger (*Sipre Num.* §157).

The widespread opposition to anger in both Jewish and extrabiblical tradition is readily understandable. Common sense and reflection reveal that anger is almost always both dangerous and foolish. Proverbs says, "Whoever is slow to anger has great understanding, but one who has a hasty temper exalts folly" (14:29; cf. 16:32). The inevitably close link between anger and sin appears from Ps. 4:4: "When you are angry, do not sin." The *Testament of Dan* dedicates three whole chapters to the problem of anger. Here we read that "there is blindness in anger" (2:2), that it is powerful enough to take over the soul itself (3:1–3), that it often joins itself with falsehood and deception (3:5–6), and that it acts senselessly (4:1). All of this seems true enough. "Anger destroys even the wise" (Prov. 15:1 LXX), for its nature is not to be controlled but controlling. It uses us; we do not use it. It moves us not to act but to react. And it typically enlarges itself: anger leads to anger. Surely this is cause for holding that "anger is evil" (3:1). It is no mystery why Horace wrote that "anger is a short madness" (*Epistle* 1.2.62), nor why anger is one of the seven deadly sins, nor why the *Sibylline Oracles* prophesy the elimination of anger in the eschatological age (8.120), nor even why Dante's *Inferno* has a place reserved for "those whom anger overcame."

But even if one sympathizes with a call to eliminate anger, how is the task to be done? Our Western religious and philosophical traditions are full of suggestions for how to subdue or eliminate anger. 4 Maccabees contends that it can be overcome with reason (see chapters 1 and 3). Seneca, in his little book on the subject, supposed that "hesitation is the best cure for anger. . . . The first blows of anger are heavy, but if it waits, it will think again. Do not try to destroy it immediately. Attacked piecemeal, it will be entirely overcome" (*On Anger* 2.29). Evagrius thought that anger can be mastered through "the singing of Psalms, by patience, and by almsgiving" (*Praktikos* 15). Dorotheos of Gaza believed that the cultivation of humility would drive out the vice (*Discourses and Sayings* 2). Thomas Manton, in his great seventeenth-century commentary on James, passed on the story of Athenodorus's advice to Augustus, that the latter should, whenever struggling with anger, recite the alphabet before doing anything, so that rage might cool and action be deliberate, not reflexive.

All of these may be understandable suggestions, but our text offers something else. Matt. 5:23–24 (leaving the gift at the altar) and 25–26 (making friends on the way to court) are both illustrations of the self-discipline of reconciliation, which is the antidote to anger. That is, the things that are condemned in 5:22—anger and insults—are in 5:23-26 overcome by the offender making peace with the offended. So what the Sermon on the Mount here envisages is not isolated individuals seeking to subdue their passions but disciples going about the often awkward task of trying to right perceived wrongs. Perhaps in this the Sermon is wisely committing us to the mean between repression and expression, between ignoring our anger and venting it. Matt. 5:21–26, which assumes that anger does not have power over us unless we consent, tells us that anger is not to be hidden or disregarded. Nor should we foolishly act upon its impulses. Anger should instead be dealt with—by becoming the opportunity for repairing broken relationships. It is when rapport and harmony are established with the objects of anger that anger disappears.

One final point. One can ask whether Matt. 5:21–26 is not potentially dangerous because it can lead to passivity in a situation of injustice. Do we really want, for instance, to tell the woman in an abusive relationship not to be angry? Would that not be a cruel and immoral imperative?

Perhaps the best thing to do here is to recognize the humanity of our text. We have gotten used to the fact, established by the historical-critical method, that the Bible is not a coherent whole but a collection of diverse documents by various authors with different opinions on a multitude of subjects. We are perhaps less used to the fact that a single book or even the redactional work of an author may not be coherent. But, as we already knew long before the deconstructionists came along, this is indeed often the case, and it seems to be the case with Matthew.

Commentators as well as Jewish readers of the New Testament have long wondered how Matthew's Jesus can tell his followers to love their enemies and yet hurl vituperations so frequently at them. Did Matthew believe Jesus exempt from certain commandments because of his status as judge? Or did he somehow think Jesus' rebukes stemmed from love and were necessary for correcting error? Did he believe that Jesus was passive with regard to injustice done to himself but active with regard to injustice committed by others? The commentaries sometimes raise these questions, but they nowhere satisfactorily answer them. The contradiction appears ineradicable.

Matters seem to be similar in Matthew with regard to the subject of anger. Despite Matt. 5:21–26 and Matthew's omission of Markan

verses in which Jesus gets angry, Matthew still relates a story in which
Jesus does violent things in the temple and a discourse—chapter 23,
the vituperations hurled against scribes and Pharisees—that is hard to
dissociate from anger. Hans Windisch described Matthew 23 as issuing
"from the agitated soul of a violently indignant prophet" (*Meaning,*
103). Matt. 23:17 in particular is problematic. For here Jesus, against
the plain sense of 5:22 ("and if you say, 'You fool,' you shall be liable
to the hell of fire"), calls his opponents "fools" ("You blind fools! For
which is greater, the gold or the sanctuary that has made the gold
sacred?"). Can anyone find the harmony here between Jesus' words
and his deeds?

Maybe we should not be looking for artificial concord but rather trying to make the best of the contradiction. Matt. 5:21–26 remains as an
appeal for self-control and kindness in word and attitude toward others.
Here Cassian and Luz are right, and the radical formulation serves to
stress the importance of such self-control and kindness. At the same
time, the biblical texts that allow justifiable anger as well as the apparent anger of Jesus in Matthew's narrative cannot be banished on the
strength of our text. They rather create a never-to-be-resolved dialectic.
The blanket prohibition of anger is a blanket prohibition, but it stands
within both Matthew and the larger biblical narrative. Within those
wider contexts, the prohibition must be qualified for the sake of the situation in which an absence of anger might lead to an absence of justice.

One can, then, agree with those who see our text as prohibiting all
anger. But when it comes to real life, none of us can be Vulcans; nor, in
view of those rare situations in which we may reasonably deem anger
the servant of good, should we want invariably to make that demand
of others. And as justification we can appeal to Matthew's Jesus, who
tells us not to be angry and not to insult others, but who also shows us,
through his encounters with his opponents and his actions in the temple, how on occasion it may be necessary to speak the harsh truth and
display the divine indignation.

LUST AND ADULTERY (5:27–30)

Jesus' prohibition of wrongful desire and its equation with adultery do
not contradict the biblical injunctions against adultery (Exod. 20:14;
Deut. 5:18), for Jesus himself speaks against this sin (5:32; 15:19; 19:9).

Rather does he pass beyond the Decalogue to require more: 5:27–30 at once upholds and supplements the law. Jesus upholds the Torah because, as Augustine had it, "The one who does not commit adultery in the heart [cf. Prov. 6:25], much more easily guards against committing adultery in actual fact. So he who gave the later precept confirmed the earlier; for he came not to destroy the law, but to fulfil it" (*Sermon on the Mount* 1.12.33). Jesus supplements the law because, while he approves the old law, which condemns the external act as evil, he declares that no less evil is the intention that brings it forth.

The text could have to do specifically with a man lusting after another man's wife, for the Greek word here usually translated "woman" (*gynaika*) may in this instance mean "wife," and the subject of the citation is adultery. There in fact may be an allusion to the tenth commandment, "You shall not covet your neighbor's wife." Matt. 5:28 uses the same verb (*epithymeō*) that the Greek translation uses for the Hebrew "covet."

It would, however, be unreasonable to narrow the scope of Jesus' imperative—as though it censures unlawful lust toward a married woman but not unlawful lust toward an unmarried woman, prostitute or not. In Matthew's world, fornication was not yet a second-class sin; it was in the same category as adultery. This is why in Matt. 15:19 fornication is ranked beside murder, adultery, and theft. When the Vulgate translated the Greek *gynaika* with the general *mulier* ("woman"), it was not twisting the sense of the text.

In at least three respects Matt. 5:27–30 must be judged conventional. First, the hyperbolic, moral equation of wrongful desire with adultery—which "suggests that no one should be regarded as a sex object" (Amy-Jill Levine in Newsom and Ringe, *Women's Bible Commentary,* 255)—cannot be reckoned as Jesus' innovation. In the *Testament of Issachar,* the patriarch at the end of his life boasts, "I have not had intercourse with any woman other than my wife, nor was I promiscuous by lustful look" (7:2). In the *Mekhilta of R. Simeon* we read that one should not commit adultery "either with the eye or with the heart" (111). And R. Simeon ben Lakish is recorded to have said, "Even he who visualizes himself in the act of adultery is called an adulterer" (*Leviticus Rabbah* 23:12). Obviously Jesus' equation in 5:27–30 not only does not contradict Moses but is at home in the Jewish tradition. There are also parallels outside that tradition. The Stoic philosopher Epictetus congratulated himself with these words:

"Today, when I saw a handsome person, I did not say to myself, Oh, that I could possess her . . . nor did I go on to fancy her in my arms" (in Arrian, *Discourses of Epictetus* 2.18). Once again, then, we must reject the idea that the Sermon on the Mount offers us some sort of novel extremism.

Second, 5:27–30 assumes that God judges not only our deeds but also our thoughts, our intentions. This too was an idea Jesus took from his tradition. According to *Pseudo-Phocylides*, a first-century book of Jewish wisdom, "it is each one's intention that is examined" (52). As the *Letter of Aristeas* puts it, even the one who thinks of doing evil will not escape (133). The rabbis could even say that "all depends upon the intention of the heart" (Babylonian Talmud *Megillah* 20a).

Third, the injunction to guard the eyes because they can arouse inappropriate desire appears in many old Jewish texts. Already Gen. 3:6 relates that Eve took forbidden fruit in part because the tree "was a delight to the eyes." In Job 31:1 we read, "I have made a covenant with my eyes; how then could I look upon a virgin?" Ecclesiasticus warns, "Turn away your eyes from a shapely woman, and do not look intently at beauty belonging to another; many have been misled by a woman's beauty, and by it passion is kindled like a fire" (9:8). The *Testament of Reuben* speaks of the spirit of hearing which brings instruction, the spirit of speech which conveys knowledge, and the spirit of seeing, "which comes with desire" (2:4–6). Obviously Jesus was far from the first to be concerned about "lustful eyes" (1QS 1:6) or the "eye full of adultery" (2 Pet. 2:14) or "the desire of the eyes" (1 John 2:16).

Despite all the parallels just cited, the very fact that Jesus' warning against lust is formulated as a solemn contrast shows it to have been needful. All too often our failures stem not from ignorance but from negligence to act upon what we already know. As Pascal put it, "All the good maxims are already current; what we need is to apply them" (*Pensées* 6, 380). This is why we read the Sermon on the Mount not once but over and over throughout our lifetimes—and also why Jesus' words were important in a first-century context even if they were not revolutionary in content.

Perhaps the most important error to guard against when reading 5:27–30 is the supposition that we have here an uninformed attack on human biology. Human beings are programmed to reproduce, and the sexual impulse is powerful. But nothing here denies those two inescapable facts. Jesus is not, so to speak, attacking hormones. He is not indicting the involuntary arrival of sexual desire. He is instead telling us that we are responsible creatures who have a choice in what we do with our natural drives. The body need not be the master.

It is crucial to observe that Matthew's construction (*pros to epithymsai*) implies that the sin lies not in the entrance of a thought but in letting it incite to wrongful passion (cf. the use of the related expressions in 6:1 and 23:5). One could translate: "Everyone looking upon a woman *in order to* lust after her . . . ." Jesus is talking not about feelings but about intentions, and so the sin he condemns lies not in the entrance of desire but in what one does with that desire. Luther got it right: "It is impossible to keep the devil from shooting evil thoughts and lusts into your heart. But see to it that you do not let such arrows stick there and take root, but tear them out and throw them away" (*Sermon on the Mount*, 88). And long before Luther, Evagrius observed: "It is not in our power to determine whether we are disturbed by these thoughts, but it is up to us to decide if they are to linger within us or not and whether or not they are to stir up our passions" (*Praktikos* 6). Matt. 5:27–30 is really about controlling the imagination—not about the eyes so much as the soul that uses them.

It is also crucial to note that when the rest of Matthew is taken to heart, we cannot construe 5:28 as frowning upon sexual desire within marriage. In 19:1–9 Jesus quotes Genesis in coming to the conclusion that "what God has joined together, let no one put asunder." Marriage is, according to this, part of the natural order, and the natural order is, despite the coming eschatological change, from God. Hence redemption does not eclipse creation. This seems to entail that the things which properly belong to marriage, including sexual intercourse, must be accepted as being from the hand of God—and thus that 5:28 outlaws not desire within marriage but unlawful desire outside it. Certainly this was the view of Paul. For although he declared that "those who belong to Christ Jesus have crucified the flesh with its passions and desires" (Gal. 5:24), he also taught that sexual desire can be properly expressed within marriage (1 Corinthians 7). As Socrates Scholasticus memorably put it, "Intercourse of a man with his lawful wife is chastity" (*Church History* 1.11).

That this was indeed the view of Matthew seems to follow from the Protestant interpretation of 1:25, where we read that Joseph had no marital relations with Mary "until she had borne a son." Roman Catholics and Eastern Orthodox, because of their belief in the perpetual virginity of Mary, have denied that this expression implies sexual intimacy later on. But Protestants, who do not hold Mary to have been ever virgin, have found implied in 1:25 the resumption of conjugal relations. On this reading it matters that Matthew labels Joseph as "righteous" (1:19), a man who does God's will. If the evangelist tells us in effect that Joseph resumed sexual relations with his wife after Jesus was born, we are prohibited from seeing anything wrong with such activity. In line with this is the generalization of Maximus the Confessor: "It is not food which is evil but gluttony, not the begetting of children but fornication, not possessions but greed, not reputation but vainglory. And if this is so, there is nothing evil in creatures except misuse, which stems from the mind's negligence in its natural cultivation" (*Four Centuries on Charity* 3.4).

This still leaves many of our questions unanswered, for Jesus tells us not what to do with inconvenient desire but only what not to do with it. This will seem particularly irksome to those whose sexual drive cannot find satisfaction in marriage. Elsewhere Matthew acknowledges the possibility of celibacy as an act of sacrifice for the kingdom of God (19:10–12), but even there he does not tell us how we are to master our instinctive impulses. Francis of Assisi once told his disciples to jump in a cold mountain stream. (Obviously he did not know that cold water increases the production of testosterone.) But Jesus says nothing of this sort. Certainly the saying about eunuchs cannot be given a literal sense. Nor does Jesus say it is necessary for men to abandon the company of women or vice versa—although monks and ascetics often drew this inference from his words (e.g., the *Philocalia*, St. Mark the Ascetic, "Letter to Nicolas the Solitary").

But if we here feel the lack of some positive counsel, Jesus' words remain highly relevant. For however we seek to come to terms with the difficulties created by frustrated sexual desire, 5:27–30 plainly implies that human beings need not be the passive victims of their natural drives; it makes plain that they are responsible for what they do with those drives. Perhaps animals are automatons when it comes to mating, but human beings have the ability to control and direct themselves. Jesus refers to an all-too-common occurrence—a man looking lustfully at another's wife—and says that it need not be. Obviously he assumes that the imagination can be rightly directed, that vigorous self-restraint is possible. If disciples must achieve a righteousness even surpassing that of the Pharisees (5:20), they must likewise exhibit a self-control surpassing that of average people.

That this is far from easy, however, appears from the vivid demands for personal sacrifice in 5:29–30 (which reappear in 18:8–9). By telling followers to pluck out their eyes and cut off their hands Jesus makes plain both how important it is to be rid of sin but also how difficult it is. He does not of course ask for literal amputation. The language is hyperbolic. Jesus knows as well as Paul that the problem is not the body as such but the sin that dwells in it (cf. Rom. 7:17, 20). As Matt. 15:17–18 has it, "Do you not see that whatever goes into the mouth enters the stomach and goes out into the sewer? But what comes out of the mouth proceeds from the heart, and that is what defiles." The Christian "amputates the passions of the soul without touching the body" (Origen, *Commentary on Matthew* 15.4). But the point still remains: "Both eye and hand are less than Christ, and when they are used as the instruments of lust and hinder the whole body from the purity of discipleship, they must be sacrificed for the sake of him. . . . When you have made your eye the instrument of impurity, you cannot see God with it" (Bonhoeffer, *Cost,* 148).

Before passing on to the next subject, one should observe that Matthew's Jesus does not simply assume that human beings have the ability to rule, or at least direct, their sexual impulses. Our Gospel even foresees a future in which human nature will seemingly be rid of its sexual component. In 22:30, in debate with Sadducees about the resurrection, Jesus affirms that, in heaven, "(Men) neither marry nor are (women) given in marriage." They will instead be "like angels." The meaning appears to be the same as the sentiment in the rabbinic source, Babylonian Talmud *Berakhot* 17a: "In the world to come there is no . . . propagation."

Sex was largely thought of as serving the purpose of procreation, not pleasure, and angels (usually conceived of as male) were thought to be deathless. It followed that intercourse for them was unnecessary and would only have been self-indulgence. So too, according to Jesus' argument, shall it then be for the righteous. They, upon gaining eternal life, will no longer need to reproduce (cf. Luke 20:34–36).

Matt. 22:30 par. has understandably not played much of a role in modern Christian thought or practice. The Reformers' rejection of the superiority of virginity, Protestantism's neglect of the angels, post-Enlightenment skepticism regarding unseen spiritual beings and even the life to come, and the modern inability to sympathize much with asceticism have made the verse and its presuppositions problematic for many. But the point here is that Matthew's Jesus can conceive of human nature apart from its sexual component. Living as we do after

Freud, who so influentially argued that we are sexual creatures through and through, we may find this an improbable thought. Yet it remains true that if we believe in any sort of life after death, it is hard to imagine that sex, which is from one point of view glands and chemicals, can have anything to do with that life. Does this not entail that at some level there is distance between the true self and its sexual nature?

DIVORCE AND ADULTERY (5:31–32)

If lust for another's spouse carries the guilt of adultery, so too does divorce. Jesus summarizes Deut. 24:1–4, where allowance is made for remarriage, and then goes on to say that (for a man) to divorce (a woman) except for *porneia* causes her (because she will remarry) to commit adultery. As it stands the text raises several questions. What is meant by "except for unchastity"? What is the reason for Jesus' prohibition? Is remarriage ever permitted? Does Jesus not here contradict the Jewish Scriptures?

Concerning the meaning of "except for unchastity," does this refer to incest, to adultery, or to something else again (a few have suggested "fornication")? In favor of seeing an exception for incest, we can envisage a situation in which Gentiles entering Matthew's community were found to be, because of marriages made before conversion, in violation of the Levitical laws of incest (see Leviticus 17). There is, however, no patristic support for the equation of *porneia* with adultery. More importantly, attention needs to be paid to the illuminating fact that Matthew itself contains a story in which the decision to divorce is made by a main character. In 1:19–25 we are told that Mary became pregnant through the Holy Spirit, that Joseph first learned of her pregnancy without learning of its supernatural cause, and that therefore he determined to obtain a certificate of divorce. In the event, he did not carry through his resolution, for the angel of the Lord appeared to disabuse him of his mistaken inference, namely, that his wife had been unfaithful.

This matters for the interpretation of Matt. 5:31–32 and 19:1–12 because the text plainly affirms that Joseph was "righteous." In fact, the statement to that effect is closely joined to the remark on Joseph's decision to divorce: "Her husband Joseph, being a righteous man and unwilling to expose her to public disgrace, planned to dismiss her quietly." Now because Matthew elsewhere allows only one exception to the prohibition of divorce, and because Joseph is a just man who decides to obtain a divorce, his circumstance must be covered by the exception clause. It is, if "unchastity" means "adultery." (Mary and Joseph were already engaged [Matt. 1:18], and under Jewish law betrothal was the legal equivalent of marriage. So Mary's theoretical unfaithfulness constitutes adultery.) If, however, one equates "unchastity" with "incest" or "fornication," then there would be a contradiction: although in 5:32 and 19:9 Jesus would make provision for a legitimate divorce, that provision would have nothing to do with the course Joseph decides to follow. But would Matthew then depict Joseph as "righteous" and so a model of behavior in accord with God's will if his actions so obviously contradicted a ruling of Jesus? It seems better to harmonize 1:18–25 with 5:31–32 and so conclude that the latter envisages adultery.

Regarding the reason for Jesus' prohibition, although 5:31–32 fails us, the lack is made up in 19:3–9, where divorce is treated at some length. Here Jesus quotes Gen. 1:27 ("male and female he created them") and 2:24 ("and they become one flesh") and argues that divorce is not consistent with monogamy, which was God's intention for human beings. Marriage creates a bond of kinship between man and wife that can no more be broken than the bond of kinship between parent and child. This explains why the force of Jesus' saying appears to be on remarriage as adultery: people who have been married remain married.

The problem of whether 19:9 allows remarriage for the innocent party (so traditionally most Protestants) cannot, as Augustine conceded (*Faith and Works* 19), finally be answered. (There is a similar debate over 1 Cor. 7:15: does this verse leave open the possibility of remarriage after abandonment?) Grammatical reflections cannot decide. One might appeal to patristic opinion, which almost universally disallowed remarriage and so understood our text accordingly. But the fathers were burdened by a less than enthusiastic view of marriage. The link with vv. 10–12, which have to do with sexual abstinence, has, however, recently been thought to uphold the patristic interpretation: the eunuchs for the kingdom of heaven are those who have separated from their spouses and do not remarry. But the saying about eunuchs is not a command but a qualified recommendation. There is also the issue of whether something like the later distinction between separation and divorce would have made any sense in

Matthew's Jewish environment. The Jewish divorce bill contained the clause, "You are free to marry again." So to obtain a divorce was to obtain permission to remarry. In line with this, 5:32 simply assumes that divorce leads to remarriage (to divorce a wife is to make her commit adultery—because she will take another spouse). The dominant interpretation in Protestant circles, which holds that one can remarry if one's spouse has been unfaithful, accordingly remains a possible reading of Matthew's text.

It has often been thought that Matthew's Jesus contradicts Moses in 5:31–32. But this is plainly wrong, for several reasons. (1) Although divorce is taken for granted in a number of Jewish texts (Lev. 21:7, 14; 22:13; Num. 30:9; Deut. 22:29 [giving a case in which divorce is not permitted]; Ezra 10; Nehemiah 13), it is elsewhere implied that something might be wrong with the action (Lev. 18:18 [?]; Deut. 24:4; Mal. 2:16 ["I (Yahweh) hate divorce"]). Moreover, Lev. 21:7 and Ezek. 44:22 prohibit priests from marrying divorcees, which suggests that divorce is at odds with holiness. (2) There is a Dead Sea Scroll which some have thought prohibits divorce (see CD 4:19–21). (3) The rabbinic school of Shammai interpreted Deut. 24:1 to allow divorce only for sexual unfaithfulness—the same teaching we find in Matthew.

(4) In 19:1–12 Jesus does not say that the teaching of Genesis is from God, that in Deuteronomy from Moses. Rather, the instructions in Deut. 24:1 were given because of Israel's moral petrification; that is, they were a "concession" to the postfallen state. Jesus distinguishes between a portion of the law that expresses God's original will for humanity, on the one hand, and, on the other, another portion in which divine instruction is a response to human failure. There is a parallel to this sort of distinction in the Hebrew Bible itself. Although Deut. 17:14–20, the law of the king, accepts kingship and promulgates divine precepts for it, other passages regard it as an imperfect institution chosen by Israel, not God (cf. Judg. 8:22–23; 1 Sam. 8:4–22). Here too then one may find divine "concessions" or "compromises."

(5) The Hebrew Bible *permits* but does not *command* divorce. The importance of this appears from Matt. 19:7–8: whereas the Pharisees ask why Moses "commanded" a certificate of divorce to be given, Jesus speaks only of Moses giving permission. This allows the view that Moses allowed divorce only as the lesser of two evils in some circumstances.

The history of the interpretation of our passage is instructive. Roman Catholic tradition, like the canons of the Church of England, has generally allowed separation but not divorce—although exceptions have been granted for cases of nonconsummation and for one of two non-Christians converting to Catholicism. Marriage has been thought legally indissoluble, at least until one partner dies. The church has and does, however, issue annulments. In these cases it is said that there was no real marriage in the first place.

Eastern Orthodox tradition has permitted divorce for many reasons, including mental illness, leprosy, and abortion. While recognizing one marriage as the norm, it has also allowed remarriage (although usually only one's first marriage is blessed in a eucharistic service; later marriages have been, until recent times, only civil affairs). Indeed, Orthodox tradition even has a few saints who remarried (e.g., the twelfth- and thirteenth-century Georgian Queen Tamar). Jesus' prohibition of divorce except for one cause has been interpreted not as an inviolate law but as a statement of the human ideal, which sinful humanity often does not live up to. So the church condescends, through its exercise of pastoral "economy," to human weakness. At the same time, it has traditionally demanded penance (usually involving abstinence from communion for a year or more) upon entrance into a second wedding. As the Sixth Ecumenical Council decreed:

> He who leaves the wife given him, and takes another is guilty of adultery by the sentence of the Lord. And it has been decreed by our Fathers that they who are such must be "weepers" for a year, "hearers" [that is, allowed to hear the sermon but not take communion] for two years, "prostrators" for three years, and in the seventh year to stand with the faithful and be counted worthy of the Oblation. (canon 87)

Protestants have tended to follow one of three courses. Most have traditionally agreed with Erasmus (who incidentally contended that King Henry VIII should be able to divorce in order to wed a woman who could give him children.). He argued that Jesus allows divorce for adultery; and further that if adultery has occurred, then remarriage can take place. A minority has differed only on the subject of remarriage: even when adultery has occurred, there can be no remarriage. Recently, however, more and more Protestants seem to be in harmony with the view of the Eastern Orthodox: Jesus' ruling should not be construed in a juridical or legalistic fashion.

Which of these approaches is the more faithful to Matthew? One can urge that Matthew himself did not understand Jesus' prohibition as a binding rule because the rest of the Sermon is not casuistic but a picturesque means of shaping the moral imagination. This would accord with the Orthodox position. And yet the appearance of "except for adultery" sounds as though we are dealing with a legal ruling. So despite the focus on virtues rather than rules, both are present: the Sermon on the Mount integrates the two. This means that the Sermon does not wholly agree with Joseph Fletcher's situational ethics, according to which Christians should not follow rules but rather do the most loving thing—something like utilitarianism, with love substituted for happiness. Rather is it closer to those Christian moral thinkers who urge that love consistently seeks the fulfillment of certain rules.

But where does this leave us? Perhaps we can here find some aid in the historical-critical method, which is here in harmony with a canonical reading that interprets Matthew in the light of other Scriptures. There are actually five different early versions of Jesus' prohibition of divorce: 1 Cor. 7:10–11; Luke 16:18 (Q); Mark 10:11–12; Matt. 5:31–32; 19:9. They appear to reflect a complex evolutionary history. Jesus' original command was probably close to the following: "Everyone who/whoever divorces his wife and marries another commits adultery" (cf. Luke 16:18a). But the teaching was clarified, expanded, and qualified in at least four different ways:

1. In view of the Roman legal situation, where women could divorce their husbands, the prohibition of a wife divorcing her husband and marrying another was added (Mark 10:11–12; 1 Cor. 7:10).
2. The saying was naturally expanded to make clear that those who married a divorcee are also implicated in adultery (Luke 16:18b).
3. Paul taught that Jesus' prohibition need not cover marriages between a Christian and non-Christian (1 Cor. 7:10–16).
4. In Matthew we find explicit notice that the rule does not cover adultery (5:32; 19:9).

What one learns from the different additions is that Jesus' ruling was both broadened (Mark, Luke) and qualified (Matthew, Paul). It is noteworthy that Paul can refer to Jesus' unqualified imperative and then immediately comment, "but if she does [nonetheless] separate . . . ." Early Christian tradition did not everywhere receive the ruling against divorce as an inviolate law to be applied literally, without imagination. Surely this fact is full of hermeneutical significance, and one may fairly view it as partial justification of the Eastern Orthodox position, which has refused to interpret the norm in a legalistic manner. Although the Eastern Church, in honor of Jesus' ruling, has consistently taught that divorce and remarriage are always the work of sin and so has discouraged divorce, it has nonetheless urged that when sin has destroyed a marriage, repentance can bring a new start.

This emphasis on repentance is in continuity with Matthew's Gospel. Although the Sermon on the Mount itself does not refer to repentance, the theme runs throughout Matthew (3:2, 8, 11; 4:17; 11:20, 21; 12:41; 21:30, 32; 27:3). Most striking of all is the remark in 27:3 that Judas himself "repented." The Greek word used here is the same as that used in 21:32, where the subject is John the Baptist's demand for repentance. Now the interpretation of 27:3 is exceedingly difficult, and we cannot enter into the exegetical details here. But it is at least possible that Judas, who not only feels remorse but also confesses and returns his ill-gotten gain, makes authentic repentance. This reading gives to the verb its natural meaning, harmonizes with Jewish texts in which suicide makes atonement for sin (e.g., *4 Macc.* 12:19; 17:1, 21; *Genesis Rabbah* on 27:27), and coheres with the praise of repentance in Judaism and Christianity: true repentance can be effective even if it comes at the last hour of life. However that may be, Matthew says nothing that would exclude the possibility of repentance for sin after baptism. Matt. 18:15–20 in fact contains directions for restoring a Christian who has sinned against a fellow believer.

Perhaps the pastoral problem of divorce can be approached through the realization that sometimes our choice is not between good and evil but between two evils. In such circumstances, which are inevitable in a fallen world, we are obviously called to choose with contrition the lesser of those two evils. Sadly, we all know of cases in which, let us say, a woman's remaining within a marriage would not only be damaging to her mental health but physically dangerous for her and her children. It would seem silly and cruel for a pastor to tell her that, whatever other wrongs her husband has committed, only the physical act of adultery will allow her to go to court and sue for divorce. The needed message is instead that the indissolubility of marriage does not cancel human freedom, and that human freedom can destroy God's intentions for marriage. In such a case it would be out of accord with the Christian tradition to say that divorce is a good thing, but it may nonetheless be regarded as the lesser of two evils. This is why the Orthodox tradition tolerates—it does not encourage—divorce and remarriage, but only with penance.

The last word on divorce, however, must be that the pastoral imperative to recognize that adultery is not the only legitimate reason for seeking divorce is fraught with hazard. Jesus originally spoke his word to a society in which perhaps many considered divorce a little thing. The rabbinic school of Hillel is said to have ruled that the "unseemly thing" of Deut. 24:1 could be enlarged to include burning a husband's food. Today things have come full circle. Within the churches as well as without, divorce has become a common fact with little stigma attached; and "irreconcilable differences" now cover a multitude of sins. "Monogamy" for many now means "serial monogamy," that is, one spouse at a time. Our freedom from casuistry has degenerated into a general permissiveness. This can hardly be in accord with the intention of Matthew, in which Jesus' word on divorce is sufficiently important so as to be recorded twice.

FOR FURTHER READING

Collins, R. F. *Divorce in the New Testament.* Collegeville, Minn.: Liturgical Press, 1992.

Deming, W. "Mark 9,42–10,12; Matthew 5,27–32 and b. Nid. 13b: A First Century Discussion of Male Sexuality." *New Testament Studies* 36 (1990): 130–41.

Garland, David E. "A Biblical View of Divorce." *Review and Expositor* 84 (1987): 419–32.

Heth, William A., and G. J. Wenham. *Jesus and Divorce: The Problem with the Evangelical Consensus.* London: Hodder & Stoughton, 1984.

Moule, C. F. D. "Uncomfortable Words I: The Angry Word: Matthew 5,21f." *Expository Times* 81 (1969): 10–13.

Saldarini, Anthony J. *Matthew's Christian-Jewish Community.* Chicago and London: University of London, 1994. Pp. 124–64.

5

Oaths, Revenge, Love
(5:33-48)

T HE NEXT THREE PARAGRAPHS on Jesus and the Torah (5:33–37, 38–42, 43–48) are harder to harmonize with the denial in 5:17–20 (Jesus did not come to abolish the Law and the Prophets) than the first three paragraphs (5:21–26, 27–30, 32–33). But if the text is to be given the benefit of the doubt and allowed to interpret itself, then it is our first task to see if harmony can be reached. Only if such cannot be achieved should we declare the text to be inconsistent with itself.

OATHS (5:33-37)

The Hebrew Bible permits oaths in everyday speech—provided they are neither false nor irreverent. But here Jesus, after summarizing the teaching found in Exod. 20:7; Lev. 19:12; Num. 30:3–15; Ps. 50:14; and elsewhere, declares that oaths are not needed. Is this not a plain contradiction of the Jewish Scriptures? The apparent discrepancy is all the greater because God and the saints swear in the Bible. In Gen. 14:22 Abraham declares, "I have sworn to the Lord, God Most High, maker of heaven and earth, that I would not take a thread or a sandal-thong of anything that is yours." In Gen. 22:16 the angel of the Lord appears to Abraham and says, "By myself I have sworn, says the Lord: Because you have done this, and have not withheld your son, your only son, I will indeed bless you" (cf. Exod. 6:8; Isa. 45:23; Luke 1:73; Acts 2:30). Theophylact could write that at the time of Moses "it was

84

not evil to swear. But after Christ, it is evil" (*Commentary on Matthew* ad loc.).

A canonical reading that, following the lead of 5:17–20, seeks for some type of harmony between Matthew and the rest of the Bible also seems problematic because some of the earliest Christian literature shows no aversion to swearing. Paul calls upon God as his witness in Rom. 1:9; 2 Cor. 1:23; Gal. 1:20; and Phil. 1:8. In Rev. 10:6 an angel "swears by him who lives forever and ever." And then there are the several extracanonical witnesses which show us that many early Christians saw nothing wrong with certain oaths. In the *Protevangelium of James*, an early infancy gospel, Anna, the mother of John the Baptist, uses the oath formula, "As the Lord my God lives" (4.1; cf. Judg. 8:19). In the apocryphal *Acts of John*, the apostle John swears with the words, "As the Lord Jesus Christ lives" (28). The *Pseudo-Clementine Recognitions* say that Jesus took an oath when he uttered John 3:5.

Matthew itself at one point seems to presuppose the validity of certain oaths. The long discussion of oaths in 23:16–22 resembles 5:33–37. For both teach that to swear by one thing is to swear by another. Indeed, both assert that to swear by heaven is to swear by God's throne. But 23:16–22 does not attack oaths without qualification; rather does their use appear to be assumed. At least no one reading 23:16–22 without 5:33–37 would conclude that the former abolishes the oath. Do we have here a genuine contradiction? Or is 23:16–22 reason for surmising that Jesus' prohibition in the Sermon on the Mount should be understood as hyperbole, not a universally binding rule?

It is not easy to figure out what we should make of the conflicting texts. One way to lessen or undo the perceived tensions is to suppose that Jesus' command does not forbid all oaths because the situation envisaged is not swearing in court but swearing in everyday speech (which according to Philo was quite common among first-century Jews [*On the Decalogue* 92]). On this interpretation, our text is a polemic only against "the evil habit of swearing incessantly and thoughtlessly about ordinary matters" (ibid.). This has historically been the view of most Roman Catholic expositors. It was also the view of Zwingli, Bucer, and Bengel. So too Luther, who wrote: "Christ is neither prohibiting nor prescribing anything for the government here, but he is letting the realm take its own course as it should and must. What he is forbidding is unauthorized, capricious, or habitual swearing" (*Sermon on the Mount*, 102). One recalls the thirty-ninth article of religion in the Book of Common Prayer: "As we confess that vain and rash Swearing is forbidden Christian men by our Lord Jesus Christ, and James his Apostle, so we judge, that Christian Religion doth not prohibit, but that a man may swear when the Magistrate requireth, in a cause of faith and charity, so it be done according to the Prophet's teaching, in justice, judgment, and truth." Already Augustine taught, "Let a man restrain himself as much as he can, since he understands that swearing is not to be counted among the things that are good, but as one of the things that are necessary" (*Sermon on the Mount* 1.17.51). Calvin for his part went so far as to judge that Jesus condemned only those oaths that "transgressed the rule of the Law" (*Institutes* 2.8.26).

One good reason for wondering whether 5:33–37 was intended to be a literal, blanket prohibition emerges from the end of the pericope. Jesus says, "Let your word be 'Yes, Yes' or 'No, No'; anything more than this comes from the evil one." This is obviously hyperbole, something most commentators recognize (although Strecker thinks it a "substitute oath": instead of swearing one uses the minimal formula, "Yes, Yes" or "No, No"). So if the latter half of our passage is not a legal ruling but an exhortation that makes use of exaggerated rhetoric, perhaps so too the first half. The argument is all the stronger in that the Sermon on the Mount is, above all, moral exhortation, not a list of enforceable rules.

Many, however, have nonetheless taken Jesus' prohibition at face value and allowed the contradiction with the rest of the canon to stand. This is historically the view of the Anabaptists. Mennonites and Quakers have also tended to avoid the oath, as did the followers of Wycliffe and several Russian sects. William Penn wrote a whole treatise on the subject (*A Treatise on Oaths*). It contains a treasure of pagan, Jewish, and Christian testimony against oaths, testimonies that consistently recognize that oaths are only necessary because people so often lie. Penn himself states that his position contradicts the law of Moses. Tolstoy, as we have already seen, went so far as to affirm that Jesus' words require the abolition of courts.

These later Christian witnesses fall in line with many from the early centuries. According to Irenaeus, Jesus "enjoined them [his disciples] not only not to swear falsely but not to swear at all" (*Against Heresies* 2.32.1). Origen included Jesus' prohibition to be among those teachings that should be taken "literally" (*On First Principles* 4.3.4). Eusebius commended Christianity with the question, "What also of the fact that men, far from perjuring themselves, have no need even of a truth oath because of learning from him to 'swear not at all,' but in all things to be guileless and true, so as to be satisfied with 'yea' and 'nay,' making their purpose to be stronger than any oath?" (*Preparation for the Gospel* 1.4 [12c]).

Matthew itself, despite chapter 23, might also be cited in this connection. For in 14:1–12 Herod takes an oath to grant the daughter of Herodias whatever she asks for; and she, to Herod's regret, asks for the head of John the Baptist. Then, in 26:69–75, Peter denies Jesus "with an oath" (vv. 72, 74). So we have two examples in Matthew itself which involve the misuse of oaths. Neither Herod nor Peter should have sworn what he did.

Is there any way of determining who is right regarding the matter of oaths, or at least whose exegesis of 5:33–37 is closer to the original intention of the text? Several observations need to be kept in mind. First, as elsewhere in the Sermon, Jesus is setting forth the ideal. Obviously there would not be any need, in a perfect world, for oaths. For the presupposition behind an oath is that there are two types of statements, one of which demands commitment (the oath), one of which does not (the statement without an oath). But ideally human beings should be invariably committed to every statement; and if they were so committed, then the device of the oath would be altogether superfluous. This seems to be recognized in the earliest extracanonical reference to our saying, namely, Justin Martyr, *Apology* 1.16.5. For the apologist takes Jesus' prohibition of swearing to mean that we should "always [be] speaking the truth."

Second, the condemnation of oaths in Matt. 5:33–37 does not stand alone; that is, it cannot be dismissed as an aberrant teaching without parallel. Again, that is, Jesus has company. Already Eccl. 5:5 says that "it is better that you should not vow than that you should vow and not fulfill it." Even more reservation appears in extracanonical sources, including Ecclus. 23:9: "Do not accustom your mouth to oaths"; Philo: "To swear not at all is the best course and most profitable to life, well suited to a rational nature which has been taught to speak the truth so well on each occasion that its words are regarded as oaths; to swear truly is only, as people say, a 'second-best voyage,' for the mere fact of his swearing casts suspicion on the trustworthiness of the man" (*On the Decalogue* 84); and the Mishnah: those who wish to fulfill the law should not be "profuse in vows" (*Demai* 2:3). Josephus tells us, regarding the Essenes, that "any word of theirs has more force than an oath; swearing they avoid, regarding it as worse than perjury, for they say that one who is not believed without an appeal to God stands condemned already" (*Jewish War* 2.135). Philo, like Coleridge later on ("The more oath-taking, the more lying"), observed that frequent swearing is really a sign of untrustworthiness (*On the Special Laws* 2.8).

Oaths were also sometimes frowned upon outside Jewish tradition. Epictetus said, "Avoid taking oaths, if possible, altogether; at any rate, so far as you are able" (*Enchiridion* 23.5). Marcus Aurelius offered that the good person has no need of them (*Meditations* 3.5). The problem with the oath appears in a couple of lines in Sophocles' *Oedipus at Colonus*. One character says, "You can count on me; I won't let you down." The other responds: "I won't swear you in like someone unreliable." To this the first character says: "You'd just have my word to go on anyway."

Third, on occasion the Jewish Scriptures enjoin swearing. In Num. 5:19–22, for example, priests are instructed to obtain oaths from a woman accused of adultery. On the other hand, Deut. 23:21–22 says that "if you make a vow to the Lord your God, do not postpone fulfilling it; for the Lord your God will surely require it of you, and you would incur guilt. But if you refrain from vowing, you will not incur guilt." This last sentence allows the possibility that some will want to refrain from making a vow—perhaps a step toward Matthew's text.

The undoubted tension between Matt. 5:33–37 and portions of the law should perhaps be relaxed—although here one is reading into Matthew rather than reading out of it—by arguing that Jesus' teaching on oaths is analogous to his teaching on divorce. In 19:1–9 Jesus admits that there is legislation for divorce, but he also asserts that "from the beginning it was not so." Moses added the legislation "because you were so hard-hearted." Just as God permitted kingship and made legislation for it even though it was less than ideal, so he allowed divorce, which is not in conformity to the perfect divine will. So if one is seeking such conformity, divorce becomes problematic. In like manner, the distinction between God's ideal will and concessions for a fallen world could be applied to oaths. One can take the text to be saying, in effect, "from the beginning it was not so." Oaths are only a concession to the fact that people lie. So those who have no place for the lie will equally have no place for the oath. The main point then would be that the oath is not a neutral thing that some use for good and others for evil; rather it is, because of its assumption that some declarations demand more commitment than others, in itself a dubious convention.

One is still perhaps left with the fact that God, in the Bible, swears.

Matthew does not address the issue. Once again, however, a canonical reading might suggest that God is not always the object of imitation but is sometimes the exception to a rule. In Rom. 12:19, for instance, Paul instructs the Roman Christians, "Beloved, never avenge yourselves, but leave room for the wrath of God; for it is written, 'Vengeance is mine, I will repay says the Lord.'" Here God alone acts in a certain way. In this matter the *imitatio dei* is rejected.

It follows from these several observations that we can assert neither that Jesus' prohibition is without parallel nor that it would have been necessarily thought to "abolish the law and the prophets." But beyond this it is very difficult to go. For in the end we cannot answer whether Jesus or Matthew understood the prohibition against oaths to forbid all oaths, including those in court, or was directed only at swearing in everyday speech. Matt. 23:16–22 inclines one to think that the latter is likely the truth. Further, at least in the next passage (5:38–42) purely personal as opposed to juridical affairs are in view. Yet any confidence on the matter is out of place.

Even if one were to conclude that Jesus' words do cover swearing in the court as well as in daily life, it would still be difficult to regard them in a legalistic fashion. This may be illustrated by the fact that, whatever the precise scope of Matt. 5:33–37 may be, all interpreters agree that the text demands invariable honesty—and yet Christian tradition has not even been able to take up this teaching without qualification. It is true that Augustine, Gregory the Great, and Thomas Aquinas, like Immanuel Kant after them, believed that one should not lie in any circumstance. But on this matter most Christians have rather sided with Plato, who permitted the prudent lie.

The thought here is that sometimes one has to choose between the lesser of two evils, and once in a while that will mean telling a lie. Origen, who actually went so far as to say that God, from one point of view, lied in the incarnation by hiding the divine nature in the humanity of Jesus, argued that Christians can lie "in such a way as to seek some great good" (preserved in Jerome, *Apology against Rufinus* 1.18). Hilary of Poitiers, acquiescing to common sense, affirmed that "there is a lie that is most necessary, and sometimes falsehood is useful, when we lie to a murderer about someone's hiding place or falsify testimony for a person in danger or deceive a sick person with respect to the chances for recovery" (*Homilies on Psalms* 10). Chrysostom, loath to denigrate Peter, implausibly urged (as did also Origen and Jerome) that the apostle and Paul conspired together, for the benefit of others, to create the instructive controversy recounted in Galatians 2. Their intention was, by having Peter play a false part, to create a dramatic means of denouncing Judaizers: the two apostles were really at one (*Homilies on Galatians* 2.11). The fifth-century monk Joseph, who thought humility demanded we lie about our spiritual achievements, contended that lying can be a medicine of last resort: one may take refuge in the lie in cases of truly critical need, "but in such a fashion that we are bitten by the guilt of a humbled conscience in a salutary way" (see Cassian, *Conferences* 2.17.17). Rahab, the harlot who lied to save the Israelite spies, is here Joseph's model, not Delilah, who told the truth to her fellow citizens but thereby dishonorably betrayed Samson. Even Augustine, who believed that the imperative to tell the truth admits of no qualification, felt uneasy condemning the person who, because thought untrustworthy, tells a lie rather than the truth in order to save a life (*On Lying* 3).

It is hard to escape the fact that sometimes people are faced not with a choice between good and evil but with a choice between two evils, and that they may accordingly on occasion feel compelled to employ what we call "a white lie," or even deceit of more consequence than that. Although the tradition tells us not to bear false witness, and does so without adding qualifiers (cf. the Decalogue and Matt. 15:19), most people recognize the sad necessity that, the world being what it is, sometimes one imperative comes into conflict with another. In such cases surely the only thing to do is mournful performance of the lesser sin, the sin that does the lesser harm to others as well as ourselves. In other words, the commandment to love one's neighbor (19:19; 22:39) must become the guiding factor—as is seemingly illustrated by Matthew itself (12:1–8).

This observation may seem out of spirit with the Sermon on the Mount, which, after all, gains so much of its power through its heedlessness of earthly contingencies. Our Gospel itself, however, offers a good example of two divine imperatives coming into conflict with each other. In 8:21 a man appears before Jesus and says, "Lord, first let me go and bury my father." In 8:22 Jesus responds with this: "Follow me, and let the dead bury their own dead." This seemingly harsh order has often been thought to contradict the Decalogue, which commands us to honor our parents. And there is no denying that Judaism included burial of one's parents within the purview of that commandment. But Jesus himself, in Matt. 15:4, rebukes his opponents for not honoring father and mother; and in 19:19 he includes the commandment to honor parents as among those leading to eternal life. So one can hardly discover in 8:22, when interpreted in its broader context, an indifference to the Mosaic law or the Decalogue. Rather, our Gospel simply depicts a situation in which two imperatives—the demand to honor one's parents and the demand to follow Jesus—are in conflict. Although the evangelist does not tell us what in this particular case the prospective disciple did, we cannot doubt that Matthew himself thought not following Jesus to be the greater sin (cf. 10:34–37). Implicit here is the notion found in an old Jewish commentary on Deuteronomy. According to this, when a prophet of God appears, "even though he bids you to transgress one of the commandments ordained in the Torah, yet according to the need of the hour listen to him" (*Sipre* on Deut. 18:15). This is just a theological version of the notion that moral imperatives can be in conflict with each other. One is reminded of Dietrich Bonhoeffer, who after writing a book on the Sermon on the Mount participated in the conspiracy to overthrow Hitler. As Georg Strecker comments, Bonhoeffer perhaps illustrates how "deviation from what is literally commanded" ("Turn the other [cheek] also," "Love your enemies") can "mean obedience in spirit" (*Sermon*, 182).

What all of this means is that however one interprets the prohibition of oaths, it, like the prohibition of divorce, must function as an ideal rather than an absolute. An ideal in this context is a rule that one must follow—until it comes into conflict with some other rule. In such a circumstance it becomes apparent that life cannot be wholly lived according to a list of imperatives. One must then instead fall back on one's moral imagination to weigh competing claims. One understands why Donald Hagner says we should not take a "biblicist approach" to 5:33–37, and why Bonhoeffer, in his *Ethics*, argued that the final moral authority for the Christian is not a set of directives but Jesus Christ himself, and why he wrote that "the will of God may lie very deeply concealed beneath a great number of available possibilities. The will of God is not a system of rules which is established from the outset; it is something new and different in each different situation in life, and for this reason . . . [one] must ever anew examine what the will of God may be" (*Ethics*, 56).

All Christian interpreters should, despite Calvin's pleas to the contrary (*Institutes* 2.8.26–27), have no trouble agreeing that there is no place for oaths in private life. That is, oaths should never be voluntarily taken. The only issue concerns being called upon to take an oath in a legal setting. Some may see no problem with this either because of the permission in the Jewish Scriptures (so, e.g., Calvin) or because Matt. 5:33–37 is thought to cover only private oaths. Such Christians may regard the rare demand to swear as an unfortunate necessity of the legal system with which one can reluctantly comply. Others may disagree and refuse to take an oath under any circumstances. Fortunately for these individuals, at least in many Western countries, legal provision has been made for their conscience. One who, for religious reasons, does not wish to swear, can instead choose to affirm.

Before passing on to the next section, a couple of final observations are in order. Some may remain troubled by Paul's use of oath formulas. Here one seems to be faced with two choices. Either Paul did not know Jesus' teaching about oaths. Or he did know it but for whatever reason did not believe it covered what he was doing. In the latter case we would perhaps have further reason for refusing to take the prohibition literally. Unfortunately for us, however, the other option is equally possible.

Lastly, modern readers are typically confused by the references to heaven, God's throne, the earth, and Jerusalem in 5:35. But in the Mishnah some authorities view oaths by heaven, by earth, and by one's own head as not binding (e.g., Mishnah *Nedarim* 1:3). This probably explains their appearance in Matt. 5:34–36—"either by heaven, for it is the throne of God, or by the earth, for it is his footstool. . . . And do not swear by your head, for you cannot make one hair white or black." If someone believed that oaths by heaven or earth or Jerusalem or one's head were, because not binding, not covered by Jesus' prohibition, 5:34–35 counters by linking heaven and earth and Jerusalem to God, thereby making all oaths binding and so nullifying any casuistic attempt to circumvent 5:34a.

REVENGE (5:38–42)

After citing the Mosaic law of reciprocation in 5:38 (see Exod. 21:24; Lev. 24:20; Deut. 19:21), Jesus goes on to offer a general principle in 5:39, "Do not resist [or: retaliate against] an evildoer." It has four illustrations: the disciple is (1) personally insulted ("if anyone strikes you on the right cheek") then (2) taken to court ("and if anyone wants to sue you and take you to court") then (3) impressed to do a soldier's bidding ("if anyone forces you to go one mile") then (4) asked to help one in need of funds ("Give to everyone who begs from you . . . who wants to borrow from you"). The brief scenes vividly represent the demand for an unselfish temperament, for naked humility and a will to suffer the loss of one's personal rights: evil should not be requited with evil. There is no room for vengeance on a personal level (cf. Rom. 12:19).

Perhaps the content of 5:38–42 is already to some extent implicit in earlier sayings in Matthew 5. In 5:3–12 Jesus blesses the meek, the merciful, the peacemakers, and those who are happy to suffer "for righteousness' sake." Would it not be incongruous for such as these to strike out at others or refuse to give when asked? Again, in 5:21–26 Jesus forbids anger, an emotion that would make the actions of 5:38–42 impossible. The continuity between the beatitudes, 5:21–26, and 38–42—which Bonhoeffer labeled "an elaboration of the beatitudes"— helps lend to the Sermon its integrity and unity.

There is also a connection with the so-called "golden rule" in 7:12. This says that we should do unto others as we would have them do unto us. Here reciprocation is commanded. In 5:38–42, however, reciprocation is forbidden. The difference is that in the former case good things are received (it is assumed that "as you would have them do to you" envisages some positive thing) whereas in the latter the things envisioned are harmful. Thus, the two texts together indicate when to respond in kind and when not to respond in kind.

In accord with 5:17–20, 5:38–42 does not appear to be a repudiation of Moses, although many interpreters have thought otherwise. The *lex talionis*, the principle of an eye for an eye (which was sometimes taken literally; see Josephus, *Antiquities* 4.280; Babylonian Talmud *Baba Qamma* 84a), is a legal principle not only in the Hebrew Bible but throughout the ancient world. It appears already in old Mesopotamian law codes and the law of Hammurabi. In the Pentateuch it belongs to the judiciary process (see especially the context of Deut. 19:21). This is not, however, the sphere of application in Matthew. That is, whereas Matt. 5:38–42 concerns personal acts of vengeance by one wronged, Deuteronomy speaks to judges about how to administer the law. It is true that 5:40 refers to the court; but Jesus is not here delivering laws for the court to follow (cf. Hagner, *Matthew 1–13*, ad loc.). He is rather speaking about interpersonal relations and declaring that it is illegitimate for his followers to apply the *lex talionis* to their private problems. So he is not overthrowing the principle of equivalent compensation on an institutional level. The subject of what is appropriate for the legal process is just not addressed. (If it were otherwise, then it would be hard to avoid Tolstoy's judgment that the Sermon on the Mount really implies the abolition of courts, for the principle of equivalent or commensurate compensation is the foundation of all legal systems. Such compensation is in fact the meaning of "justice.")

In this connection it should be observed that elsewhere Matthew's Gospel indeed retains the principle of equivalent compensation. In 10:32–33 Jesus says that those who acknowledge him before others will be acknowledged by the Son of man before the Father in heaven, and that those who deny him before others will be denied by the Son of man before the Father in heaven. Here the divine activity corresponds to the human activity. The law of reciprocity also operates within the Sermon itself, in 6:14–15: "For if you forgive others their trespasses, your heavenly Father will also forgive you; but if you do not forgive others, neither will your Father forgive your trespasses." So for Matthew there is no contradiction between rejection of the *lex talionis* in one sphere of activity and retention of it in another. Matt. 6:14–15 and 10:32–33 are proof that 5:38–42 is not an utter repudiation of the *lex talionis* across all of life but rather a prohibition of its application to one particular area (so also Rom. 12:19).

One is further encouraged to seek for harmony between 5:38–42 and the Hebrew Bible because the latter itself has sentences that approach the former. Exod. 23:4–5 instructs Israelites to return an enemy's ass if it has gone astray or assist it if its burden is too heavy. In Lev. 19:18 we read, "You shall not take vengeance or bear a grudge against any of your people, but you shall love your neighbor as yourself." Prov. 20:22 says, "Do not say, 'I will repay evil'; wait for the Lord, and he will help you." Prov. 24:29 enjoins, "Do not say, 'I will do to others as they have done to me; I will pay them back for what they have done.'" Isa. 50:6 refers to the mysterious servant who says, "I gave my back to those who struck me, and my cheeks to those who pulled out my beard; I did not hide my face from insult and spitting" (cf. Lam. 3:30). Even in the Hebrew Bible itself the *lex talionis* is probably intended to restrain vendettas: once equivalent compensation has been extracted, the matter is ended. This fact allowed Augustine, *Sermon on the Mount* 1.19.56, to urge that if Jesus goes on to prohibit revenge, there is no real contradiction. Furthermore, it goes without saying that one who performed the actions of Matt. 5:39–42 would break no Mosaic law.

The text quoted from Isaiah in the previous paragraph is, as already argued in chapter 1, alluded to not only here, in 5:38–42, but also in the passion narrative, where Jesus takes up the role of the servant. This is just one way in which Matthew presents Jesus himself as the out-standing example of his own teaching. Throughout the Gospel he gives to those who ask from him (8:5–13; 9:27–31; etc.). He does not retaliate when struck (26:67–68). He does not defend himself against false charges when accused before the authorities (26:57–68; 27:11–26). That Jesus is mostly silent after his arrest is an eloquent illustration of what it might mean not to resist or retaliate against evildoers.

It should be stressed that Matthew's teaching on non-retaliation, although it goes against human instinct, does have its parallels. There is a rabbinic passage that declares, "Our rabbis taught: Those who are insulted but do not insult, hear themselves reviled without answering, act through love and rejoice in suffering, of them Scripture says, 'But they who love him are as the sun when he goes forth in his might'" (Babylonian Talmud *Shabbat* 88b). Plutarch tells the story of how Pericles accepted in silence for an entire day a hooligan's abuse and reviling and, afterward, when darkness fell, commanded his servants to take a torch and escort the man home (*Pericles* 5). Texts such as these—and there are others—show that, despite the recurrent protest that turning the other cheek is impractical, Jesus' teaching on nonretaliation is not isolated wisdom. Indeed, Greco-Roman literature shows a developing tendency to speak against revenge. (It must be admitted, however, that in the Greek and Roman world nonretaliation was generally based on the desire for tranquillity and command of the passions.)

Throughout church history Matt. 5:38–42 has been read in two very different ways. Many Christian interpreters have found here the justification for pacifism. Before Constantine, Christian leaders rejected participation in the Roman army and cited our text as sufficient reason. Edward Gibbon could even argue that the Roman Empire fell in part because Christianity eviscerated the military spirit. Much later, many early Anabaptists, the Quakers, and other groups insisted, on the basis of the Sermon on the Mount, that one cannot be both a disciple of Jesus and a soldier, for a soldier cannot turn the other cheek.

Christian pacifists have not only cited Matthew 5–7 but also 26:47–56, the story of the arrest of Jesus. Here an unnamed disciple draws a sword and cuts off an ear of the slave of the high priest. Jesus commands him to put his sword back into place, "for all who take the sword will perish by the sword." And Jesus himself does not resist arrest. Consistent with this is his entry into Jerusalem on a donkey instead of a war horse (21:5), which exemplifies meekness. Beyond this, it seems highly likely that Matthew himself, writing after A.D. 70, could not have avoided seeing political meaning in 5:38–42. For the failed war against Rome had made it plain that the road to revolution led to tragedy. From Matthew's perspective, 5:38–42 must, at the very least, have represented ideological distance from the cause of those, such as the Zealots, who took up arms against Rome in the hope that God would bring them victory.

Augustine, on the other hand, believed in the possibility of a "just war" in which Christians could participate. If the state itself is Christian, then it may be necessary, for the common good, to engage in "benign violence." One can do this and at the same time internalize Jesus' teaching (*Epistle* 138.2). Indeed, Augustine still insisted that private self-defense had no place in Christian life (*Problem of Free Choice* 1.5).

We find something similar in Calvin. In arguing against the Anabaptists, the reformer claimed that "in the Apostolical writings we are not to look for a distinct exposition of those matters [concerning the state], their object being not to form a civil polity, but to establish the spiritual kingdom of Christ" (*Institutes* 4.20.12). Calvin found strong justification for his position in the fact that in the Hebrew Bible warfare is sometimes carried on under God's direction.

There is force in Calvin's view. For if indeed Matthew understood 5:38–42 to enjoin an absolute pacifism and so to outlaw participation in all wars, it is very difficult to see how he could have included in his Gospel 5:17–20, with its strong affirmation that Jesus did not come to abolish the law.

One can also, on the basis of the commandment to love (7:12; 19:19; 22:37–39), question the pacifist's interpretation. Each situation envisioned in 5:38–42 is one in which the disciple alone is insulted or injured. But what does one do if others are being insulted or injured? Although this is a crucial question to which Matthew returns no explicit answer, in the parable in 18:23–35 a king, out of mercy, releases a servant from debt. But when that servant mistreats another, the king intervenes with punishment. In this story the king lets himself suffer wrong; but when it is another who suffers, mercy gives way to justice. Could it be that a similar sort of distinction should be read into 5:38–42?

There are additional reasons for wondering whether 5:38–42 justifies a consistently pacifistic stance. If by pacifism is meant inactivity and submission, our text is clearly about something else. Walter Wink has offered that 5:38–42 does not simply enjoin passive longsuffering. Jesus does not say, Do not strike back, or Give the garment asked for, or Go a mile willingly. He rather says, Turn the other cheek, Give an additional garment, Go an extra mile. These activities do not constitute straightforward compliance but show "how the oppressed can recover the initiative, how they can assert their human dignity in a situation that cannot for the time being be changed. The rules are Caesar's, but how one responds to the rules is God's, and Caesar has no power over that" (Swartley, *Love of Enemy*, 111). In other words, Jesus was propounding a "subversive assertiveness" intended to open "a way by which evil can be opposed without being mirrored, the oppressor resisted without being emulated, the enemy neutralized without being destroyed" (ibid.). There may be some truth in this analysis, which would entail that simple passivity (the sort of thing Augustine thought appropriate for the individual Christian) is not being commended. Our text rather calls for a creative, nonviolent activism.

Such activism cannot be the subject of casuistry. "Do not resist [or: retaliate against] an evildoer" is a general principle, and it is followed not by case law but by striking illustrations, by concrete pictures intended to awaken the imagination to unexpected possibilities. It is, furthermore, even possible that the pictures offer impractical advice. If, after being struck on the right cheek with a back-handed insult from an enemy's right hand, one were literally to turn the other cheek, the slapper would either have to switch hands to give a back-handed insult or use a fist. And if one were to give away one's undergarment as well as one's overgarment, the result would be nudity. The very strangeness of these images warns that we may have here exaggeration or hyperbole.

Even if one were, against the drift of my argument, inclined to a pacifistic interpretation of 5:38–42, we would still, as elsewhere in the Sermon on the Mount, face the problem of a choice between two evils. Non-retaliation is one idea embodied in our text; but what if the equally important imperatives for justice or defense of the innocent appear to demand the exercise of force? What do we do when there is a conflict between love of neighbor and love of enemy? Our text offers no rule for such conflicting situations because none can be offered. Augustine asked whether one should give money simply because one is asked, even when it is obvious it is going to a bad cause—for example, the injury of innocents. Most of us, agreeing with Aristotle that we should give "to the right people, the right amounts, at the right time"

(*Nicomachean Ethics* 1120a), would answer that one should not, even if this literally contradicts the imperative in 5:42. We would rather be inclined to think that, despite the silence of the Sermon on the subject, we must distinguish between different sorts of people who want or need our money.

The history of the interpretation of our text illuminates how the same text may function differently in different contexts. Jesus and Matthew and the pre-Constantinian Christians were outsiders or belonged to minorities, as have most proponents of pacifism. Now outsiders and minorities are not, by definition, responsible for the institutions of society. This circumstance makes it easier for them to promulgate ideals that seemingly take little or no account of the conflicts that inevitably arise when the follower of Jesus becomes involved with such institutions. But others, in contrast to Jesus and Matthew, have found themselves both Christians and members of governmental organizations; and they have necessarily found new ways of understanding 5:38–42. Rather than condemning the exegetical changes brought by the Constantinian revolution we should regard them as inevitable and consistent with the fact that the Sermon on the Mount offers examples that call the moral imagination into play. "It is necessary on the basis of the exemplary nature of the text to take one's own situation into account. The history of influence testifies to this necessity of change and the freedom which is given by the text itself" (Luz, *Matthew 1–7*, 335).

One last point. Commentators have often asked why disciples should turn the other cheek. Various responses have been given. Some have thought that non-retaliation might turn enemies into friends (although the passion narrative gives the lie to this interpretation). Bonhoeffer opined: "The only way to overcome evil is to let it run itself to a standstill because it does not find the resistance it is looking for. Resistance merely creates further evil and adds fuel to the flames. But when evil meets no opposition and encounters no obstacle but only patient endurance, its sting is drawn, and at last it meets an opponent which is more than its match" (*Cost*, 157–58). However beautiful the sentiment, it is not clear it appears in Matthew. The Sermon on the Mount does not promote utilitarianism.

Others have suggested that the weaker simply has no recourse when compelled by a stronger, so prudence dictates cooperation. Still others have supposed that God will take vengeance soon enough, or that non-retaliation is part of a spiritual discipline designed to mortify the ego.

But Jesus says none of this. Throughout 5:38–42 no motive is given for acting in the peculiar manner Jesus desires. This strange fact, which leaves his commands as it were hanging in the air, means that the question of whether or not the world will be transformed by such action is just not addressed. *Testament of Benjamin* 4:1–5:4 may teach that evil people, when confronted with unexpected mercy, will be turned to the good. Matthew's text, however, hints at no pragmatic motive. It simply demands, without explanation, that those who do Jesus' bidding will provocatively go the extra mile. The only reason forthcoming appears in the next paragraph, which invokes the imitation of God. But such imitation is theology, not pragmatism. We must not forget that the speaker, who embodies his imperatives, ends up on a cross.

LOVE OF ENEMY (5:43–48)

Matthew 5:43–48, on love of enemy, is the final and climactic paragraph of the six paragraphs introduced by 5:17–20, and it contains the most important and most difficult commands. As Cyril of Alexandria said, "Our mistaken preconceived ideas and the heavy tyranny of our passions render it a thing difficult for our minds to accomplish . . . the natural person does not admit of these things, regarding as folly and mere impossibilities the oracles of the Spirit" (*Commentary on Luke* 29).

Jesus opens with Lev. 19:18 ("Love your neighbor"). He will again quote—and uphold—this imperative in 19:19 and 22:39. So obviously he does not speak against it here. What he does oppose is the sentiment, "hate your enemy." This bit of common folk wisdom (which could conceivably mean "do not love your enemy"; cf. 6:24) does not appear in the Hebrew Bible. There are, however, related sentiments—as only to be expected, for the maxim accurately describes ordinary human behavior. The reader may consult 2 Chr. 19:2; Pss. 5:5; and 139:21 and the story of Elisha calling down bears upon young taunters in 2 Kgs. 2:23–25. But the closest parallels occur in the Dead Sea Scrolls. In 1QS 1:10 the members of the sect are to "hate all the sons of darkness," and Josephus tells us that they swore "to hate always the unjust" (*Jewish War* 2.139). Obviously they did not hate the sin and love the sinner: they rather hated both.

Jesus quotes Lev. 19:18 not to contradict it but to enlarge it. The
Pentateuch, like subsequent Jewish tradition, understands "neighbor"
to be Israelite (see Lev. 19:17), and this reading allows one to confine
love to one's own kind, or even to define neighbor in opposition to
enemy. Jesus, however, gives "neighbor" its broadest definition. If one
loves even one's enemies, who will not be loved? One is inevitably
reminded of the story of the Good Samaritan, who is good to an
Israelite, his enemy (Luke 10:29–37). Love must prove itself outside
the comfortable world of family, friends, and associates. The solidarity
of the clan is forever gone. "Jesus is appealing for an experience of solidarity with humankind, an experience that is non-exclusive, an experience that is not dependent upon reciprocity because it includes even
those who hate you, persecute you or treat you badly" (Nolan, *Jesus,*
76).

Not only does Jesus not here set out to contradict the Hebrew Bible,
but the latter has several texts that foreshadow 5:43–48. Exod. 23:4–5
says this: "When you come upon your enemy's ox or donkey going
astray, you shall bring it back. When you see the donkey of one who
hates you lying under its burden and you would hold back from setting
it free, you must help to set it free." 1 Samuel recounts how David
spared Saul, even though Saul was seeking his life. Job 31:29 appears to
distance the speaker from delight over the ruin of his enemies (cf. Ps.
7:4). In Ps. 35:13–14 the psalmist declares how he mourned and prayed
for those who repaid him evil for evil. Jer. 29:7 recommends that Jewish exiles assist the Babylonian state that has removed them from their
homeland.

The context of Jesus' command to love enemies equates them with
those who persecute the faithful ("and pray for those who persecute
you"). This means those enemies are not just one's personal opponents
but God's opponents—who are elsewhere said to hate the saints (10:22;
24:9, 10). This is dramatic. We have here the potential for what we see
in Luke 23:34, where Jesus forgives those who crucify him (cf. Acts
7:60, where Stephen forgives his executioners).

What is meant by "love"? This is clarified by what follows. One is
to pray for enemies and do good to them and greet them. Clearly Jesus
is not talking about emotions but instead is speaking of actions that
benefit others. He is not dictating to our fickle feelings but commanding what can be commanded—our will to do this rather than that.

In loving the enemy the disciple is only imitating God, who causes
the sun to shine and the rain to fall upon all, not just the righteous (cf.

Ps. 145:9 and Prov. 29:13—God gives light equally to oppressor and poor). God's generous actions break the rule of reciprocity and cost/benefit analysis. In accord with this, in 5:43–48, as in the preceding paragraph, God's kindness does not convert the wicked. On the contrary, God is good to them notwithstanding their continued unrighteousness. The same is true for the faithful disciple. Jesus does not say that kindness will end enmity or bring reconciliation. Although as a matter of experience this may happen from time to time, the text actually seems to presuppose just the opposite situation: despite the goodness God has brought to people through the creation, there are nonetheless wicked people. But the rain still comes down upon all, just as the sun still shines upon all. God's goodness can be without apparent effect. The lesson is manifest: to act in the hope of reconciliation would be to do less than God does; it is just what everyone else as a matter of fact does. So Jesus asks the disciple in this instance to act on principle without attention to the consequence. There is no guarantee of getting this for that, kindness for kindness. Nothing is said about breaking the cycle of revenge, or about bringing the enemy into the fold of faith. One doubts, then, whether the Sermon on the Mount really suggests that love of enemies is "the way to lasting peace on earth" (Moltmann, *Way,* 131).

Our text assumes, in accordance with the biblical tradition, that God makes the sun rise and the rain fall. That is, natural processes are here directly assigned to God. This way of looking at nature—which, to judge from my student samples, is still alive and well with farmers but close to dead among city dwellers—makes it easy to draw inferences about God's character from the natural order. For if both the natural realm, on the one hand, and the moral and spiritual, on the other, have God as their author and sustainer, there must be genuine affinity between the two. Recall that the death of Jesus—a religious event—is accompanied by events in the natural world—darkness and an earthquake.

Although the succinct, arresting, and memorable imperative "Love your enemies"—which has been called "the Magna Charta of Christian ethics" (Schwager, *Scapegoats,* 174)—appears to be the distinctive invention of Jesus' own mind, it has, as already observed, some parallels of a sort in the Jewish Scriptures. One can also cite related texts from outside the Jewish tradition, so once again we cannot dismiss Jesus with the observation that his words are wholly at variance with the moral sensibilities of humanity. Already an ancient Babylonian document contains this advice: "Do no evil to your opponents; recompense with good the one who does evil to you; let justice be done to your enemy." Epictetus instructs Cynics that if they should find themselves flogged as an ass, then they must love the one who flogs them (in Arrian, *Discourses of Epictetus* 3.22). According to Seneca, "If you are imitating the gods, you say, 'then bestow benefits also upon the ungrateful, for the sun rises also upon the wicked, and the sea lies open to pirates . . .'" (*On Benefits* 4.26).

Jesus' imperatives may be especially compared with two thinkers outside his Jewish world—Socrates and Buddha. Socrates appears to have fought discrimination against personal enemies. In the *Crito,* Socrates tells Crito that we must not do any wrong at all (49Bff.). He goes on to say that this holds even when we have been wronged. To injure when ill-treated is not right, although the many hold it to be. Rather, "it is never right to do any injustice, or to do injustice in return, or, when one is evilly treated, to defend oneself by doing evil in return." Socrates, however, seemingly did not extend his generosity to social inferiors. That is, non-Athenian citizens and especially slaves were not included in his advice to forgo revenge and to do good to enemies. Unlike Jesus, Socrates confined forgiving and active love to his own kind. He thus took a step toward Jesus' position, but he was not quite there.

Probably the closest parallels to Jesus' teaching appear in old Buddhist texts. How far these actually represent the view of the historical Gautama no one knows; but they remain very striking all the same. The *Songs of the Brothers and Sisters,* for instance, says that love should be a friend and companion to all, and that one's love should be "infinite," that is, without any bounds. The *Dhammapada* teaches that hatred cannot overcome hatred, that hatred ceases only through love. The *Maha-Vagga* tells a story in which a man forgives the one who has killed his father and mother. The moral is that hatred can only be undone by nonhatred. The difference here from Jesus seems to be twofold: in the Buddhist texts love's pragmatic dimensions are usually explicitly commented upon, and compassion extends not only to human enemies but also to the animal kingdom.

Notwithstanding the interesting parallels, there can be no question that Jesus' radical demand for acts of love has had a special impact on human history. The first Christians not only remembered that Jesus demanded loving actions (cf. Rom. 12:14, 17–20; 1 Cor. 4:12–13; Justin, *Apology* 1.14.4) but sometimes they even behaved accordingly. Early

Christian apologists thought the love of Christians for their enemies to be an exceptional thing (*2 Clement* 13; Athenagoras, *Supplication for the Christians* 12.3). One sociologist has recently urged that early Christianity succeeded in part because believers, in obedience to the demand for love, often took care of the sick when plagues afflicted the cities, whereas the pagans often ran away. The result was that, every time a place suffered pestilence, a higher percentage of Christians than pagans survived (because even just blankets and water greatly improved one's chances of survival). Not only was the eventual result statistically significant in terms of the general population, but a religious interpretation in terms of the power of the Christian God was inevitable (see Stark, *Rise of Christianity*).

Yet this last sort of love, however admirable, was not love of enemy; and the truth is that throughout church and exegetical history there has been, against the obvious sense of our passage, a very strong tendency to restrict the scope of 5:43–48. Many of the early citations or allusions to the materials behind Matt 5:38–48 par. omit any explicit mention of "enemy" (note Rom. 12:14; 1 Pet. 3:9; see Kuhn, "Liebesgebot"). Some interpreters have confined Jesus' imperatives to so-called personal or private enemies instead of public enemies. This makes Jesus' words irrelevant for public life, including service in the police force or military. Others have sought to confine them to inner sentiments: one can hurt others, even kill them, yet all the while not hate them inside one's heart. This was, I remember reading somewhere, the view of C. S. Lewis, who thought he could love and shoot an enemy at the same time. Origen argued that, since our text, in contrast to the usual formulation of the command to love neighbor, does say to love one's enemies "as oneself," one can rightly love enemies less than neighbors (*Homily on the Song of Songs* 2.8). Thomas Aquinas argued that whereas all Christians should love their enemies when necessity demands it, such love is not necessary for salvation and will be exhibited in other situations only by the perfect (*Summa* 2.II q. 25 art. 8–9).

Recently a problem has arisen regarding our text. Feminists have called our attention to the fact that the imperative to love enemies, when taken in conjunction with the blessing of the persecuted (5:11–12), the call not to be angry (5:21–26), and the imperatives to turn the other cheek (5:39) and to go the extra mile (5:41), can and have sometimes encouraged passivity in victims of violence, especially women in situations of abuse: the verses have become an excuse, a coping mechanism for those who do not feel permission to escape their oppression. Elisabeth Schüssler Fiorenza has even declared that the texts cited "construct a sacred canopy that compels victims to accept their sufferings without resistance" (*Violence,* xvi). She admits, however, that the original intention of the Sermon on the Mount may have been quite different, and in this she is correct. That is, we are dealing here with the incorrect use of a text. Matthew's Jesus, who embodies the meekness and passivity of his own imperatives, at the same time fights the evils of his time by prophetically denouncing injustice and impiety and by compassionately ministering to the poor and needy. He does not, that is, tolerate oppression but promotes freedom. So too is it with the disciples, who share in the work of Jesus for the same ends (see chapter 10). Moreover, and as observed earlier, the strange imperatives of Matthew 5 may well return some dignity and the initiative to the sufferer. Certainly the Sermon on the Mount is not about acquiescing to evil but rather precisely about refusal to participate in the violence that evil breeds.

According to the traditional English translations of 5:48, Jesus asks his followers to be "perfect." What does this mean? "Be perfect" can have nothing to do with sinfulness. For one thing, nothing else in Matthew points to such an idea, and the Lord's Prayer, in which one asks for daily forgiveness, points directly away from it. For another, with the words, "if you, then, being evil, know how to give good gifts to your children" (7:11), Matthew's Jesus displays his concord with Paul and the author of 1 John: there is none that is righteous, and if we say we have not sinned, we deceive ourselves.

How then do we understand 5:48? The first pertinent observation is that although the verse concludes 5:43ff., it is also the fitting culmination to all of 5:21ff. Now throughout this section Jesus has asked for a sort of perfection—not the perfection of being without sin but the perfection of what we might call completeness. He demands that all anger and adulterous thoughts be eliminated. He enjoins a comprehensive dedication to the truth that makes oaths otiose. And he commands a love that is universal in scope. In each case Jesus orders something that cannot be surpassed. What more can be done about lust if it has been driven from one's heart? And what more can one do about integrity of speech if one always speaks the truth? And who else is left to love after one has loved the enemy? Jesus' call to perfection is a call to completeness, to do certain things utterly.

This is confirmed by 19:16–30, the story of Jesus' encounter with a rich man. This individual asks Jesus what is needed for eternal life. Jesus cites commandments from the decalogue and Leviticus's imperative to love neighbor. When the man says he has kept these and asks what he still lacks, Jesus tells him that if he wishes to be "perfect" he should sell all that he has, give the money to the poor, and follow Jesus as a disciple. Here, as in 5:48, perfection has nothing to do with sinfulness. Rather, once more the central idea is completeness. If in 5:48 it is the completeness of love, here it is the completeness of commitment and obedience. The man is being summoned—this is really a call story, like those in 4:18–22 (Peter and Andrew and James and John) and 9:9 (Matthew)—to the life of full-time discipleship, to wholehearted obedience to Jesus Christ. To answer that summons would mean giving up everything.

This idea of "perfection" as completeness is also confirmed by Jewish texts outside the Bible. The people who composed and copied the Dead Sea Scrolls were to be "perfect in all that has been revealed of the law" (1QS 8:1); that is, perfection for them was full obedience to the norm revealed to the community, and failure to observe all the rules meant exclusion. Certainly they did not equate perfection with sinlessness, for one of the apocryphal psalms found at Qumran describes David as "intelligent and perfect in all his ways before God and men." Now the Bible makes it more than abundantly clear that David was not without sin, and that cannot be the meaning of the psalm's words. They rather point to David's overwhelming and undivided desire to serve God.

Before quitting this chapter two final remarks need to be made. First, we may observe that, in a way reminiscent of Matt. 5:43–48, other texts bring together the themes of love, sonship, and imitation of God. Eph. 5:1–2 has this: "Therefore be imitators of God, as beloved children, and live in love, as Christ loved us and gave himself up for us . . . ." 1 Pet. 1:13–25 tells Christians that they are "obedient children" of the divine Father; as such they are to be holy, for he is holy; and they are to love one another deeply. The pattern appears once more in 1 John 4:7–12, which begins with these words: "Beloved, let us love one another, because love is from God; everyone who loves is born of God and knows God. Whoever does not love does not know God, for God is love." We evidently have here a pattern common to early Christian moral teaching: because Christians are the offspring of God they must behave as does God, which means above all loving others.

Second, Jesus' teaching on nonresistance and love of enemies has played an important part in the writings of Rene Girard. Girard has explored in great detail the scapegoat mechanism and its role in human history. It is, he argues, our natural tendency not to take responsibility for our guilt and failings but rather to lay blame at the door of someone else, and also our natural tendency to go further and turn that someone else into a scapegoat, the recipient of our frustration, anger, and violence. This is true not only on the individual level but also on a collective level: human institutions often incorporate a legitimized violence that satisfies the human need for scapegoats. But Girard urges that this mechanism is undone by Matt. 5:38–48. Here our enemy is not the recipient of our pent-up violence but the object of our love. In that circumstance there can be no scapegoat.

FOR FURTHER READING

Horsley, R. A. "Ethics and Exegesis: 'Love Your Enemies' and the Doctrine of Non-Violence." *Journal of the American Academy of Religion* 54 (1986): 3–31.

Klassen, William. *Love of Enemies: The Way to Peace.* Philadelphia: Fortress, 1984.

Kuhn, Heinz-Wolfgang. "Das Liebesgebot Jesu als Tora und als Evangelium." In *Vom Urchristentum zu Jesus: Für Joachim Gnilka,* edited by Hubert Frankemölle and Karl Kertelge, 194–230. Freiburg: Herder, 1989.

Minear, Paul S. "Yes or No: The Demand for Honesty in the Early Church." *Novum Testamentum* 13 (1971): 1–13.

Schottroff, Luise, et al. *Essays on the Love Commandment.* Philadelphia: Fortress, 1978.

Schwager, Raymund. *Must there be Scapegoats? Violence and Redemption in the Bible.* San Francisco: Harper & Row, 1987.

Swartley, Willard M., ed. *The Love of Enemy and Nonretaliation in the New Testament.* Philadelphia: Westminster/John Knox, 1992.

Wink, Walter. "Beyond Just War and Pacifism: Jesus' Nonviolent Way." *Review and Expositor* 89 (1992): 197–214.

6

Almsgiving, Prayer, Fasting (6:1–18)

F OLLOWING THE LONG PASSAGE on Jesus and the Torah (5:17–48),
which highlights demands intended to go beyond the Torah and
so beyond common Jewish teaching, Matthew offers Jesus' teaching on the Christian cult, which outlines behavior that stands in
marked contrast to both the "hypocrites" in the synagogues and pious
pagans (6:1–18). Together the sections set forth exactly what is both
characteristic and distinctive of the followers of Jesus.

In addition to their similar functions, 5:17–48 and 6:1–18, as we saw
in chapter 2, feature several formal agreements. Both open with a general introduction employing the word "righteousness" (5:17–20; 6:1).
The examples of proper behavior are in both formulated as contrasts;
that is, Jewish tradition or practice is in each case set over against
Jesus' teaching. And while Jesus' imperatives in 5:21–48 are introduced with "But I say to you," those in 6:2–18 are introduced with
"Amen I say to you."

If 5:17–48 and 6:1–18 resemble each other in several particulars,
they are different in that whereas the former has primarily to do with
actions, the latter has largely to do with intention. One can even argue
that 6:1–18 is a sort of commentary on what precedes it. The section
on the Torah tells the disciples *what* they are to do while the section
on Christian piety tells them *how* they are to do it.

Formally, 6:1–18 exhibits much parallelism. The sections on almsgiving, prayer, and fasting all have the same outline:

1. Negative prohibition
     "Whenever you . . . do not . . ."
     "As the hypocrites do . . ."
     "That they may be seen/glorified . . ."
     "Amen I say to you they have their reward"
2. Positive injunction
     "But when you . . ."
     Description of deed in secret
     "your Father in secret"
     "your Father will reward you"

The neat scheme is interrupted by 6:7–15, the section on the Lord's Prayer, which, like the irregular last beatitude, therefore calls attention to itself.

The teaching in 6:1–18 has remarkably close parallels in 23:1–12. These include the following: (1) In both sections Jewish religious behavior, cited first, serves as a foil for proper Christian behavior; that is, positive imperatives follow negative descriptions. (2) The synagogue is in view (6:2, 5; 23:2–3). (3) The chief sins are hypocrisy and piety for show. (4) "To do/they do in order to be seen by others" (6:1; 23:5) appears. (5) 6:1 speaks of the "Father in heaven," 23:9 of "the heavenly Father." (6) "But you" (6:3, 6, 17; 23:8) marks the transition from negative description to positive exhortation.

Whether or not one explains these similarities as stemming from Matthew's editorial hand or instead from a source Matthew used, on a literary level the repetition makes for emphasis: it is the important things that are repeated. So if chapter 23 returns to the themes of 6:1–18, that can only drive home the gravity of what Jesus has to say about private piety.

Sometimes the extreme privacy in religious matters demanded by 6:1–18 has been thought to be in tension with 5:16, where works are to be done before others so that the Father in heaven may be glorified. Despite a difference in emphasis, however, harmony may be found in this, that whereas 6:1–18 "deals with specifically cultic performances . . . 5:16 speaks of good deeds generally; and 5:16 has as its goal to lead the people to praise God, while 6:1–6, 16–18 criticizes religious observance done ostentatiously and leading to the glorification of humans, something in and of itself improper" (Betz, *Commentary*, 347).

ALMSGIVING (6:1–4)

The section opens with a verse whose function vis-à-vis 6:2–18 is the same as that of 5:17–20 vis-à-vis 5:21–48: we have here a heading for the subsequent paragraphs. This heading announces the topic—right deeds must be accompanied by right intention, condemns improper practice—true piety is not for show, and speaks of eschatological loss—"you have no reward from your Father in heaven." One is inevitably reminded of Rom. 2:28–29: "For a person is not a Jew who is one outwardly, nor is true circumcision something external and physical. Rather, a person is a Jew who is one inwardly, and real circumcision is a matter of the heart—it is spiritual and not literal. Such a person receives praise not from others but from God." As 1 Sam. 16:7 has it, "the Lord does not see as mortals see; they look on the outward appearance, but the Lord looks on the heart."

Matthew 6:2–4 concerns almsgiving, which perhaps is mentioned before prayer and fasting because it is, for obvious reasons, more difficult than they. (Many ministers so dread preaching sermons on tithing and asking for pledges because few people are happy to part with their income. Sermons on prayer are much easier to deliver.) It is in any case clear that Jesus does not call almsgiving itself into question, only its misuse for self-glorification. The problem is not whether but how, not the thing but the intent (Chrysostom, *Homily on Matthew* 19.2). The teaching is in line with those rabbinic texts that praise almsgiving but demand it be hidden. "R. Eleazar said: One who gives charity in secret is greater than Moses our teacher" (Babylonian Talmud *Baba Batra* 9b; cf. *Ḥagigah* 5a; Mishnah *Sheqalim* 5:6). The rabbis knew as well as Matthew that those who make their names great lose their names (Mishnah ʾ*Abot* 1:13) and that, as Bonhoeffer put it in our own time, "love is always self-forgetful" (*Cost*, 178).

Even though the synagogues had trumpets, the words, "do not sound a trumpet before you, as the hypocrites do in the synagogues and in the streets," are probably figurative. "To blow a trumpet" is a common metaphor (cf. our English "to trumpet abroad" and perhaps Matt. 24:31); it is a picturesque way of indicating the making of an announcement or the calling of attention to oneself. But there could be some connection with the "sophar chests" that were set up in the temple and the provinces (Mishnah *Sheqalim* 1:3; 2:1; 6:1–5; Tosefta *She-*

qalim 2.16). If these trumpet-shaped receptacles could be made to resound when coins were thrown into them, thereby calling attention to the giver, our verse may have been a polemical barb at this practice.

Matthew speaks of "hypocrites." Throughout his Gospel they are usually identified with the scribes and Pharisees (15:7; 22:18; 23:13, etc.), and those groups are probably the implicit subject of 6:2–6, 6–18 as well. The scribes and Pharisees are hypocrites because they say one thing and do another (23:23–28) and because their hearts are wrong even when they outwardly do observe Torah (23:1–15, 23–28).

When writing of the "hypocrites" who sound trumpets before themselves, the church father Jerome applied the words to vain Christians who make a show in the churches (*Letter* 22.27, 32). That is, he did not contrast Jewish practice with Christian practice but wrong Christian practice with right Christian practice. Origen did the same (*Commentary on Matthew* 11.5). We may take these patristic applications as precedent, even though Matthew himself would have had in mind real Jews in "the synagogue across the street" (Stendahl). Both the sad history of Christian anti-Judaism and the distance of so many Christians today from flesh-and-blood Jews make it inappropriate to use Jewish piety as an effective counterexample; and certainly church members have sinned more than enough to supply us with an inexhaustible list of illustrations of the vices countered in Matt. 6:1–18.

In 6:3–4 we turn from the negative to the positive. Some, remarking on the Arabic use even today of the left hand to denote a close friend, think the exhortation is to hide one's good works from one's neighbors. Others think more literally: to use one hand is to be discreet, to use two is to call attention to oneself (so Gundry). But most commentators are probably correct to suppose that 6:3 is "hyperbole of language" (Theodoret). It pictorially exhorts one not to think too highly of one's own almsgiving—which of course also implies leaving others in ignorance. One should not "accept glory from one another" but instead "seek the glory that comes from the one who alone is God" (John 5:44). Augustine caught the meaning: "Do not let your desire for human praise mix with your consciousness when you strive to fulfill the divine command in regard to giving alms" (*Sermon on the Mount* 2.8). (Neither Augustine nor Matthew's Jesus takes into account the possibility raised by Amma Sarah in the *Apophthegmata Patrum:* "It is good to give alms for others' sakes. Even if it is only done to please people, through it one can begin to seek to please God.")

Our text speaks of God as "your Father who sees in secret" (cf. 5:6,

18). God's practical omniscience is assumed, as it is already in the Hebrew Bible (see, e.g., Psalms 33 and 139). This is part and parcel of the theology of our Gospel. God sees everything, which is why human beings will have to give account for every word they utter (12:36). God even knows all things beforehand, which explains how the Scriptures could foresee events before they happened (1:23; etc.).

PRAYER (6:5–6)

"When you pray" may presuppose the three hours of prayer—morning, afternoon, and evening (cf. Acts 3:1; 10:30; *Did.* 8.3). "Stand and pray" reflects the fact that Jews regularly prayed while standing (cf. 1 Sam. 1:26; Neh. 9:4; Jer. 18:20; Mark 11:25; Babylonian Talmud *Berakhot* 29b; the Eighteen Benedictions are known as the *Amidah*, which is from the verb "to stand"). Typically they bent their knees or prostrated themselves only on solemn occasions or during times of trouble (1 Kgs. 8:54; Matt. 26:39; Acts 20:36; 21:5).

"In the synagogues" and "at the street corners" take us indoors and outdoors, so what is in view is prayer in every public place. But, against a few of the old German Pietists, the point cannot be condemnation of public worship or public prayer as such. For in 21:13 Jesus affirms the public temple as a place of prayer; and the Hebrew Bible, whose continuing force is declared in Matt. 5:17–20, assumes the validity of public prayers (e.g., 1 Kings 8 [Solomon's prayer of dedication of the temple]). So what the Sermon on the Mount must be condemning is prayer aimed at being conspicuous, prayer that is addressed not solely to God, or less to God than to those looking on (so rightly Calvin, *Commentary*, ad loc.). In Hans Dieter Betz's words, "the 'performers' do it, in the final analysis, because they love themselves. Prayer, supposedly the most intimate expression of love to God, has turned into its very opposite, preoccupation with oneself . . ." (*Commentary*, 362).

"Go into your inner [or: storage] room and shut the door" is not a mystical way of speaking of prayer within the heart (so Ephrem, *Faith* 20.6, and other fathers, including most of the Syrian tradition) but instead hyperbole, just a way of saying that prayer is not a performance for a human audience. Chrysostom rightly commented that one who went into an inner room to pray only after telling others about it would hardly win Jesus' approval (*Homily on Matthew* 19.3). So once again we need to pass beyond the literal language to see the point, which is, in the words of a rabbinic text, that "all depends upon the intention of the heart" (Babylonian Talmud *Megillah* 20a). If the intent is right, then one can pray before others—as Jesus does in 11:25–30 (public thanksgiving); 14:19 (public blessing); 15:36 (public blessing); and 26:36–46 (Gethsemane; but contrast 14:23, where he prays alone). One should recall 18:19–20, where group prayer is presupposed, as well as first person plurals of the Lord's Prayer: obviously this is a communal text. (Was it inserted after 6:5–6 precisely to make the point that communal prayer is not being attacked?) I quote Theophylact: "Should I not then pray in church? Indeed I should, but with a right mind and not for show. For it is not the place which harms prayer, but the manner and intent with which we pray. For many who pray in secret do so to impress others" (*Commentary on Matthew* ad loc.). Bonhoeffer said the same thing: "In the last resort it is immaterial whether we pray in the open street or in the secrecy of our chambers" (*Cost*, 183).

THE LORD'S PRAYER (6:7–13)

The Lord's Prayer is directly introduced by 6:7–8. These verses, in contrast to 6:5–6, where Jewish misbehavior is in view, command Jesus' followers not to pray as the Gentiles. The effect is to suggest that the Christian way of prayer should rise above the errors of both Jewish and Gentile traditions. (We shall see, however, that every phrase of the Pater Noster has parallels in Jewish texts, biblical and postbiblical. From beginning to end it is utterly Jewish, which is why it has recently been the subject of ecumenical discussion between Christian and Jew.)

The Lord's Prayer has not seven petitions (so Augustine, at least in *Sermon on the Mount* 2.9–10, and *Enchiridion* 116, also Juan de Valdés, Bengel, and others, all counting "Do not lead us into temptation" and "but deliver us from evil" separately) but six (so Origen, Chrysostom, Gregory of Nyssa, most Protestant commentators, and the Roman Catholic Rudolf Schnackenburg). In a way reminiscent of the Decalogue and Matt. 22:34–40, which command first Godward duties and, second, duties to fellow human beings, the first three petitions of the Lord's Prayer relate directly to God the Father or heavenly things, the last three (which are sometimes said to pertain, in order, to the past, the present, and the future) to our situation or earthly necessities. Another way of putting this is that the first half offers expressions of piety, the latter half petitions in the proper sense. The following outline may be offered:

i) The address

ii) Three petitions regarding God's lordship
"Hallowed be your name"
"Your kingdom come"
"Your will be done"

iii) Three petitions regarding human need
"Give us this day our bread"
"Forgive us our debts"
"Do not bring us to the time of trial"

Aquinas relates the structure to 6:33: by praying first for heavenly matters and then afterwards for earthly blessings we seek first the kingdom of God and then know that earthly things will be added to us (*Lord's Prayer* 1:3).

There was originally no doxology (we would expect one in a Jewish prayer), although the lack was made up by later liturgical insertions into the manuscript tradition (whence the well-known closing, "For yours is the kingdom and the power and the glory forever. Amen" [cf. 1 Chr. 29:11]; note that this adds to the triads of the Lord's Prayer). The poetic qualities of the Lord's Prayer are nonetheless manifest, and despite its simplicity, Betz calls the unit "a literary masterpiece." The first three petitions are formally similar. Each consists of three items— verb + definite noun + "your." The third, like the last beatitude, is irregular because longer and so closes the opening sequence. The triads and parallelism (contrast Luke's version) are characteristic of Matthew's whole Gospel.

The last three petitions, whose language is less solemn than the first three (Lohmeyer), are less unified. Matt. 6:11 (the petition for bread) opens not with a verb but with an object (the noun "bread") in order to signal a new series. The series continues by introducing the last two petitions with the conjunction "and" (*kai*):

"Our bread for tomorrow give us today"
"And forgive us . . ."
"And do not bring us . . . but . . ."

The jarring "but" (*alla*) marks the close of the whole prayer, which ends with a sort of antithetical *inclusio:* the prayer commences with "Father" and concludes with "(the) evil (one)."

How or if the second three petitions are to be related to the first three is unclear. Perhaps there is no thematic connection. Some, however, have imagined that the petition for bread links up with God's status as Father (cf. 7:7–11), that the prayer for forgiveness is appropriately addressed to God in God's capacity as king, and that the entreaty to be delivered from trial and (the) evil (one) is fittingly related to the doing of God's will. Whether that be so or not, Karl Barth was correct to observe that whereas the first three petitions announce God's lordship, the last three reveal that the frail human creature depends on that lordship: we cannot live without God to feed us, forgive us, and save us.

The balanced and symmetrical arrangement of the Lord's Prayer is often thought to reflect the liturgical practice of Matthew's church. That is a possibility. But it is worth noting that the literary scheme apparent in 6:9–13 appears on a larger scale in chapter 13. There, after reproducing the sower and its interpretation as they appear in Mark, Matthew goes his own way and gives us six parables. They fall into two groups in a way that mirrors the two parts of the Lord's Prayer. This can be seen at a glance:

The Lord's Prayer	*The Parables in 13:24–50*
first sequence of three	first sequence of three
triple use of formula	triple use of formula
verb + noun + you	"Another parable he put before them"
verb + noun + you	"Another parable he put before them"
verb + noun + you	"Another parable he put before them"
second sequence of three	second sequence of three
triple use of a different formula	triple use of a different formula
"our" petition	"The kingdom of heaven is like"
"and" + "our" petition	"Again, the kingdom of heaven is like"
"and" + "our" petition	"Again, the kingdom of heaven is like"

Turning to 6:7, Jesus says one should not "heap up empty phrases." The criticism is not novel but conventional. One can find similar polemic in many ancient sources. Ecclus. 7:14 declares, "Do not prattle in the assembly of the elders, nor repeat yourself in your prayer." *Mekhilta* on Exod. 15:25 says that the prayer of the righteous is "short." According to Babylonian Talmud *Berakhot* 61a, "One's words should always be few toward God" (appropriately followed by a quotation of Eccl. 5:2: "Never be rash with your mouth, nor let your heart be quick to utter a word before God"). In *Berakhot* 33b a man is rebuked for piling up praises (cf. *Megillah* 18a). The emperor Marcus Aurelius counseled people to pray in a "simple and frank fashion" or not to pray at all (*Meditations* 5.7). The temptation to hope that the deity will hear if words are sufficiently multiplied or time amply protracted (cf. the priests of Baal in 1 Kgs. 18:20–29) is evidently built into human nature, whence the need—met in the previous quotations—to be reminded that before God words are neither efficacious in themselves nor magical. (It is ironic that the Lord's Prayer itself came to be used as a mechanical, magical formula, as is shown by its frequent appearance on early Christian amulets.) With prayer it is, so to speak, a question of quality rather than of quantity.

The broad generalization that the Gentiles pray as they do because they believe that "many words" will improve their chances of being heard probably refers chiefly not to time spent in prayer but to verbosity. For in Gethsemane Jesus prays very few words, but the time involved seems considerable (26:36–46; cf. the behavior of Hannah in 1 Sam. 1:12).

Throughout the Synoptics, although Jesus often repeats himself (as in Gethsemane) and spends long hours in prayer, he consistently utters terse prayers; and his model prayer, the Our Father, is noticeably brief and compact as compared with most of the standard Jewish prayers that have come down to us. Only in John does one find lengthy petitions addressed to God (e.g., John 17). But here the purpose is not to impress God but to teach the disciples; the long prayers are actually discourses uttered for the benefit of the disciples. The fact is made plain enough in 11:42, where Jesus subjoins to his prayer these words: "I have said this for the sake of the crowd standing here, so that they may believe that you sent me." (Martin Bucer argued that what is true for Jesus in John is true for believers in general: words in prayer are only really necessary for public services in order to edify others; they are not needed when one is alone: *Enarrationes perpetuae in Sacra quatuor Evangelica* fol. 63r).

Jesus says that many words are unnecessary because "your Father knows what you need before you ask him." God hears the heart, not the voice—or, as Augustine put it, God hears not many words but "fervent attention" (*Letter* 130). This judgment, which is consistent with the thrice-repeated refrain that God "sees in secret" (6:4, 6, 18), is conventional common sense (although why the observation does not eliminate prayer altogether is a problem not taken up). Isa. 65:24 promises (as part of an eschatological scenario) that "Before they call I will answer, while they are yet speaking I will hear." *Exodus Rabbah* on 14:15 asserts that God knows what is in the heart before one speaks. One also thinks of Xenophon, *Memorabilia* 1.3.2: Socrates prayed simply, "Give me that which is best for me," for he knew that the gods know what the good things are. The extreme brevity of the Lord's Prayer harmonizes with this sentiment.

Much of the recent work on the Lord's Prayer has focused on the extent to which the prayer is eschatological. Many believe that it is thoroughly concerned with the last things. "Hallowed be your name," "Your kingdom come," and "Your will be done on earth as it is in heaven" are all ways of asking God to usher in the final state. "Give us this day our bread for tomorrow" is a plea for the heavenly manna, the bread of life to be bestowed in the end time. "And forgive us our debts, as we also have forgiven our debtors" has in view the coming judgment, when God will judge and remit sins. One might also think that in the background is the common conviction that the redemption has been delayed because of human sin. "And do not bring us to the time of trial" is a request for preservation during the great tribulation that introduces the kingdom.

Although many remain unpersuaded, the eschatological interpretation of the Pater Noster has much to commend. Not only does ancient Judaism supply us with a number of prayers that are thoroughly eschatological in orientation (e.g., *2 Bar.* 21:19–25 and the so-called *Alenu*), but the thematic unity that is thus given to the prayer is impressive. There is also the important fact that the prayer goes back to Jesus himself, and he was an eschatological prophet whose proclamation partly centered on an eschatological scenario.

The prayer opens with an address, "Our Father in heaven" (cf. 12:50; Mark 11:25; medieval exegetes, however, read the Latin as meaning: "Our Father who is. In heaven hallowed, etc."). These words, which connote intimacy and authority at the same time, are presumably a liturgical enlargement (by Matthew himself?) of Luke's simpler "Father" (behind which lies the Aramaic *ʾabbaʾ*, a word used in Mark 14:36; Rom. 8:15; and Gal. 4:6). No prayer in the Hebrew Bible opens with this address, although the idea that God is the father of faithful Israel, his children, is certainly well attested (see especially Isa. 63:15–

16; Jer. 31:20; Hos. 11:1–4). The Mishnah, however, does use the phrase, "Our Father in heaven" (*Soṭa* 9:15; *Yoma* 8:9; cf. *Mekhilta* on Exod. 20:25), and extrabiblical Jewish prayers do have invocations with "Father." Examples include 4Q372 frag. 1 line 16 ("My father and my God" as the opening address in an apocryphal prayer of Joseph); 4Q460 frag. 5 line 6 ("my father" in the conclusion of a prayer); Wisd. 14:3 ("O Father" in words of Solomon to God; cf. 2:16; 5:5); Ecclus. 23:1 and 4 ("O Lord, Father and Ruler of my life"); 3 Macc. 6:3 and 8 (the priest Eleazar twice uses "Father" in a plea for deliverance); Mishnah *Berakhot* 5:1 ("the ancient Hasidim spent an hour [in reflection before praying] in order to direct their hearts to their Father in heaven"); the *Ahabah Rabbah* ("O our Father"); Babylonian Talmud *Taanit* 25b ("Our Father, Our King" in a prayer ascribed to Rabbi Akiba); and *Taanit* 23b ("When the world was in need of rain, the rabbis used to send school-children to him [Hanan] who seized the train of his cloak and said to him, Abba, Abba, give us rain! He said to God: Lord of the universe, render a service to those who cannot distinguish between the Abba who gives rain and the Abba who does not"). Perhaps we should also remember that the Greeks could invoke Zeus as "Father."

In the light of all the parallels, especially the Qumran texts, it is unwise to insist (as so many have when writing on the Lord's Prayer) that Jesus' use of *"Abba"* was unique, or (in the overblown words of J. C. Lambert, "Lord's Prayer," 61) that Jesus' words "mark a new epoch not only in the history of prayer, but in the history of revelation." Above all, there is no room here for the sort of anti-Judaism found in the expositions of Tertullian and Augustine, who said that God could never command the disobedient Jews to call him "Father." At the same time, it remains true that early Christian sources speak of God as Father much more frequently than contemporary Jewish sources; and since Mark 14:36; Rom. 8:15; and Gal. 4:6 transliterate the Aramaic *ʾabbāʾ* into Greek, there is a good chance that the address was thought special because characteristic of Jesus.

Regarding how "Our Father in heaven" functions in Matthew, several things merit observation. First, as in Jewish liturgical texts with the first person plural (which is used throughout the rest of the prayer) stress is on the communal dimension. We have here a prayer for the church, for those who have become, through Jesus, brothers and sisters as children of God (cf. 5:45). Within the immediate context, namely, 6:1–18, the public character of the Lord's Prayer counterbalances the emphasis upon purely private piety in 6:1–8, 16–18 and so prevents the impression that all true piety is purely personal. Cyprian appropriately commented:

> Before all things the teacher of peace and the master of unity would not have prayer to be made singly and individually, as for one who prays to pray for himself alone. For we say not "My Father, which art in heaven," nor "Give me this day my daily bread," nor does each one ask that only his own debt should be forgiven him; nor does he request for himself alone that he may not be led into temptation, and delivered from evil. Our prayer is public and common; and when we pray, we pray not for one, but for the whole people, because we the whole people are one. (*On the Lord's Prayer* 8)

One is reminded of the rabbi who reportedly was wont to pray not "lead me in safety" but "lead us in safety" (Babylonian Talmud *Berakhot* 29b–30a). Aquinas said that to pray "Our Father" is to express our love of our neighbor (*Lord's Prayer* 1:4), and Juan de Valdés commented:

> [one should] remember that by this word ["Our"] he [Jesus] demonstrates that all who call upon this same name . . . are his brothers. Then he should examine himself closely whether all his acts toward them are fraternal and whether his love for them as brothers is heartfelt. If he should find himself defective on this spot, he should implore God with earnest tears, not only of the eyes but also of the heart, to give him a loving spirit towards his brothers. (*Dialogue on Christian Doctrine* fol. 76v)

Second, whereas Jesus instructs his disciples to say "Our Father," throughout Matthew he speaks of God as "my Father" and seems thus to distinguish himself from others (cf. the distinction in John 20:17). He is the Son of God in a sense other human beings are not (3:17; 17:5; etc.).

Third, Matthew often speaks of God being "in heaven." We must reckon seriously with the possibility that the evangelist, as well as Jesus, understood the words spatially—although already the Hebrew Bible knows that God cannot be contained (1 Kgs. 8:27; Isa. 66:1; in 3:17 a divine voice comes "from heaven"). But there is much more to the expression. "Heaven" and "earth" together denote the whole of creation (5:18; 24:35; 28:18). The former is characterized by its adherence to God's will (6:10), whereas the latter is the realm of sin and conflict (6:19; 10:34; 23:35). And the effect of putting God in heaven is to underline that, for the present, although God is with the saints, yet God's rule is not fully effective in our world. The sparrow falls and the saints are persecuted. So despite the intimacy communicated by praying "Our Father," there is, as Gregory of Nyssa poignantly saw in his exposition of our words, paradoxically a great gulf between the divine world and the human reality (*Lord's Prayer* 2).

Fourth, elsewhere Matthew's Gospel is aware that sometimes followers of Jesus will find themselves at odds with their biological families (8:22; 10:34–37; 19:29). The community in such a case stands in as a sort of replacement, a surrogate family, which is why we so often meet in Matthew the term "brother(s)." As it says in 12:50: "Whoever does the will of my Father in heaven is my brother and sister and mother." So there is a potential social dimension to our text. Those who have experienced familial conflict because of discipleship will find a new family; and in that context they will reserve the word "father" for God (23:9).

Fifth, our Gospel never instructs believers to pray to Jesus (contrast John 14:14). It seems rather everywhere to presuppose that prayers should be directed to God the Father. Perhaps the evangelist would have approved of Origen's formulation: prayer is to the Father through the Son (*On Prayer* 15.1–4).

Sixth, when Jesus himself prays to God as "my Father" in 26:39, this is only one of three items in the story of Gethsemane (26:36–46) recalling the Lord's Prayer:

The Lord's Prayer	Jesus in Gethsemane
"Our Father"	"My Father"
"Your will be done"	"Your will be done"
"Do not bring us to the time of trial"	"Pray that you not come to the time of trial"

These parallels (as comparison with his source, Mark, show) come from Matthew's deliberate design. Here once more Jesus embodies his speech: he prays as he asks others to pray.

(Incidentally, ecclesiastical commentators have often been quick to claim that Jesus himself could not have prayed the Lord's Prayer. He rather intended the prayer for others. They have done this because of the petition for forgiveness: the doctrine of Christ's sinlessness would make this awkward on his lips. But however one comes to terms with this theological difficulty, the parallels in Matthew between Gethsemane and the Lord's Prayer strongly imply that our evangelist had no difficulty in thinking of Jesus using his own prayer.)

Finally, granted the eschatological orientation of the Lord's Prayer, and the circumstance that becoming a son or daughter of God is an

eschatological hope in 5:9 (as elsewhere in Jewish and Christian literature; cf. *Jub.* 1:24–25), 6:9 may involve an element of "realized eschatology": disciples already know themselves to be adopted children of
God. Certainly Christians through the centuries have thought it an
astounding privilege to address their prayers to God as Father. The
Greek liturgies preface the Lord's Prayer with "boldly dare (*meta par-
rhēsias . . . tolman*) to call upon You, the heavenly God, as Father," just
as the Roman liturgies use "we are bold" (*audemus*) for the same purpose. Cyril of Jerusalem wrote: "O most surpassing loving-kindness of
God! On them who revolted from him and were in the very extreme of
misery has he bestowed such complete forgiveness of their evil deeds,
and so great participation of grace, as that they should even call him
Father" (*Mystagogical Catechesis* 5.11). Thomas Watson's *Body of
Divinity*, in expounding the Lord's Prayer, offers twenty encouraging
paragraphs that begin with "If God be our Father" and then relate how
God takes care of the faithful in a parental fashion.

Many moderns are uncomfortable with addressing God as "Father."
Is this not an outdated, patriarchal way of thinking and speaking that
has had and continues to have oppressive consequences? This is not the
place to enter into discussion of this difficult issue. For what it is worth,
I am inclined to agree with Jan Milič Lochman. With only a little exaggeration, he observes that "the Father of Jesus Christ is a wholly non-
patriarchal Father" (*Lord's Prayer*, 20–21). By this he means that, in the
Gospels, Jesus' Father is not an oppressive authoritarian but is rather
the good giver of gifts (7:7–11) who lets his children go their own way
and still welcomes them home when they have sinned against him
(Luke 15:11–32).

Following the address, the first petition asks for the hallowing of
God's "name." "Name" is a reverential way of speaking of God as
revealed to us; perhaps the meaning is here close to our own "reputation." But Matthew may have thought more specifically in terms of
the revealed name of power (Exod. 3:13–15) which the Father shared
with Jesus and the Spirit—"the name of the Father and of the Son and
of the Holy Spirit" (28:16–20; cf. John 17:11; Phil. 2:9).

The solemnity of this first request ensures that the intimacy conveyed by the address "Father" will not degenerate into presumptuous
familiarity. The passive construction probably has, against Augustine
(*Sermon on the Mount* 2.5.19), and perhaps most commentators, not
human beings but God as the implicit subject: the Father is being
called upon to act, as in John 12:28: "Father, glorify your name." We

have here a request for God to fulfill the eschatological promise of
Ezek. 36:23: "I will sanctify my great name." What is envisaged is
God's universal rule, when God, because of the redemption of the
saints and the restoration of paradise, will be fittingly honored by both
Israel and the nations. There will be an end to the state in which "all
day long my name is despised" (Isa. 52:5, quoted in Rom. 2:24).

"To hallow" or "sanctify" God's name should be reckoned as a traditional way of speaking (Isa. 29:23; *1 Enoch* 61:12; Babylonian Talmud
Yebamot 79a); it denotes the opposite of "to profane" the name (Lev.
18:21; 22:32; Ezek. 36:20). Jesus may indeed have taken "hallowed be
your name" from a traditional Jewish prayer. For the earliest form of
the Kaddish prayer, which was prayed in synagogues after the sermon,
was something close to the following:

> Exalted and hallowed be his great name
>   in the world which he created according to his will.
> May he let his kingdom rule
>   in your lifetime and in your days and in the lifetime
>   of the whole house of Israel, speedily and soon.
> Praised be his great name from eternity to eternity.
>   And to this say: Amen.

The nearness of this to the beginning of the Lord's Prayer is undeniable, so if it was already known in the first century (unfortunately an
uncertain issue) one would be inclined to suppose that it influenced
the composition of the Lord's Prayer. But even if the Kaddish was not
known before Matthew's time, its content nonetheless shows us that
the Lord's Prayer belongs to the Jewish tradition.

Despite the eschatological meaning of "hallowed be your name," it
should be added that church tradition has not been wholly wrong in its
regular stress upon a present application: human beings should now
glorify God's name. For one can hardly ask God to hallow the divine
name and then turn around and do things to profane it. Thus the truth
in Cyril of Jerusalem's interpretation: God's name "becomes holy in
us, when we become holy, and do things worthy of holiness" (*Mystagogical Catechesis* 5.12). Theodore of Mopsuestia (*Catechetical Homilies* 11.10) could associate "hallowed be your name" with 5:16, which
calls disciples to do what will "give glory to your Father in heaven."

"Your kingdom come," the second petition, is plainly eschatological. For while elsewhere in Matthew the kingdom has already entered
the present, it still remains hidden (13:31–33); and its full manifestation—which will mean the hallowing of God's name and the doing of

God's will on earth as in heaven—belongs only to the end of things (Dan. 2:44). As Aquinas wrote: "God by his very essence and nature is Lord of all. And Christ is Lord of all. . . . Consequently all things ought to be subject to him. However, they are not subject yet, but will be at the end of the world: 'He must reign until he has put all his enemies under his feet' (1 Cor. 15:25). Therefore, it is for this that we pray when we say, 'Your kingdom come'" (*Lord's Prayer* 5:1). (But Aquinas also says that praying for the kingdom is to pray for deliverance from sin even now, so that when we are given such deliverance Matt. 5:4 is fulfilled—"Blessed are the meek, for they will inherit the earth"; cf. Maximus the Confessor, *Lord's Prayer* 4.)

In the background may be the ancient Near Eastern idea of kingship, which was soteriological. The sovereign, "with the power given him by God . . . puts an end to the chaotic period when there is no king, so that also the weak, widows and orphans also have human rights and can exist as human beings" (so Alfons Deissler, in Petuchowski and Brocke, eds., *Lord's Prayer*, 8). In the Lord's Prayer God is similarly envisaged as becoming the eschatological king (cf. Isa. 52:7–10; Ezek. 20:33). This is something only God can do, and something human beings can only pray for.

But why then pray at all for the kingdom's coming if the power to bring it is beyond us? Luther wrote that "the kingdom of God comes indeed without our prayer, of itself; but we pray in this petition that it may come unto us also" (*Small Catechism*). Ancient Jewish and Christian sources, however, preserve the conviction that prayer might hasten the coming of the kingdom (e.g., Luke 18:1–8; Babylonian Talmud *Baba Meṣia* 85b). Is this the presupposition of our text? Certainly every other petition in the Lord's Prayer is uttered in the hope that the Father in heaven hears and answers the requests of his people. Even in our own century Dietrich Bonhoeffer expressed the belief that God uses "prayers to hasten the coming of the End" (*Cost*, 185).

Christian exegetical tradition has much more often than not interpreted "your kingdom come" in terms of the presence of God's kingdom (and sometimes of the liturgical experience itself). Here it has, from an exegetical point of view, not been on target (although again the implication of praying for God's good future is that one must, as much as possible, live in accord with that future). Calvin also missed the main point when he commented that "God reigns when people, in denial of themselves, and in contempt of the world and this earthly life, devote themselves to righteousness and aspire to heaven" (*Institutes* 3.20.42).

It is interesting that soon after the invocation of God as Father the subject becomes the kingdom (cf. Matthew's distinctive expression, "the kingdom of my Father," as in 13:43; 26:29). Well-known Jewish prayers address God both as Father and King (e.g., the fifth and sixth of the Eighteen Benedictions and Rabbi Akiba in Babylonian Talmud *Taanit* 25b) and also ask for God's reign to arrive (e.g., the Kaddish and the eleventh of the Eighteen Benedictions). So even if one cannot find any Jewish prayer that makes "kingdom" the subject of the verb "come" (cf. Matt. 16:28), it is obvious that Jesus' prayer again belongs to the tradition of Jewish petition.

The prayer that God's will be done on earth as it is in heaven (absent from Luke's version) is, as Luther saw, a variant of the first two petitions; that is, when God's name is hallowed and the kingdom has come, then God's will will be done on earth as in heaven (*Small Catechism*). In one sense, then, our line "contains nothing new" (Calvin, *Institutes* 3.20.42).

Even though "your will be done" is to be given eschatological sense, its use by Jesus in Gethsemane shows that it can also have a broader meaning in accord with traditional expositions of our line. When Jesus negates his will before the will of his Father in heaven, he illustrates that "your will be done" is a comprehensive principle. That is, even though human beings may ask for specific things, in the end they must submit to the inscrutability of the divine will, whatever it may be. "Annul your will in the face of his will" (Mishnah *ʾAbot* 2:4). God will be what God will be (Exod. 3:14); the divinity is not determined by our petitions. This is why R. Eliezer ben Hyrcanus is purported to have prayed: "Do your good pleasure in heaven above and give composure of spirit to those who revere you here below, and what is good in your sight, do" (Babylonian Talmud *Berakhot* 29b). Immanuel Kant once observed that whoever prays for daily bread must also submit to God's wisdom, and "it may perhaps comport better with this wisdom to let the suppliant die today for lack of bread" (*Religion*, 184). Maybe even the structure of the Lord's Prayer hints at this sort of recognition, for the heavenly requests, as the more important, come before the earthly requests, which must be subordinated to the former. One must "strive first for the kingdom of God" (6:33).

"On earth as it is in heaven" resembles certain rabbinic texts. In Babylonian Talmud *Berakhot* 17a we read, "May it be your will . . . to establish peace in the upper family and in the lower family." In *Berakhot* 29b there is this: "Do your will in heaven and give rest of spirit to them that fear you below." Matthew's line can and has been interpreted in line with these Jewish prayers: both heaven and earth are spheres in which God's will is not yet done. If humans sin on earth, there are also "spiritual forces of evil in the heavenly places" (Eph. 6:12).

But the more likely interpretation has it that heaven is here the standard for earth: what is now true of the former should become true of the latter. The church fathers typically thought of God's "ministers that do his will" (Ps. 103:21), the good angels (Augustine, *Sermon on the Mount* 2:6:20; Cyril of Jerusalem, *Mystagogical Catechesis* 5.14; Chrysostom, *Homily on Matthew* 19.7; this then becomes tied in with the common patristic exhortation to imitate the angels: Cyril of Alexandria, *Commentary on Luke* 74; Maximus the Confessor, *Lord's Prayer* 4; etc.). So too Calvin: "We are thus enjoined to pray that as everything done in heaven is at the command of God, and the angels are calmly disposed to do all that is right, so the earth may be brought under his authority, all rebellion and depravity having been extinguished" (*Institutes* 3.20.43; some have added that the glorified saints should be included along with the angels). This is the more probable interpretation because (1) throughout Matthew "heaven" has positive connotations and (2) 18:14 and 22:30 speak of angels in heaven. (Betz, *Commentary*, 395, who contrasts the singular "heaven" of 6:10 [which he takes to mean "sky"] with the plural "heavens" of 6:11 [which he associates with God's transcendence], relates the former to the obedient courses of the heavenly spheres—sun, moon, stars. But as ancients believed the stars to be angelic beings, this is not really an alternative interpretation.)

"On earth as it is in heaven" is most often taken as a qualification of the third petition. But Origen (*On Prayer* 26.2) and the so-called *Opus Imperfectum* on Matthew take it to qualify the first and second petitions as well. This fits the eschatological interpretation and could be correct. Lancelot Andrews (*Private Devotions*, 281) arranged the first three petitions this way:

1		name	be hallowed
2	thy kingdom		come
3		will	be done,
			as in heaven
			also in earth

With the request for bread, the most controverted and difficult of the six petitions, we turn from issues of God's lordship to human need "on earth." What is meant by "daily bread"? The Greek word translated "daily" (*epiousios*) is an unresolved puzzle. No modern discovery has put the lie to Origen's observation that the term "is not used by the Greeks, neither does it occur with the scholars, nor does it have a place in the language of the people. It seems to have been invented by the Evangelists" (*On Prayer* 27.7). It could mean (1) "needful" (cf. Prov. 30:8) or (2) "for the current day" (cf. Luke 11:3) or (3) "for the coming day." The last possibility may be best choice. For not only is it linguistically the most plausible, but it has very early support (e.g., the *Gospel of the Nazaraeans*, according to Jerome, *Commentary on Matthew* ad loc. ["our bread of tomorrow—that is, of the future—give us this day"]; cf. Origen, *On Prayer* 27.13); and it seems to be reflected in the Boharic and Sahidic versions. Further, probably in the background is the story in Exodus 16, where Israel is given manna (called "bread" in Num. 21:5 and elsewhere) for the day to come.

The link with Exodus is recognized in the tradition. Luke's "daily" (*to kath' hēmeran*) appears in the story of the manna in Exod. 16:5 LXX. Tertullian saw the story of the manna as the interpretive key to Matt. 6:11 (*Against Marcion* 4.26.4). Lancelot Andrewes's use of "angels' food" in his paraphrase of the Lord's Prayer alludes to Ps. 78:25, where the manna of the desert is called "the bread of angels." More recently Jan Milič Lochman, in commenting on 6:11, says he is "reminded of the story of the manna in the Old Testament" (*Lord's Prayer*, 92). J. Duncan M. Derrett has observed that just as Moses commanded there to be no hoarding of the manna, so the Lord's Prayer "renounces the possibility of hoarding" (*Ascetic Discourse*, 48). Perhaps the final petition also has a background in the wilderness traditions, where the theme of temptation is so prominent (Houk).

But then what concretely is meant? Are we to think of the things that the body requires for the coming day (cf. 7:9)? So Cyril of Alexandria, *Commentary on Luke* 75; Calvin, *Institutes* 3.20.44, and Bonhoeffer, *Cost*, 185. Luther's *Small Catechism* takes "bread" to include "everything that belongs to the support and wants of the body," including food, drink, clothing, shoes, house, field, cattle, money, goods, a pious spouse, pious children, pious servants, pious rulers, good government, good weather, peace, health, discipline, honor, good friends, and loyal neighbors! Common, however, has been the objection that such mundane or this-worldly interpretations conflict with

6:25–34, where Jesus tells his followers not to worry about food and drink and such matters. As Maximus the Confessor observed, "It is obvious that he [Jesus] did not enjoin us to ask in the prayer what he had exhorted us not to seek in his commandment" (*Lord's Prayer* 4; cf. Peter Chrysologus, *Sermons* 67).

Most Catholic exegetes have thought rather of the Eucharist. This is the view enshrined in Jerome's Vulgate, where *supersubstantialem* ("of a higher substance") is the translation, and it is the dominant patristic tradition (Chrysostom and Cyril of Alexandria being exceptions). It is perhaps significant that the Lord's Prayer is already associated with the Eucharist in *Didache* 8–9, a text presumably close in time and space to Matthew. The eucharistic interpretation found in "daily" a reason to take communion every day (cf. Ambrose, *On Sacraments* 5.4).

Other interpreters have thought of spiritual sustenance in general (cf. Prov. 9:5; Matt. 4:4; John 6 and see Origen, *On Prayer* 27), or of the preaching of the word of God (so the early Luther in the *Explanation of the Lord's Prayer* [1519]), or of Jesus himself, who is "the bread of life" in John's Gospel (Maximus the Confessor, *Lord's Prayer* 4; Peter Chrysologus, *Sermons* 67) or of the messianic banquet, specifically the heavenly manna or bread that God will give to the redeemed at the consummation (cf. Luke 14:15; Rev. 2:17; *2 Bar.* 29:8; *Liber Antiquitatum Biblicarum* 19.10; *Mekhilta* on Exod. 16:25). Some have tried to hold to more than one interpretation at the same time. Cyprian took the petition to be about literal food as well as the Eucharist (*Lord's Prayer* 18–19).

Given the eschatological outlook of the other petitions, one is inclined to accept the last alternative, which fits so nicely with Jerome's comments on the *Gospel of the Nazaraeans*. Also in its favor is the emphatic position of "today" (at the end of the sentence). But here, as Cyprian, Aquinas, and so many others have correctly seen, acceptance of one interpretation to the exclusion of the others would be foolish. A text can have multiple layers of meaning. The feedings of the five and four thousand, for instance, have several. Both Matt. 14:13–21 and 15:29–39 allude to the messianic banquet, the Last Supper, the story of Elisha in 2 Kgs. 4:42–44, and the gift of the manna in the wilderness. It may be similar with the Lord's Prayer, especially given the rich symbolism surrounding "bread" in the biblical tradition. Certainly if one expects God to reward the faithful at the messianic banquet, both our Gospel and the rest of the Bible make it plain that God sustains them in every way, physically and spiritually, even now. This is the plain teaching of 6:25–34 and of numerous other passages of Scripture (e.g., Pss. 104:14; 132:15). So the Christian who prays "Give us this day our daily bread" can with justice think simultaneously of all daily needs being met as well as of the coming consummation, which is anticipated in the Eucharist.

The fifth petition speaks about both divine and human forgiveness: we ask God to forgive us our "debts"—the meaning is "sins" (cf. 6:14–15)—as we have forgiven others. The ubiquity of human sin is presupposed (cf. 7:11). That there is an eschatological dimension to this is obvious (cf. Polycarp, *Epistle* 6:1–2). For elsewhere in Matthew forgiveness of sins is something to come at the last judgment (5:23–25; 18:23–35). One thinks of Luke 6:37: "Do not judge, and you will not be judged [at the last judgment]; do not condemn, and you will not be condemned. Forgive, and you will be forgiven."

Matt. 6:12 implies that God's forgiveness is, from one point of view, conditional. God does not bestow grace in an antinomian fashion but rather demands that we act in accord with the mercy shown toward us. The point is made plainly in the parable in 18:23–35, which concludes with the lesson that God's mercy will be withdrawn "if you do not forgive your brother from the heart." But even closer to hand is 6:14–15, which immediately follows the Lord's Prayer and so stresses, precisely in connection with that prayer, the necessity of forgiving others. Not only is asking God's forgiveness in vain if we do not forgive others, but the praying of the Lord's Prayer is likewise vain without such (cf. also 5:21–26). We cannot expect God to do for us what we will not do for others. It is the merciful who receive mercy (5:7). "As often as you are merciful, the All-merciful has pity on you" (Tosefta *Baba Qamma* 9.30).

The meaning of all this is not that forgiveness can be earned or made part of a crude bargain, an idea that would make the Lord's Prayer contradict Paul. Among other things, God's forgiveness of us and our forgiveness of others are hardly commensurate. In Helmut Thielicke's words, God forgives us for "hitting him with a club" while we typically are called only to forgive "the pinpricks we get from our fellows, our neighbor, our boss, our subordinates" (*Our Heavenly Father,* 112). Matt. 6:12 is not about some worthiness earned through our pale imitation of divine forgiveness; it is about our desire. God's forgiveness, although it cannot be merited, must be received, and it will not, Jesus affirms, be received by or become effective in (either now or at the last judgment) those without the will to forgive others (cf. 1 John 4:20).

One should not press the tense of "have forgiven," as if God must wait to forgive us until we have forgiven others. Our line is not a precise statement of theology but parenesis, moral exhortation, and 18:23–35 teaches that God's mercy comes before ours. Maybe Calvin was close to the truth:

> The condition of being forgiven as we forgive our debtors is not added because by forgiving others we deserve forgiveness, as if the cause of forgiveness were expressed; but by the use of this expression the Lord has been pleased partly to solace the weakness of our faith, using it as a sign to assure us that our sins are as certainly forgiven as we are certainly conscious of having forgiven others . . . and partly using as a badge by which he excludes from the number of his children all who, prone to revenge and reluctant to forgive, obstinately keep up their enmity. . . . (*Institutes* 3.20.45)

Although Jewish prayers very often, and communal prayers typically, contain pleas for forgiveness (e.g., Exod. 32:32; Ps. 25:18; the sixth blessing of the *Shemoneh Esreh*; the *Abinu Malkenu*), it is not clear that any makes God's forgiveness of us dependent on our forgiveness of others. Perhaps Jesus first put that sentiment into a prayer (cf. Mark 11:25). Whether or not that is so, the sentiment itself is common enough in non-prayer texts, both Jewish and Christian. A sampling: Ecclus. 28:2: "Forgive your neighbor the wrong done and then your sins will be pardoned when you pray"; Col. 3:13; Mishnah *Yoma* 8:9 (the Day of Atonement effects atonement only if one has forgiven others); Babylonian Talmud *Shabbat* 151b: "The one who is merciful to others, mercy is shown to that one by Heaven, while the one not merciful to others, mercy is not shown to that one by Heaven"; *Rosh HaShanah* 17a: "Who is forgiven iniquity? One who passes by transgression (against himself)."

How does the conventional teaching about forgiveness relate to the rest of Matthew, in which Jesus dies for others? God, in the biblical tradition, forgives under the image of father (Ps. 103:13; Matt. 18:35; Luke 15:11–32). But this forgiveness does not exist in a vacuum, unrelated to the rest of life or religion. In the Jewish Scriptures it is associated with the covenant, with the temple cult, and with repentance. In the New Testament it is similarly related to the new covenant (Luke 22:20; 1 Cor. 11:25), to the death of Jesus (which in Hebrews and elsewhere functions in such as way as to replace the temple cult), and to repentance (cf. Luke 17:3–4; Acts 5:31). The generalization holds for Matthew. Although our Gospel offers no theory of the atonement, it plainly teaches that God's forgiveness of human beings is mediated through the new covenant (26:28) by means of Jesus' death (20:28) and requires repentance (3:2; 4:17; 9:13). So even though it was different with the pre-Easter disciples, for the Christian who prays Matt. 6:12 with the rest of the Gospel and the canon in mind, "Forgive us our debts" cannot but be related to the soteriological dimension of Christ's work. "He will save his people from their sins" (1:21) stands over the whole Gospel, including the Sermon on the Mount and the Lord's Prayer.

The final and climactic petition, which underlines the frailty of human nature and the need for the preceding line about forgiveness, has two complementary parts, one negative, one positive. The first, like many Jewish prayers (e.g., Babylonian Talmud *Berakhot* 60b), asks God not to let us fall victim to "temptation" or "the time of trial." The latter translation (preferred now by the NRSV) assumes that the eschatological birthpangs or messianic woes (cf. 24:8; Rev. 3:10) are primarily in view: one hopes not to succumb to apostasy in the latter days. (Cf. perhaps the related hope that the final tribulation might be shortened for the sake of the elect [Mark 13:20].) But since in the Synoptic tradition and elsewhere in early Christian literature the great tribulation has already entered the present (cf. 10:34–36; Mark 13:3–23; 1 Cor. 7:26; 2 Thess. 2:7; Rev. 7:9–17), there is no antithesis between eschatology and everyday life. All temptation belongs to the latter days.

When Jesus is in Gethsemane, he instructs the disciples to pray that they not enter into the time of trial or temptation. How does this illuminate 6:13? One might argue that it speaks against the eschatological interpretation, for Gethsemane does not appear to be an eschatological event. In fact, however, in Matthew (as in Mark) Jesus' passion and resurrection constitute a sort of end-of-the-world in miniature. If Jesus predicts that the end will feature the temple's demise (24:3), betrayal and martyrdom (24:9–10), "falling away" (24:10), heavenly darkness (24:29), resurrection of the dead (12:41–42), and the fulfillment of the vision of Daniel 7 (24:30), all of these things have their parallels in Jesus' death and vindication. See 27:51 for the tearing of the temple's veil, chapters 26–27 for betrayal and martyrdom, 26:31–35, 56, and 69–75 for "falling away," 27:45 for darkness, 27:51–53 for resurrection, and 28:18 for the fulfillment of Daniel 7 (cf. Dan 7:13–14). The last days of Jesus either foreshadow or belong to the last time, and Gethsemane may be interpreted accordingly.

In Jas. 1:13 we read that God tempts no one. Our text can be read as "a flat contradiction" of this (Betz). But how likely is it that the author of James, who so often alludes to the Jesus tradition, either did not know the Lord's Prayer or wished to dispute it? Here the ecclesiastical commentators on James may be helpful. They show us several possible strategies, most involving a distinction between two types of trial or temptation. The eighteenth-century Baptist John Gill, for instance, wrote that we should not rejoice over the temptations brought by Satan or stirred up by sin, which can only be matters of grief, but only over "afflictions and persecutions for the sake of the Gospel . . . because they are trials of the faith of God's people . . ." (*A Practical Body of Divinity* 3.6). Similarly Oecumenius (*Catholic Epistles* ad loc.) and Theophylact (*Catholic Epistles* ad loc.) asserted that we can rejoice in the trials sent to us by God (cf. James) but, when temptations to sin arise from within ourselves, we need to ask for deliverance (cf. the Lord's Prayer). John Cassian, on the other hand, differentiated between being tempted and being overcome by temptation.

> [From] "Lead us not into temptation" . . . comes a problem that is not a minor one. If we pray that we be not permitted to be tempted, where will that constancy come from for which we are to be tested? There is the scriptural statement that every one who has not been tempted has not been approved of. There is "Blessed is the man who endures temptation." So this cannot be the sense of "Lead us not into temptation." It is not "Do not allow us ever to be tempted" but rather "Do not allow us to be overcome when we are tempted." (*Conferences* 9.23; cf. Aquinas, *Lord's Prayer* 9:3)

Dionysius of Alexandria said something similar: God tempts us but does not actually lead us into, that is, make us succumb to sin: the blame for that lies with the devil and ourselves (Fragment on Luke 22:42ff.). Cyril of Jerusalem, however, found yet another way of establishing harmony between the Lord's Prayer and Jas. 1:2: Jesus' words have to do with being overwhelmed by temptation, Jas. 1:2 with bettering it: "But perhaps the entering into temptation means being overwhelmed by temptation? For temptation is, as it were, like a winter torrent difficult to cross. So those who are not overwhelmed in temptations pass through, showing themselves excellent swimmers, while those who are not such, enter into them and are overwhelmed." He goes on to cite Judas as an example of one who was overcome by temptation, Peter as an illustration of one who overcame it (*Mystagogical Catechesis* 5.17). Perhaps in this connection we can cite, from Matthew itself, the story of Jesus' own temptation (4:1–11). For here the Spirit leads him to the wilderness, but it is the devil who assaults him with temptations. One recalls the story of Job, where God permits Satan to have his way with an individual.

Support for this interpretation comes from 2:17 and 27:9. Many times in his narrative Matthew associates an event in the life of Jesus with a prophetic passage from Scripture. When he does so he uses a formula: "All this took place in order to fulfill what had been spoken by the Lord through . . . ." Twice, however, this formula is altered to the simpler "Then was fulfilled." On both occasions something terrible has happened—the slaughter of infants in Bethlehem (2:17) and Judas's suicide (27:9). It seems pretty clear that the substitution of "then" (*tote*) for "in order to" (*hina*) reflects a studied desire to dissociate God from evil. Some things God foresees and brings to pass; others God foresees and permissively wills (cf. the theological distinction between God's active and passive will). The point for us is that an author sensitive enough to make this sort of distinction is unlikely to have intended 6:13 to implicate God in human sin. For Matthew, evil comes not from God but from sinful humans and the devil (see also 13:1–30, 36–43; and cf. the reflections in Ecclus. 15:11–20).

Unlike Luke's version of the Lord's Prayer, Matthew's concludes with "rescue us from the evil one" (so Eastern church tradition) or "from evil" (so most Western church tradition, with Tertullian, Calvin, and Reformed commentators, including Barth, being exceptions). The Greek can mean either. For the neuter, see Luke 6:45 and Rom. 12:9; for the masculine, John 17:15; Eph. 6:16; and 2 Thess. 3:3. Both translations can also cite for support Jewish parallels. If 11QPs^a 19:15–16 ("Let Satan not dominate me, nor an unclean spirit; let pain and the evil inclination not possess my bones"); 4QLevi^b ar frag. 1 ("Let not any satan have power over me"); and Babylonian Talmud *Berakhot* 16b ("Rabbi prayed, 'May it be your will O Lord our God . . . to deliver us . . . from the destructive Accuser") are prayers for deliverance from the devil, *Berakhot* 60b ("Do not bring me into the power of sin or into the power of iniquity or in the power of temptation . . .") is a plea for deliverance from evil in general. Unfortunately one cannot come to a firm decision on this matter. For in Matthew *ho ponēros* is sometimes masculine (13:19, 38), sometimes neuter (5:39; 12:35).

*   *   *   *   *

Originally, with Jesus himself, the Lord's Prayer was probably intended not for the public at large but particularly for the itinerant missionaries who helped in his work (cf. Luke 11:1). One might even speculate that Jesus intended them to subjoin his prayer to the appointed daily prayers. Certainly later rabbis composed prayers for this end. That Jesus' prayer was intended to be uttered after other prayers would help explain why it has no praise, no thanksgiving, no blessing: it was never intended to be comprehensive or to cover all things needful. Rather was it a prayer with very specific and limited needs in mind. (Cyprian was quite incorrect in trying to make the Lord's Prayer "a compendium of heavenly doctrine" [*Lord's Prayer* 9], and Tertullian's description of it as "an epitome of the whole gospel" [*On Prayer* 1] is equally tendentious. How could a compendium or summary of Christian faith pass over Jesus' life, death, resurrection, and lordship? The Lord's Prayer is not even, despite the far-flung habit of speaking of it as such, a breviary of Christian prayer, or akin to the Ten Commandments, which summarize the law. Too much of importance is missing.)

How was the Lord's Prayer used in the early church? Matt. 6:9 says, "Pray then in this way." These words could imply, despite the nearly universal practice of Christendom, that the Lord's Prayer is more an example of how to pray than a formula to be mechanically repeated. This was the view of Theodore of Mopsuestia (*Catechetical Homilies* 11.3, 5), as well as, in dependence on him, the eighth-century Nestorian bishop Isaac of Nineveh:

> If someone says that we should recite the prayer uttered by our Saviour in all our prayers using the same wording and keeping the exact order of the words, rather than their sense, such a person is very deficient in his understanding. . . . Our Lord did not teach us a particular sequence of words here; rather, the teaching he provided in this prayer consists in showing us what we should be focusing our minds on during the entire course of this life. (Isaac of Nineveh, *The Second Part* 14.36)

Such was also the view of Gill: the Lord's Prayer is "not prescribed as a set form, in so many words . . . since then it would not have been varied, as it is by the two evangelists, by whom it is recorded." Might this help explain why, although there seem to be pieces of the Lord's Prayer scattered throughout the New Testament (e.g., Mark 11:25; John 17:15; Acts 21:14), it is formally cited only in Matthew and Luke? Origen labeled it a "form" or "outline" of prayer (*On Prayer* 2), and Tertullian suggested one add private petitions to it (*On Prayer* 10; cf. the sequence in *Acts of Thomas* 144–49). Some rabbis even objected to fixed prayers without extemporizing because they thought them potentially without sincerity (Mishnah *ʾAbot* 2:13; *Berakhot* 4:3–4; Babylonian Talmud *Berakhot* 29b).

Tertullian's advice to add one's own petitions recalls the rabbinic counsel to append personal prayers after completing the Eighteen Benedictions (Babylonian Talmud *Abodah Zarah* 7b), and one wonders if the Lord's Prayer early on took the place of the *Shemoneh Esreh,* the common daily prayer of Judaism. There are some parallels between the *Shemoneh Esreh* and the Lord's Prayer (e.g., requests for forgiveness, food, and eschatological fulfillment) as well as between the Lord's Prayer and abbreviations of the former (see especially Babylonian Talmud *Berakhot* 29a). Moreover, the central portion of the Eighteen Benedictions, just like the Lord's Prayer, falls into two distinct parts (in the first half the petitions are for individuals, in the second half for the nation); and early Christian tradition instructs believers to say the Lord's Prayer three times a day (*Did.* 8.3) while standing (*Apostolic Constitutions* 7.24)—which precisely parallels what the rabbis demanded for the Eighteen Benedictions. (By the time of Ambrose in the fourth century, however, we find the advice to pray the Lord's Prayer only once a day, either upon rising or upon retiring [*On Virginity* 3.4].)

Whatever the practice of the early Jewish Christians, later Christians associated the Lord's Prayer (in its Matthean, not Lukan form) especially with the liturgy. It was the first prayer uttered by the newly baptized (*Apostolic Constitutions* 7.45), and it has from very near the beginning been almost invariably closely associated with celebration of the Eucharist (see, e.g., Cyril of Jerusalem, *Mystagogical Catechesis* 5; Augustine, *Letter* 59). The Lord's Prayer has also been a traditional part of catechisms, both Catholic and Protestant. The 1924 Book of Common Prayer, for instance, requires that, before confirmation, one be able to recite the creed, the Ten Commandments, and the Lord's Prayer.

One final word on the Lord's Prayer. Sometimes Christian apologists have sought to stress its uniqueness. As we have seen, however, for every detail we can find Jewish parallels. Lancelot Andrews even constructed six different "paraphrases of the Lord's Prayer from the Old Testament," two from phrases in the Pentateuch and one each from lines in Job, the Psalms, works attributed to Solomon, and Isaiah through Ezekiel (*Devotions,* 285–87). The truth would seem to be this. The themes of the Lord's Prayer should be regarded as characteristic of Jewish prayers. In its eschatological outlook it is indeed distinctive, but, as noted above, this does not make it unique. Even the one point at which some critical scholars are still tempted to think it truly novel, namely, its brevity, is problematic. For some of the substitutions for the full Eighteen Benedictions are equally short (see, e.g., the prayer of

Rabbi Joshua in Mishnah *Berakhot* 4:4, or that of Eliezer in Babylonian Talmud *Berakhot* 29b); and rabbinic texts know the saying, "the prayer of the righteous is short" (*Mekhilta* on Exod. 15:25). While some rabbis said that the short substitutes should be prayed only in an emergency, others used them in daily practice (Mishnah *Berakhot* 4:3). So some time before the composition of the Mishnah at least some Jews regularly prayed very short prayers. Jesus' prayer should probably be placed in that context. Through and through, then, the Lord's Prayer breathes the spirit of Jewish piety, and it should be a never-ending reminder of the debt of the Christian church to Judaism. A Jew wanting to have nothing to do with Jesus could still pray the Our Father.

FORGIVENESS (6:14–15)

This little appendix to the Lord's Prayer elaborates upon the fifth petition, recalls 5:21–26, and anticipates 18:23–35 (which, by way of a parable, warns us of the dire consequences if the teaching of 6:14–15 is neglected). It says that if we forgive others, we will be forgiven, and that if we do not forgive others, we will not be forgiven.

Teaching on prayer is also followed by teaching on forgiveness in Mark 11:23–25 and Luke 17:3–6. There appears to have been a traditional connection between the two topics, to wit: prayer is not efficacious unless the members of the community are reconciled to each other. One thinks in this connection of Matt. 5:21–26, where the religious act of sacrifice is to be put off until one is reconciled to a brother or sister. The "kiss of peace" in the traditional liturgies, a sign of reconciliation preceding communion, has been a traditional expression of this idea that religious acts without concord with others are done in vain (cf. Cyril of Jerusalem, *Mystagogical Catechesis* 5.3). One recalls *Didache* 14.2: "But let not anyone having a dispute with a fellow be allowed to join you (in the assembly) until they are reconciled, so that your sacrifice not be defiled."

FASTING (6:16–18)

Matthew 6:1–18 concludes with a section on fasting (a discipline which pagans, despite its recommendation by certain philosophers, thought of as characteristically Jewish). Whether there is any direct connection with prayer (as in so many later monastic and ascetical texts) is not clear. In any event probably in view is voluntary private fasting (as in Dan. 9:3; Matt. 4:2 [Jesus' temptation in the wilderness]; Mark 2:18; Luke 18:12; and *Did.* 8.1), something that provided special opportunity to call attention to oneself, not prescribed public fasting (as for the Day of Atonement: see Lev. 16:29–31; Num. 29:7). The verses must seem nearly irrelevant to most of us who are Protestants, for we, like the people behind *Gospel of Thomas* 14 and those opposed in *Apocalypse of Elijah* 1:13–14, no longer practice fasting. (This explains why the older Protestant commentaries on Matt. 6:16–18 usually condemn Lenten fasting, explain that many early Christians had an exaggerated estimate of the value of fasting, and warn even of the dangers of occasional private abstinence.) But to Eastern Orthodox and Roman Catholics who still, in accord with Matt. 9:15 (cf. Acts 13:2–3; 14:23), occasionally fast, the text may yet have something to say.

Almsgiving (6:2–4) is obviously done for the sake of others, and prayers (6:5–13), at least of the petitionary kind, can be offered on behalf of one's neighbor. Fasting, however, we think of as self-directed. It is a discipline traditionally thought to teach humility, discipline, self-knowledge, and dependence on God (cf. Ecclus. 24:36; Philo, *Special Laws* 2.195; *Apocalypse of Elijah* 1:15–22). Thus, it is particularly heinous when this act of piety is turned into religious display. But "the spirit of vainglory is most subtle and it readily grows up in the souls of those who practice virtue," for, as Evagrius knew, "what you do to destroy it becomes the principle of some other form of vainglory" (*Praktikos* 13, 30).

Fasting was often accompanied by external signs, such as sackcloth, ashes, and the rending of clothing (note Dan. 9:3; Jonah 3:5; Jth. 8:5). So here Jesus can speak of those who "disfigure" themselves—is the meaning "go unwashed" or "cover with ashes" or "make pale"?—in the attempt to proclaim to onlookers that they are fasting. He, however, commends oil to those who fast. This is not just literal instruction for fasting but a "figurative illustration" that appeals "to creative fantasy and to the liberty of the listener"; that is, "the listener himself or herself has to determine what 'washing and anointing' means tangibly" (Luz, *Matthew 1–7*, 361). The general principle is clear: the inner state should not be advertised by artificial signs, for humility demands secrecy, and the goal of fasting is not enhanced reputation. The actual application—which covers not only fasting but all piety— is left to the reader.

Most commentators now find in "put oil on your head and wash your face" a reference to everyday hygiene, so that the meaning is this: when fasting you should look just as you do normally. To this interpretation there is a striking parallel in *Testament of Joseph* 3:4: "For these seven years I fasted, and yet seemed to the Egyptians like someone who was living luxuriously, for those who fast for the sake of God receive graciousness of countenance."

Perhaps, however, we should follow Theophylact, who took "put oil on your head and wash your face" to signify a special occasion of gladness (*Matthew* ad loc.). Anointing the head with oil was sometimes a sign of rejoicing (as in Ps. 23:5 and 104:15), so our text might be suggesting that one even mislead others: one pretends to rejoice in the middle of the affliction of fasting. Such deception for the sake of humility became common among Christian ascetics (see, e.g., Theodoret, *Religious History* 26.5 [Simeon Stylites hid and lied about his ascetic tortures]).

On the surface our text can be read to mean that one should hide one's fasting from everyone. But William Law observed that a husband or wife can hardly fast without the rest of the family knowing it. His conclusion was this: "the privacy of fasting does not suppose such a privacy as excludes everybody from knowing it, but such a privacy as does not seek to be known abroad" (*A Serious Call to a Holy and Devout Life*, chapter 15). This is the sort of ad hoc, interpretative clarification that a text as dense, figurative, and brief as the Sermon on the Mount constantly requires.

Our verse ends, as do the little subsections on almsgiving and fasting, with the promise of reward: the Father will reward the pious. Moderns, particularly after Kant, often show embarrassment over this sort of language. Ulrich Luz calls it "troubling." The suspicion is that the Sermon on the Mount is a disguised hedonism: one gives up the praise of others not to seek God for God's sake but in order to gain heavenly reward. Should we not rather find more congenial the prayer of the Sufi mystic Rabiʾa, who prayed, "If I worship you in fear of hell, burn me in hell. And if I worship you for hope of paradise, exclude me from paradise. But if I worship you for your own sake, withhold not your everlasting beauty"? Do we not think praiseworthy the maxim of Antigonos of Soho: "Be not like servants who serve the master on condition of receiving a gift, but be like servants who serve the master not on condition of receiving" (Mishnah ʾAbot 1:3)?

Whatever our own predilections, on the matter of rewards the Sermon on the Mount does not anticipate Kant. We do not here read of doing the good for its own sake. The Sermon rather takes for granted the human hope for happiness and promises that it will find fulfillment in the kingdom of God. In this it is realistic. Just as a tree by nature has roots that draw nourishment to itself, not others, so human beings are unavoidably centered in themselves. The Sermon on the Mount knows this. It accordingly does not overestimate human nature but confronts it in its self-centered reality with fear and hope.

Having said all this, it should be added that Matthew is too sophisticated to have a mechanical idea of reward. The parable of 20:1–16 clearly teaches that eschatological rewards will be full of disproportionate grace and so surprising. So there can be no calculation of this reward for that act. Moreover, because love, which is the basis of reward (25:31–46), is not quantifiable, judgment is not made with a scale of balances.

FOR FURTHER READING

Barth, Karl. *Prayer.* 2nd ed. Philadelphia: Westminster, 1985.

Betz, Hans Dieter. *Essays on the Sermon on the Mount.* Philadelphia: Fortress, 1985. Pp. 55–69.

Brown, Raymond E. *New Testament Essays.* Garden City, N.Y.: Doubleday, 1967. Pp. 217–53.

Harner, P. B. *Understanding the Lord's Prayer.* Philadelphia: Fortress, 1975.

Houk, Cornelius B. "ΠΕΙΡΑΣΜΟΣ, the Lord's Prayer, and the Massah Tradition." *Scottish Journal of Theology* 19 (1966): 216–25.

Lambert, J. C. "Lord's Prayer." In *A Dictionary of Christ and the Gospels,* edited by James Hastings, 2:60–63. Edinburgh: T & T Clark, 1908.

Lochman, Jan Milič. *The Lord's Prayer.* Grand Rapids: Eerdmans, 1990.

Lohmeyer, Ernst. *The Lord's Prayer.* London: Collins, 1965.

Mangan, C. *Can We Still Call God "Father"? A Woman Looks at the Lord's Prayer Today.* Wilmington: Glazier, 1984.

Petuchowsky, Jakob J., and Michael Brocke, eds. *The Lord's Prayer and Jewish Liturgy.* New York: Seabury, 1978.

Thielicke, Helmut. *Our Heavenly Father: Sermons on the Lord's Prayer.* New York: Harper & Row, 1960.

7

Social Obligations
(6:19–7:12)

HAVING GIVEN TEACHING vis-à-vis Torah (5:17–48) and issued commandments concerning almsgiving, prayer, and fasting (6:1–18), Matthew's Jesus next addresses social issues (6:19–7:12). The instruction falls into two sections. The first, 6:19–34, teaches that one should disregard mammon (6:19–24) and that the one who does this can rely on the heavenly Father's care (6:25–34). The second is about not judging others (7:1–6) and, again, about the heavenly Father's care (7:7–11). The entire section ends with the golden rule (7:12).

The three small paragraphs in 6:19–24 and the long paragraph in 6:25–34 are structurally similar, as can be seen at a glance:

thesis statement or introduction		22a	24a	25
two (supporting) observations in antithetical or compound parallelism	19–20	22b–23b	24b–c	26, 28–30
concluding remark(s)	21	23c–d	24d	32–34

The formal parallelism helps underline the unity of theme. There is, nonetheless, a transition between 6:24 and 25. The first three units all function as imperatives. The last functions less to add new demands

138

than to comfort those who choose to live under the Sermon's harsh demands.

TREASURE ON EARTH AND IN HEAVEN (6:19–21)

Jesus tells his followers not to store up treasures on the earth (6:19; cf. Luke 12:33). "The exhortation presupposes that this is precisely what everyone normally does" (Betz, *Commentary*, 433). Jesus' first reason for his demand is the commonsense observation that such treasures perish: moth and rust consume them and thieves carry them away (cf. Jas. 5:2–3, which may allude to our saying). The unarguable sentiment was common enough in the ancient world (and is not common enough today). Like the happiness it brings, and like the grass of the field, which is alive today and tomorrow is thrown into the oven (6:30), earthly possessions are bound to pass away. Money is "a matter unstable" (Menander, *Dyskolos*, frag.). "Prosperity is unstable" (*Pseudo-Phocylides* 27). All the things people typically strive for stand under the sentence, "heaven and earth will pass away" (24:35; cf. 5:18).

The second reason (given in perfect antithetical parallelism) for not storing up treasures on the earth passes beyond common sense and appeals to eschatological doctrine: one's efforts are better put into storing up treasure in heaven, in a realm that is not touched by time, chance, and decay (6:20; cf. 5:12; Ecclus. 29:10–11; *Psalms of Solomon* 9:5; *2 Bar.* 24:1; Babylonian Talmud *Baba Batra* 11a; in Tosefta *Peah* 4.18 a king gives away much wealth in order to have "imperishable treasure for the age to come"). Once the assumptions are granted— there is an afterlife and what one does here matters there—the argument cannot be questioned. How can one invest in the temporal and unstable when it is possible to invest in that which is stable and endures? Only an unabashed materialism could annul the logic.

Like 6:4, 6, and 18, our text does not here specify what is meant by "treasure in heaven." But by this point in the Sermon there is no need for specification. The beatitudes have already expanded on that concept in detail.

Our text also does not tell us *how* to lay up treasures in heaven. But this too is plain from the rest of the Sermon on the Mount. Good deeds make for reward in the afterlife. One should probably think especially of the teaching about alms or giving to others (6:2–4). One gains by giving away.

Some enthusiastic believers have taken these and other words of Jesus to entail the renunciation of all belongings. Origen, Cyprian, Anthony of the Desert, Francis of Assisi, and countless others have rid themselves of all property in order to live lives fully committed to their religious convictions (note also Acts 2:43–47). But it is far from clear that voluntary poverty accords with the spirit of Matthew. Matt. 6:19 speaks about "treasure," not earthly goods in general; and the verb "store up" (so NRSV; the Greek is literally, "treasure up") refers to accumulation, not simple possession. Further, as Isaac the Syrian observed, those who own nothing cannot give alms; but in 6:2–4, which follows upon the command to be perfect (5:48), there is certainly no hint that those who obey Jesus and give alms are in any way inferior (*Ascetical Homilies* 21). (This is one of the arguments of Clement of Alexandria's *Who Is the Rich Man Who Shall Be Saved?*, and it is a good one.) There is also the striking fact that Matthew can call Joseph of Arimathea both "a rich man" and "a disciple of Jesus" (27:57). Seemingly Matthew would not have gone even as far as the Pelagians, the Eustathians, and the Manichees, who taught only that the richest should give up their wealth (cf. *Pseudo-Clementine Homilies* 15.9). The sort of poverty that Matthew demands is "poverty of spirit," that is, humility (5:3).

Having said all this, our Gospel, in which there is no hint of the belief that wealth is a sign of divine favor (contrast *Testament of Job* 44:5 and Babylonian Talmud *Nedarim* 38a), offers little comfort for the rich. Here, as 5:17–20 should lead us to expect, there is agreement with the Hebrew prophetic tradition (see especially Amos). Matthew contains stories in which people give up their earthly lives and possessions (4:18–22; 8:18–22; 9:9). Moreover, 19:16–30, which has so many interesting parallels with the Sermon on the Mount, is a narrative illustration of 6:19–20, and here the rich man, who cannot give up his goods, does not enter the kingdom, whereas the disciples, who have "left everything," are told they will receive "a hundredfold and inherit eternal life" (19:29). The lesson, reinforced by the saying about a camel going through the eye of a needle, is plain: God's kingdom is hard to reach if one is rich, for one is almost inevitably inclined to trust in the security of wealth rather than in God alone (cf. 13:22; also Prov. 15:16–17; Ecclus. 31:5–7; 1 Tim. 6:9–10; *Pseudo-Phocylides* 42–47; *Sibylline Oracles* 2.109–18). Empty hands reach out for God; full hands are clutched to the self.

Perhaps one should compare Matthew with what we find in Ben Sira, namely, warnings of the dangers of wealth (18:32; 31:5; 34:20–22) juxtaposed with praise of the rich who are devout (13:24; 31:8; 40:18). It may also be reasonable to hold that Matthew foreshadows the teaching of Clement of Alexandria's *Who Is the Rich Man?*, even though the philosophical idiom is foreign to our Gospel. For Clement, "salvation does not depend on external things, whether they be many or few, small or great, illustrious or obscure, esteemed or disesteemed; but on the virtue of the soul, faith, hope, love, brotherliness, knowledge, meekness, humility, and truth . . ." (18). Clement does not deny that riches are seductive and dangerous, that they are an obstacle on the way to God: quite the contrary. But he observes that many other things are also obstacles, and "it is no great thing or desirable to be destitute of wealth, if without special object" (11). Wealth is therefore not to be eliminated on principle but rather used according to the needs of the hour: "make friends for yourselves by means of unrighteous mammon" (Luke 16:9).

The problem, of course, as Clement well knows, is that those who seek to use wealth for good ends so often become not its master but its slave. As it says in 13:22, "the cares of the world and the lure of wealth choke the word." Bernard of Clairvaux wrote of the rich man in Matthew 19: he "did not own his possessions: they owned him; if he had owned them, he could have been free of them" (*Commentary on the Song of Songs* 21.4[8]). So, according to Clement, what is demanded of the faithful is neither ascetic renunciation nor acceptance of a communistic ideal but *freedom for obedience,* that is, the freedom to do what God "wishes, what he orders, what he indicates" (*Who Is the Rich Man?* 26). The rich typically do not have such freedom—whence the hyperbole in Matt. 19:24: "it is easier for a camel, etc." The so-called perfect, however, do have such freedom; for while they neither hate wealth nor love poverty, they are profoundly indifferent toward worldly goods; and such indifference, generated by a consuming love for God and spiritual things (cf. Matt. 6:33), enables them to do what the rich man could not, namely, respond in wholehearted obedience to the demands of Christ.

Matt. 6:21 follows the couplet about treasure with a sentiment about the heart: "For where your treasure is, there your heart will be also." There is more than a catchword connection. That upon which one's heart and mind are set is where one's treasure will be. The athlete whose entire focus is bent on triumph in a contest will, if suc-

cessful, be rewarded in the arena. In like manner, the disciple with
heart or mind set on the things above, not on the things below (cf. Col.
3:2), will, if successful, be rewarded above. Just as deeds reveal intentions, so one's treasure tells the tale of what one is really all about.

THE EYE IS THE LAMP OF THE BODY
(6:22–23)

"The eye is the lamp of the body" is difficult. For us the eye is a win-
dow: as a transparent medium it lets light in. We do not think of the
eye as a lamp, that is, as its own light source. It was different in antiquity. Not only did Greek philosophers believe the eye to have its own
light (Empedocles frag. 84; Plato, *Timaeus* 45B–46A; Philo, *On Abraham* 150–57): so did the general populace (cf. Aristotle, *On Sensation*
437a: "everyone" believes the organ of sight to consist of fire). The
same generalization holds for ancient Jewish texts, which speak of
"the light of the [or: my] eyes" (Ps. 38:11; Prov. 15:30; Tob. 10:5; 11:13
(S); Bar. 3:14; cf. Prov. 19:13). While many commentators, on the basis
of Tob. 10:5 and 11:13 (S) and modern figurative usage, give the biblical expression metaphorical meaning, there are old texts in which eyes
are said to be dimmed or darkened and literal loss of eyesight is the
subject (Gen. 27:1; 48:10; Deut. 34:7; 1 Sam. 3:2; *Sibylline Oracles*
3.420; Babylonian Talmud *Ḥagigah* 16a). So when the eye is compared
with the sun (Bar. 2:18; Ecclus. 23:19; *Joseph and Aseneth* 14:9; *3
Enoch* 26:6) or with torches (Dan. 10:2–9 LXX) or, as in our saying, with
lamps (cf. Zech. 4:1–10; *2 Enoch* 42:1; Babylonian Talmud *Shabbat*
151b), we should think of the belief that "rays shine through the eyes
and touch whatever they see" (Augustine, *On the Trinity* 9.3.3; cf.
1 Enoch 106:2, 5, 10; *4 Bar.* 7:3; *3 Enoch* 1:7–8).

"The eye is the lamp of the body," which has a proverbial ring,
clearly does not set forth a novel idea. It is simply a statement of the
common premodern understanding of vision—which is how Matt. 6:22
was understood by, for example, Clement of Alexandria (*Teacher*
3.11.70) and the sixth-century Syrian monk Martyrius in his *Book of
Perfection* 8 §§55–56. (Most of church tradition, however, wrongly
equates the eye and lamp of our saying with the mind and so goes
another way altogether.) Confirmation comes from the variant in

Gospel of Thomas 24, where the "light within a man of light" dispels darkness and "lights the whole world." The picture is of light going out.

"If your eye is healthy your whole body will be full of light" continues to unfold the common theory of vision. The meaning is not (notwithstanding our modern inclination) that a good eye illuminates the body's interior. Rather, when an eye is sound, this shows there is light within (cf. the logic and structure of 12:28, where the "if" clause names the consequence of the "then" clause). A good eye is the proof of inner light, for the condition of the former is the existence of the latter. Inner light makes eyes shine.

Thus far everything could be read in physiological terms. But our saying ends with a moral observation: "If then the light in you is darkness, how great is the darkness." Moreover, the expression in 6:23 translated by the NRSV as "unhealthy" is literally "bad" or "evil," and "bad eye" comes from the ethical vocabulary of Judaism. It expresses the antithesis of generosity—selfishness, covetousness, an evil and envious disposition, hatred of others (Deut. 15:9; Prov. 22:9; Tob. 2:10; *Testament of Issachar* 4:6; Mishnah *'Abot* 2:9, 11; cf. the "dark eye" of *Testament of Benjamin* 4:2). The locution is used again in Matt. 20:15: "Am I not allowed to do what I choose with what belongs to me? Or is your eye evil because I am good?" This last means, as the NRSV translates, "Or are you envious because I am generous?"

Once one sees that our saying is a sort of riddle that can be read on two different levels, as a statement either about vision or about moral principles, then it becomes obvious that the "healthy eye" of 6:22 has double meaning. It refers not only to the physical eye but also to moral intention. In Judaism "good eye" meant generosity (Prov. 22:9; Ecclus. 32:8, 10; *Testament of Issachar* 3:4; Mishnah *'Abot* 2:13). So Matt. 6:22–23, read on its deeper level, says that just as a "good eye," a proper disposition toward others, is an effect of the light within, so similarly is a bad eye, that is, a selfish, ungenerous, miserly spirit, the companion of inner darkness. That is, one's moral disposition correlates with an inner darkness or light within.

What does it mean to be full of light or full of darkness? It is unnecessary to suppose a well-developed and carefully considered dualism such as that found in Zoroastrianism or the Dead Sea Scrolls. Nor need one look to Greek philosophy for an explanation. Already the Hebrew Bible says that God dwells in light (Ps. 104:2; Dan. 2:22; Hab. 3:3–4), has a countenance of light (Pss. 31:16; 44:3; 67:1; 89:15; 90:8), and gives light to the saints (Job 29:2–3; Ps. 4:6; 18:28; 43:3). And although light is sometimes an eschatological hope (Isa. 60:20; cf. Rev. 21:23; 22:5), God's children are even now illuminated by the light of life (Ps. 56:13) and they possess wisdom, which is light (Wisd. 7:10, 26). Indeed, the righteous are sometimes even called light (Isa. 42:6; 49:6; cf. Matt. 5:14)—and it is light that determines the direction of all their activities. They "walk in the light of the Lord" (Isa. 2:5).

So it was natural enough for ancient Jews to speak occasionally of an inner light. Already Prov. 20:27 says that "the human spirit is the lamp of the Lord, searching every innermost part." Among the Dead Sea Scrolls is 4QHoroscope (4Q186), in which individuals are made up of various parts of light, and 1QS 4:2 refers to the "giving of light to the heart of man." In 2 Cor. 4:6 Paul says that God "has shone in our hearts to give the light of the knowledge of the glory of God in the face of Christ." The author of Eph. 1:18 can speak of God "enlightening the eyes" of believers' hearts. Our saying belongs with these texts, in which those who have within themselves the divine light share the divine life and know salvation (Ps. 27:1).

What does it mean to be in darkness? It means separation from God—which is why first Hades and then later on hell (despite its fire) are dark places (Job 10:21-22; Matt. 8:12; 22:13). As it says in Job, "Surely the light of the wicked is put out, and the flame of their fire does not shine. The light is dark in their tent, and the lamp above them is put out" (18:5–6). Inner light leads to loving one's neighbor, inner darkness to illiberality and selfishness. 1QS 4:9–11 naturally enough associates a greedy mind with blindness of eye.

Matthew 6:22–23 ends with a frightening observation: "If then the light in you is darkness, how great is the darkness." This recalls Jewish laments or prophecies of judgment: Job 3:4 ("let that day be darkness"); 10:24 (in the land of death "light is like darkness"); Zeph. 1:15 ("a day of darkness and gloom"); 1QH 5:32 ("the light of my countenance is darkened to deep darkness"); *Testament of Job* 43:6 ("his lamp, extinguished, obliterated its light; and the splendor of his lantern will depart from him"). The listener is called to self-examination. Am I filled with light or with darkness? Has my spirit become darkened? And how do I know one way or the other? Is my eye good, or is it bad?

In its entirety, 6:22–23 moves one to ponder the relation between outward acts and inward states (see also 7:15–20; 12:33–34; 15:10–20; 23:27). The proof of right religion resides in deeds, for that which is within is the source of that without. This is why the healthy eye and inner light are found together and why the bad eye and inner darkness entail one another. ("The light in you" is not identical with the lamp of the body that is the eye. Our saying is rather about the relationship between these two distinct things.) Darkness and light are contrary powers with opposite effects. Light without unselfish good deeds is darkness. So one can discern whether within the self there is darkness or light by looking at the character of one's deeds.

It should now be obvious why 6:22–23 is in its present context. On either side are sayings about money—about not treasuring up treasure on the earth (6:19–21) and about serving God instead of mammon (= money). Matt. 6:22–23 is also about money, or rather about what one does with it. The person with a "healthy" eye is the one who, through generosity, thereby serves God instead of mammon and stores up treasure in heaven. The person with an "unhealthy" eye is the one who, because of selfishness, thereby serves mammon instead of God and stores up treasure only on the earth.

God and Mammon (6:24)

Matthew 6:24 (cf. Luke 16:13) has exactly the same structure as the preceding unit, 6:22–23. Both are quatrains that consist of a thesis statement followed by two expository sentences in antithetical parallelism followed by the conclusion or application. But the formal similarity is less important than the thematic connection just noted. The "healthy eye," interpreted as generosity, serves God. The "unhealthy eye," interpreted as selfishness, serves mammon. ("Mammon" is a Semitic loanword meaning "money" or "possessions." Whether or not it already had pejorative connotations in Jesus' time is unclear. But perhaps the tradition transliterated instead of translating because it functioned like the name of an idol.)

In general one cannot serve two masters (Rom. 6:16); that is, one cannot really serve two masters well, because their demands will not always be compatible. But where, in particular, is the incompatibility between God and mammon? God, who commands an exclusive obligation, demands charity, that is, the giving away of mammon. But mammon invites one to serve oneself through the accumulation of goods, with the result that one comes to trust in something other than God. The idea was far-flung in antiquity. "It is impossible for love of the world to coexist with the love of God" (Philo, frag. 2:649). "It is not

possible . . . to attach yourself both to things mortal and to things
divine" (*Poimandres* 4.6b). This is why, "with the question of money,
human existence as such is at stake" (Luz, *Matthew 1–7*, 398). "You
must put God first, or nowhere" (Gore, *Sermon*, 145).

ANXIETY AND THE FATHER'S CARE
(6:25–34)

Those who do not store up treasure on the earth (6:19–21), who are generous with what they have (6:22–23), and who serve God instead of
mammon (6:24) are inviting anxiety. For life in the world demands that
we have and use things. Jesus inveighs against such anxiety (cf. 10:19).
That sincere religious commitment might create anxiety was also recognized by the rabbis. In *Mekhilta* on Exod. 16:4 Rabbi Simeon ben
Yoai says: "How can a man be sitting and studying when he does not
know where his food and drink will come from nor where he can get
his clothes and coverings?" If it is true, as Hillel purportedly said, that
"the more possessions, the more care" (Mishnah *'Abot* 2:7), it can also
be that the fewer possessions the more care. But recognition of God's
providence and wisdom concerning temporal things should encourage
a spiritual equanimity. "Do not worry about anything" (Phil. 4:6).

Our section opens with a command not to worry about food, drink,
or clothing (6:25a) which is followed by supporting argumentation: "Is
not life more than food, and the body more than clothing?" (6:25b).
The force of the rhetorical question is not perfectly clear (which is why
some have thought the last part of 6:25 to be a secondary addition).
Augustine believed Jesus to be reasoning theologically from the lesser
to the greater: God, "who gave us life will much more easily give us
meat. . . . Similarly, you are to understand that he who gave the body
will much more easily give raiment" (*Sermon on the Mount* 2.15; cf.
Matt. 10:28–31 and 1 Pet. 5:7: "Cast all your anxieties upon him, for
he cares for you"). But it is equally possible that we have here "a warning against excessive concern: What does a person have in life if he or
she constantly drudges or worries?" (Luz, *Matthew 1–7*, 404–5).

Encouragement to be free of anxiety, which amounts to a call to
tranquillity, comes in the form of several illustrations. The first has
to do with the birds of the air (6:26). They neither sow nor reap nor
gather into barns; and God, who feeds them, will the much more take
care of disciples. Much theology is here enfolded. In the background

is the rich biblical tradition that God feeds God's people—and not just through mundane, natural processes. There are the stories of Israel's wilderness wanderings, during which the people were sent manna and quail and given water. There is the jubilee legislation, which calls Israel to depend on Yahweh's catering hand during the Sabbath-year fallow (Lev. 25:18–24). There is 2 Kgs. 4:42–44, which tells of God, through Elisha, multiplying bread. Our Gospel also contains the theme, for twice Jesus miraculously feeds crowds (14:13–21; 15:32–39).

There is also theology in the assertion that God the Father feeds the birds (in which connection readers do not think of miracles but of the everyday course of nature). Not only did God create the world at some point in the past, but God is actively involved in its workings at present. The sentiment appears often in the Bible and Jewish tradition. God "provides the raven its prey, when its young ones cry to God, and wander about for lack of food" (Job 38:41). God "gives to the beasts their food, and to the young ravens which cry" (Ps. 147:9). "Birds and fish you [God] nourish" (*Psalms of Solomon* 5:9–10). One may even cite the *Qur'an*: "There are countless beasts that cannot fend for themselves. Allah provides for them and for you" (29:60). Perhaps the most interesting parallel appears in Mishnah *Qiddushin* 4:14, where Simeon b. Eleazar observes that wild animals and birds practice no craft yet are sustained without care. He goes on to mourn that human beings, who have a higher purpose than the animals, are not sustained without care, for through their evil deeds they have forfeited their right to such sustenance. Although Simeon's conclusion (based on Gen. 3:17–19) is the opposite of the Sermon on the Mount, the manner of argument is strikingly similar.

There is yet a third theological component to our verse. Because 6:26 draws an inference about God from the birds, it also offers a sort of simple natural theology: Jesus gathers something about God's dealings with humanity by looking at how God works in the natural world (cf. Job 12:7–8; Prov. 6:6–11). Because God (to borrow from Wordsworth) "rolls through all things," it is possible to learn about the divine nature through informed contemplation of the natural world (cf. 5:45). One should recall the intertwining of nature and human affairs in the narrative of the magi and the star (2:1–11) and in the story of Jesus' passion, in which the earth quakes (27:51–53). These accounts reflect belief in a cosmic piety: all of creation, not just humanity, is directly related to the creator. Because God is Lord of all, no sphere is beyond the pale of religious discourse, and there must be lessons to be had everywhere.

The final theological lesson in 6:26 is that, in accord with Jewish tradition, human beings are more valuable than the birds. The idea, which is reiterated in 10:31 and 12:12, is clear in Adam's lordship over the beasts (Gen. 1:28–31; cf. Matt. 21:1–3) and implicit in the entirety of the biblical history.

Jesus refers to birds later in our Gospel in ways that potentially enlarge the meaning of 6:26. In 8:20 he says (seemingly in an ironic allusion to Psalm 8) that while the birds of the air have nests, the Son of man has nowhere to lay his head—which tells us that even though 6:25–34 assures us that God takes care of the faithful, this assurance covers nothing more than the basic necessities. God does not give luxuries. In 10:29 Jesus speaks of sparrows being sold and falling to the ground, which entails that God's care of them does not guarantee their physical safety. In 13:4 birds, as part of a series of unfortunate events, eat seeds that fall along the path. As 13:19 identifies the birds with "the evil one," one might draw a homiletical link with 5:45, where God sends the sun and rain to the evil as well as the good. Matt. 13:31–32 tells of the birds of the air coming to nest in the great shrub that began as a mere mustard seed. Here is an illustration of God providing shelter for animals.

Passing on to 6:27, the verse offers a second supporting argument for not being anxious, namely, that worrying accomplishes nothing. "Can any of you by worrying add a single hour [or: cubit] to your span of life [or: height]?" Whether or not we are to look beneath the question and think about God, the one who can lengthen life or stature (so Augustine), the meaning of the rhetorical question is straightforward: anxiety accomplishes nothing, or at least nothing desirable. One could cite a dozen proverbs to this effect, and we all know this truth from experience, but our inability to live according to what we know requires that we be reminded again and again.

Jesus' third supporting argument is put forward in 6:28–30, which is so reminiscent of 6:26:

6:26	6:28–30
Look at the birds	Consider the lilies
they do not sow/reap/gather	they do not toil/spin
the Father feeds them	God clothes the grass
Are you not of more value?	will he not much more?

Matthew 6:28–30 says the same thing as 6:26 but with a different illustration. The repetition is, however, not redundancy. It rather adds force, which is required because the text is addressing an anxiety deeply rooted in human nature.

In the Hebrew Bible the comparison of the human being to flower or grass often underlines the brevity and fragility of human life. "All people are grass, their constancy is like the grass of the field. The grass withers, the flower fades . . ." (Isa. 40:6–7; cf. Job 8:12; 14:1–2; Pss. 37:1–2; 90:5–6; etc.). But in the Sermon on the Mount it is otherwise. The brave show of the flora, which is soon over, and their decoration of the grass, which is used to fire the baking oven, do not convey how fleeting life is but how much care God invests in them despite their short existence. So 6:28–30 seems to turn a traditional motif on its head—just as 6:26 may, if the sentiment expressed in Mishnah *Qiddushin* 4:14 (quoted above) was conventional. Perhaps a first-century Jew would have found Matt. 6:26ff. ironic and provocative because it draws conclusions from the birds and the flowers opposite to those others had sometimes drawn.

In 6:29 Jesus says that even Solomon's glory cannot compare with the flowers of Galilee. The text might slightly disparage Solomon's excessive splendor. David's son was remembered as one who "exceedingly plumed himself upon his riches" (Clement of Alexandria, *Teacher* 2.10.102), and 11:8 has sometimes been thought to depreciate the "soft robes" of Herod's courtiers. By contrast, God clothed Adam and Eve with simple garments of skins (Gen. 3:21); and the disciples of Jesus, who is greater than Solomon (Matt. 12:42), have only coat and cloak (5:40).

The argument winds down in 6:31–33. The Gentiles, who do not trust the God of Israel, strive for food, drink, and clothing (cf. the parable of the rich fool in Luke 12:16–21). But those who trust this God need not so strive, for God "knows that you need all these things" and will therefore supply them (perhaps through human servants; see 10:10). The reader is reminded of 6:7–8, where the Gentiles vainly heap up empty phrases whereas Jesus' followers can speak little because their Father knows their needs. Perhaps indeed the reader is supposed to go back to the Lord's Prayer and realize that the one who prays in faith for bread need not worry about food or drink.

Matthew 6:30 refers to the disciples as people of "little faith" (cf. 8:26; 14:31; 16:8; 17:20). One wonders if the expression was not traditionally tied to anxiety over earthly necessities, for *Tanḥuma Beshal-*

laḥ 117b has this: "R. Elazar of Modiᶜim said: If one has food for the day but says, 'What shall I eat tomorrow?,' he is deficient in faith. R. Eliezer the Great said: He who has yet bread in his basket and says, 'What shall I eat tomorrow?,' belongs to those of little faith" (cf. *Mekhilta* on Exod. 16:4, 19, 27; Babylonian Talmud *Soṭa* 45b). In any case it is comforting that, according to Jesus, God takes care of those with a broken or insufficient faith.

Matthew 6:33 exhorts disciples to seek first the kingdom because then "all these things" will be supplied. Those who take care of God's business will be taken care of by God—which is why Mark the Ascetic taught that if one seeks the kingdom above all there will not only be no anxiety about particular things but not even any need to pray for them specifically (the *Philocalia*, St. Mark the Ascetic, "No Righteousness by Works," 166). But what does "strive first for his kingdom" mean? Probably the thought is that the kingdom, which has already begun to manifest itself in Jesus and the church, can be entered not only in the future but in the here and now, and since entering the kingdom is synonymous with salvation, one should make it one's overriding concern.

On this reading, striving for the kingdom means in practice the same thing as striving for righteousness. For this last does not mean God's eschatological vindication of the saints or divine justice but the conduct God requires to enter the kingdom. So to seek the kingdom is to seek righteousness, which is its precondition, and to seek righteousness is to seek the kingdom, to which it leads.

The section closes with 6:34, probably an addendum of Matthew himself. It is a two-part proverb drawn from the well of ancient Near Eastern wisdom. "Do not prepare for tomorrow before it is come; one knows not what evil may be in it" and "Do not spend the night in fear of the morrow. At dawn what is the morrow like? One knows not what the morrow is like" are both found in old Egyptian sources. Prov. 27:1 and the rabbinic corpus (e.g., Babylonian Talmud *Berakhot* 9b; *Sanhedrin* 100b; *Yebamot* 63b) and still other sources (e.g., *Pseudo-Phocylides* 116–21; *Sentences of Syriac Menander* 385–86; Seneca, *Letter* 101.4) offer similar sayings. But these sayings all sound pessimistic or stoical and counteract worry by appealing to unelaborated common sense (cf. Matt. 6:27; 1 Cor. 15:33). In Matthew, however, the traditional proverb is, through its new context, given a fresh sense. With God one can be content with what is at hand (Luke 3:14; Heb. 13:5); and anxiety for tomorrow is foolish because the compassionate

Father in heaven is Lord of the future. If sufficient for the day is the evil thereof, God is more than sufficient in the midst of that evil. (Monastics made the true observation that the presence of anxiety in the soul would prevent it from examining the things that truly matter; see, e.g., the *Philocalia,* St. Mark the Ascetic, "No Righteousness by Works," 224.)

*   *   *   *   *

Matthew 6:25–34, which is not obviously filled with common sense, has struck many as exceedingly problematic. How can one not seek food, drink, and clothing, things necessary for existence? Is this not a religious flight from solid reality? How can one depend on God to provide in a world where evil all too often triumphs? How can one see God's hand in a nature that is red in tooth and claw and dominated by the never-ending struggle for the survival of the fittest? How could anyone take no thought for tomorrow? Would the result not be disaster? And, finally, does the passage not encourage people to belittle or abandon work? (The Messalians, against whom Augustine wrote *On the Work of Monks,* used our text to justify abandoning manual labor, and Anthony the Great found in 6:34 reason to give away the remainder of his money and property: Athanasius, *Life of Anthony* 2).

Some of these problems are partly answered by the Gospel itself. For example, 6:34 cannot mean utterly neglecting the future, for throughout Matthew Jesus asks his disciples to think about what the future holds (see especially chapters 24–25). Again, 10:29 proves that our Gospel offers no romantic view of nature while 5:10–12; 10:16–23 and the last days of Jesus eliminate a sanguine view of what providence permits to come upon the saints. Other problems seem much less pressing when one realizes that probably for Jesus and the tradition before Matthew our text was not formulated as general religious instruction: most of the material now gathered in 6:25–34 originally functioned as consolation for itinerant missionaries. That is why the hearers are compared to the birds who neither sow nor reap nor gather into barns: the original addressees were not regular workers.

It remains true, nonetheless, that 6:25–34 is part of the Sermon on the Mount and, in Matthew's editorial intention, impinges upon all faithful readers. Probably the best way to make use of the passage today is to explore the general theological principles that it enshrines. Our text requires one to think about providence, about the special value of human beings, about what it might mean for us to depend on

God, and about the possibility that God, despite appearances, is active in the world. Our text should also stimulate serious deliberation on the problem of anxiety within a Christian context. Barth urged that "all evil begins with the fact that we will not thankfully accept the limitation of our existence where we should hope in the light of it, and be certain, joyously certain, of the fulfillment of our life in the expectation of its end. The root of all evil is simply, and powerfully, our human care." He went on to argue, drawing up Matt 6:25–34, that the Christ-event removes the ground for all anxiety and that "we may be anxious, but we cannot provide for our anxiety the object which it must have if it is to have any final seriousness. We cannot give it an absolute character. We can only deceive ourselves and others if we think that there is good reason for it, and that we achieve anything by it. Our care is empty and futile. By it we can only realize and reveal our sin and shame" (*Church Dogmatics* IV.2.65.2).

PROHIBITION OF JUDGING (7:1–2)

The reader now turns from one social issue, what to do with and about mammon, to another, how to treat one's neighbor. The command not to judge and the notion that one will be judged as one has judged others were popular in early Christianity (Rom. 2:1; 14:10; 1 Cor. 4:5; 5:12; Jas. 4:11–12; 5:9; *1 Clem.* 13.2; etc.). But what precisely do they mean here?

Simple ethical judgments cannot be in view, and believers are not being instructed to refrain from critical thinking. There is also no reason to entertain Tolstoy's idea that here the state's judicial activities are proscribed: that would be a flat contradiction of the Hebrew Bible and so a flat contradiction of 5:17–20. Rather, 7:1–2 enjoins mercy, humility, and tolerance between individuals. These qualities are inconsistent with taking on a role reserved for the only capable judge, God (cf. 13:36–43, 47–50, where the sorting out of good and evil awaits the last judgment). "Do not judge" means "do not condemn," and so one could translate our saying: "Do not condemn, so that you may not be condemned at the last judgment." T. W. Manson appropriately commented:

> The whole business of judging persons is in God's hands, for He alone knows the secrets of men's hearts. This does not mean that we are not to

use all the moral insight we possess in order to discover what is right and wrong; but that we are to confine ourselves to that field and refrain from passing judgment on persons. For our judgment is itself a factor in shaping their lives, and a harsh judgment may help a fellow-creature on the road to perdition. (*Sayings*, 56)

The monk Moses, according to the *Apophthegmata Patrum*, said: "The monk must die to his neighbor and never judge him at all, in any way whatever."

THE SPECK IN ONE'S EYE (7:3–5)

The concrete 7:3–5 clarifies the abstract 7:1–2, but the former also adds a new element, the theme of hypocrisy. The thought is very close to Rom. 2:1: "Therefore you have no excuse, whoever you are, when you judge others; for in passing judgment on another you condemn yourself, because you, the judge, are doing the very same things." One also recalls the story of David and his anger upon hearing Nathan's parable about the rich man who had taken the poor man's little ewe lamb: the king did not realize that what made him angry in another was his own fault (2 Sam. 12:1–5). Because human beings unhappily possess an inbred proclivity to mix ignorance of themselves with arrogance toward others, the call to recognize one's own faults is a commonplace of moral and religious traditions (cf. John 9:41; 1 John 1:8). "The abuse of brotherly correction is the normal thing one expects, and . . . the proper use is the exception" (Betz, *Commentary*, 488).

"Splinter" (not "mote") stands for small moral defects, "beam" for sizable moral defects. The image is intended to be comedic (and may have been proverbial; cf. Babylonian Talmud *Baba Batra* 15b: "If the judge said to a person, 'Take the splinter from between your teeth,' he would retort, 'Take the beam from between your eyes'"). It is just as absurd as the picture of a camel going through the eye of a needle (19:24) or someone straining at gnats and swallowing a camel (23:24).

In 7:3 one simply sees (*blepein*). In 7:5 one sees clearly (*diablepein*). In the latter instance one sees in order to help (cf. Irenaeus, *Against Heresies* 4.30.3). The stare to find fault becomes the genuinely friendly eye of a brother or sister who is a servant. Some commentators fail to discern in 7:3–5 any instruction concerning fraternal correction. For them, the text prohibits judging altogether. But Matthew shows a special concern elsewhere for the proper procedures for dealing with sin in others; see 18:15–20, a passage that our evangelist thinks consistent with unlimited forgiveness (18:23–25; cf. Lev. 19:17, where love and reproof of neighbor go together). Moreover, Matthew usually uses "brother" to mean Christian "brother," so it is natural to see here intraecclesiastical activity (so Augustine, Bengel, and most of Christian exegetical tradition).

PEARLS BEFORE SWINE (7:6)

This verse has a very colorful history of influence that has consistently ignored its present literary context. Augustine argued, like many after him, that the verse instructs the faithful not to reveal important esoteric teachings to outsiders who will only fail to appreciate them (*Sermon on the Mount* 2.20.67–70; cf. *Pseudo-Clementine Recognitions* 2.3; 3.1; one can cite as a parallel Jesus' practice of restricting certain teachings to the disciples: 13:36–52; 15:15–20). Evagrius thought in terms of spiritual masters dispensing only a little truth at a time to spiritual novices (*Capita practica ad Anatolium*); Elchasai, of sectarian teachings being trampled upon by the orthodox (Hippolytus, *Refutation* 9.12); Origen, of temporarily abandoning for their own good lapsed Christians (*On First Principles* 3.1.17). The *Didache* found in 7:6 a rule prohibiting giving communion to the unbaptized (9:5; so also Tertullian, Jerome, and many others). John of Damascus took Matt. 7:6 to prohibit the giving of communion to heretics (*The Orthodox Faith* 4.13; cf. the equation of "dog" and "pig" with heretic in 2 Pet. 2:22). Some modern scholars, identifying the dogs with Gentiles (cf. 15:26–27), have found a prohibition against the Gentile mission (cf. 10:5–6). Others have posited a mistranslation from the Aramaic: Jesus originally said (in dependence on Prov. 11:22) not to put a ring or earring in the nose of a dog (although this hardly illuminates the saying as it stands in Matthew). Dietrich Bonhoeffer, following Luther, assumed that our text is an admonition about the necessity to limit the time and energy directed toward the hard-hearted. The gospel goes out to all; but when it is not received the proclaimers must move on (cf. 10:14; so too Hagner). Ulrich Luz has recently declined to interpret the logion in its Matthean context: the evangelist simply took it over from his source without imparting any meaning to it.

Against all these suggestions, "Do not give to dogs what is holy"— originally a priestly rule about sacrificial meat (Mishnah *Temurah* 6:5;

etc.), but here used metaphorically—fits very nicely into its present setting. Matt. 7:1–5 has commanded that there be not too much severity. Matt. 7:6 follows up by saying that there should not be too much laxity. That is, the text anticipates a problem and searches for a balance, for moral symmetry. The principles in 7:1–5 are not to be abused. They do not eliminate the use of critical faculties when it comes to sacred concerns. As 18:15–20 shows, it is sometimes necessary to deal with the faults of others.

This interpretation admittedly remains general, and it is possible that Matthew had something more specific in mind (cf. the suggestions recounted above). But the general point is clear: one must not be meekly charitable against all reason.

THE GOOD FATHER (7:7–11)

Matthew 7:7–11 (cf. especially John 16:23–24) has been almost as pliable in the hands of interpreters as has 7:6. Augustine thought of one asking for the truth kept from the dogs and swine of 7:6 and of the strength to live in accord with that truth (*Sermon on the Mount* 2.21.71). Others have drawn a line back to 7:1–5: the disciple prays for wisdom to take the mote out of another's eye (so Bonhoeffer, who also harks back to 6:25–34: disciples "have to learn that their anxiety and concern for others must drive them to intercession" [*Cost*, 208]). Still others have gone further back to the Lord's Prayer: 7:7–11 encourages those who pray the Lord's Prayer to know that their prayers will be heard. Robert Gundry links 7:7–11 with the golden rule, which immediately follows: just as God gives us good things, so we should give good things to others. Hans Dieter Betz finds in 7:7–11 the recommendation of "a general approach to life, an approach based on the assumption that one can trust life as good. . . . The basic approach to life . . . should be that of the quester, the seeker, the knocker on doors. One should not yield to misanthropic pessimism, introverted seclusion, or withdraw into the group of the like-minded" (*Commentary*, 507). Betz supports this interpretation by claiming that "all the sayings in the SM from 6:19 on have to do with the question of whom and what to trust" (ibid.). Some modern commentators, however, have seen no connection with the surrounding material and have accused Matthew of creating a messy amalgam (Hill, *Matthew*, 148). Already Luther interpreted 7:7–11 as for all practical purposes an isolated admonition to pray. For him the paragraph instructs us that in addition to knowing right doctrine and correct behavior (cf. the rest of the Sermon on the Mount) we ought also to pray.

But the key to understanding 7:7–11 is probably its parallelism with 6:25–34. As observed on pp. 34–36, both sections come after an exhortation (6:19–21; 7:1–2), a parable on the eye (6:22–23; 7:3–5), and a second parable (6:24; 7:6). Both also agree in arguing from the lesser to the greater and contain supporting illustrations that take the form of rhetorical questions. The parallelism in form coincides with a parallel in function. Matt. 7:7–11 is, like 6:25–34, intended to bring encouragement to those who stand under the harsh imperatives of the Sermon on the Mount: the heavenly Father cares for them.

Matthew 7:7–11 is a drawn-out argument: 7:7 ("Ask, and it will be given you, etc.") contains the thesis. 7:8 ("For everyone who asks receives") supplies the justification. 7:9–10 (the child asking for bread, the child asking for a fish) offers two illustrations. 7:11 ("how much more will your Father in heaven give good things to those who ask him") makes the concluding inference. The whole is nicely united by a chiastic inclusion:

> Ask (*aiteite*)
>
> 7
>
> and it will be given (*dothēsetai*) you
> give (*dōsei*) good things
>
> 11
>
> to those who ask (*aitousin*) him

"Ask" (the key word of our section; it appears five times here) refers to prayer, as do "seek" and "knock" (cf. Isa. 55:6; Jer. 29:13–14; Babylonian Talmud *Megillah* 12b; interpreters, however, have often found different applications for each verb). Theophylact wrote: "In what has preceded the Lord has commanded us to do great and difficult things. Here he shows us how these things can be accomplished: through unceasing prayer" (*Commentary on Matthew* ad loc.).

The picture in 7:9 of a child asking for bread from a father sends the attentive reader back to the Lord's Prayer; and one also recalls that 6:25–26, 31–33 is about how God feeds the faithful. That the force of the concluding and climactic 7:11 lies in an inference about God's care demonstrates where the real thrust of the entire unit lies. Matt. 7:7–11 is less a collection of yet more imperatives than it is a way of telling hard-pressed disciples to take heart. The Father in heaven will give "all good things"—not the Holy Spirit (cf. Luke 11:13) or the kingdom but all that is required for the difficult life of faithful discipleship—to those who depend on him. "All good things" should not be restricted: it includes spiritual gifts (cf. Chrysostom, *Homily on Matthew* 23.4) as well as the food, drink, and clothing of 6:25–34—everything that is necessary to fulfill Jesus' demands (cf. the *Opus imperfectum* ad loc., which speaks about gaining the grace necessary to live the Sermon on the Mount).

In what is almost an aside, 7:11 refers to human beings as "evil." The Sermon on the Mount takes for granted a strong biblical doctrine of human corruption: all swirl about in the abyss of sin. Sinners persecute saints (5:10–12, 38–48). People kill (5:21), get angry (5:22–26), commit adultery (5:27), divorce their spouses to marry others (5:31), and take oaths because the lie is so prevalent (5:33). They use religion for their selfish glorification (6:1–18), occupy themselves with storing up earthly treasures (6:19–21), fail in generosity (6:22–23), serve mammon (6:25), foolishly worry about secondary matters (6:25–34), and pass judgment on others (7:1–5). But implicit here is not only a strong doctrine of sin but a strong doctrine of grace, for as John of Karpathos observed, "The Lord promised these 'good things' not to the righteous but to sinners, saying: 'If you then, being evil, know how to give good gifts to your children, how much more will your heavenly father give the Holy Spirit to those that ask him?' (Luke 11:13). Ask, then, unremittingly and without doubting, however poor your efforts to gain holiness, however weak your strength; and you will receive great gifts, far beyond anything that you desire" (the *Philocalia*, St. John of Karpathos, "For the Encouragement of the Monks in India" 45).

The Sermon on the Mount, although it refers to prayers that are presumably not answered (6:5, 7), offers no explicit reflection on the problem of unanswered prayer (contrast Jas. 4:3; *Pseudo-Clementine Homilies* 3.56 emends our passage to make it clear that only those who do God's will are heard). Elsewhere Matthew contains a story in which the disciples fail because they do not have enough faith and in which Jesus rebukes them accordingly (17:14–21). But this is as much hindrance as help, for is not the unbounded confidence of 17:21 (on moving mountains by faith; cf. 18:19—if two or three agree it will be done for them) just as much pious illusion as 7:7–11? We seem to have in Jesus' teaching on prayer an expectation as unrealistic as the moral imperatives of the Sermon on the Mount.

One may seek to diminish the difficulty by finding hyperbolic speech in 17:21. Even more helpful, however, is the story of Gethsemane (26:36–46). Here Jesus himself utters a prayer ("Let this cup pass from me") that is not answered. The implication is twofold. First, the prayers of the righteous will be overlooked if they do not accord with God's intention (7:11 itself restricts God's answers only to "good things"). Second, all prayer has to be offered under the proviso "yet not what I want but what you want" (26:39).

THE GOLDEN RULE (7:12)

The so-called golden rule—a relatively modern expression that has not been documented before the eighteenth century—appears also in Luke 6:31. In its Matthean context it sums up in brief the right conduct toward others and so appropriately closes 6:19–7:11, a section on social behavior. But 7:12 also brings to a climax the entire central core of the Sermon on the Mount, 5:17–7:11. Mention of "the Law and the Prophets" takes us back to 5:17 and establishes an *inclusio.* This indicates that "in everything do to others as you would have them do to you" is, in rabbinic fashion, a general rule that is not only the quintessence of the Law and the Prophets but also the quintessence of the Sermon and so of Jesus' moral teaching in general.

Despite the importance the golden rule receives from its literary function in Matthew, it is far from being a dramatically new sentiment. Rabbinic sources tell us the following story about the rabbi Hillel, a contemporary of Jesus: "A certain heathen came before Shammai and said to him, 'Make me a proselyte, on condition that you teach me the whole Torah while I stand on one foot.' Thereupon he repulsed him with the builder's cubit which was in his hand. When he went before Hillel he said to him, 'What is hateful to you, do not do to your neighbor: that is the whole Torah, while the rest is commentary on it; go and learn" (Babylonian Talmud *Shabbat* 31a). One can easily collect dozens of additional parallels—not just from Jewish (e.g., Tob. 4:15; *Targum Yerushalmi I* on Lev. 19:18; *2 Enoch* 61:1–2) and Greco-Roman (e.g., Herodotus 3.142; 7.136; Isocrates, *Nicocles* 61; Diogenes Laertius

5.21) sources but also from Buddhist, Confucian, and Islamic texts. The *Analects* of Confucius contains this: "Tzu-kung asked saying, Is there any single saying that one can act upon all day and everyday? The Master said, 'Perhaps the saying about consideration: Never do to others what you would not like them to do to you'" (15:23).

Sometimes Christians have argued that there is a substantial difference between the negative (do not do as you would not have others do to you) and the positive (do as you would have others do to you) formulations of the golden rule, and that it is important that Jesus took up the latter (so, e.g., Hagner). But the ancient sources, including Christian sources, do not betray any awareness of a difference on this matter. Moreover, the negative formulation need not presuppose a calculating attitude with its own selfish ends in view: it too can be rooted in a genuine concern for others. The lesson to be drawn is that the truth of Jesus' teaching does not hinge upon its novelty. Here indeed the Sermon on the Mount incorporates what Augustine called a "common proverb" (*Letter* 157.3.15). (One has no doubt that if Jesus had used the negative formulation Christian apologists would have been quick to show how it is superior to the positive formulation. They would, for instance, have observed that convictions about what ought not be done are more uniform across any society and more readily recognized than other convictions.)

The golden rule is said to be "the Law and the Prophets." This does not mean that one can deduce all of the commandments from 7:12 (obviously a falsehood in any case). Nor does it mean that one can use the verse to determine the validity of differing commandments (5:17–20 says they are all valid). Rather is 7:12 a fundamental demand which states the true end of the Torah, which remains in force.

Many have found in 7:12 an implicit promotion of self-centeredness ("as you would have them do unto you"). Some think this a good thing: Jesus did not oppose self-love or negate self-esteem. Others, however, have found here a naive narcissism or enlightened self-interest—and have sometimes gone on, for this reason, to deny that Jesus, who was otherwise so radical, could have taught the golden rule.

Two things need to be said. First, the golden rule is an open principle that needs to be filled with proper content; it is an abstract maxim that presupposes virtue. Early Christians recognized this, as Augustine reported:

a number of translators have added the words "good things" in their translation, rendering the passage thus: "Whatever good things you will that one should do to you." This was because they imagined it advisable to guard against the chance of anyone's wishing to have dishonorable things done for him by others—the provision of extravagant banquets, for example, to say nothing of more discreditable possibilities. (*City of God* 14.8; cf. *Sermon on the Mount* 2.22.74)

There is, however, no need to add "good things" when the golden rule is interpreted within the Sermon on the Mount. The Sermon makes it plain that acting according to 7:12 will involve obedience to God's revealed will (5:17–18) and an exceptional "righteousness" (5:20) and will include within its purview even one's enemies (5:43–48). In Matthew it is thus no longer "common sense" (so wrongly Theophylact [*Commentary on Matthew* ad loc.], who takes 7:12 to be a way of getting others to do good to us). Context determines meaning, and within its present context 7:12 is not a formula for making the world better for oneself, nor even a formula of justice, but rather a formula of exceptional benevolence. Luz is right: "the Golden Rule is radicalized by the Sermon on the Mount. Everything, without exception, which is demanded by love and the commandments of Jesus you should do for other people" (*Matthew 1–7*, 430).

Second, the implicit egoism of 7:12 actually runs throughout the Sermon on the Mount. How else can one understand the appeal to rewards and punishments? Jesus asks people to behave in a certain way in order to enter the kingdom of heaven and avoid eschatological condemnation. But this realistic concession to human nature as it is paradoxically serves the purpose of taking people beyond themselves: again and again, although it promises reward, the Sermon on the Mount crucifies the ego. It is the same in 7:12. One begins with the ego as the reference point, but one immediately moves beyond it. It is accordingly wrong either to disparage the golden rule as too self-centered or to applaud it because it promotes self-esteem. The truth rather is that it is simply a way of asking one to do good to others. The formulation may be conventional, and related sentences may sometimes involve little more than self-centered cost/benefit analysis (e.g., Tosefta *Megillah* 4.16: "Do that they will do to you"). But in Matthew the golden rule is another way of delivering the demand to love one's neighbor. One should observe that both Jewish and Christian sources (such as *Did.* 1.2; *Targum Yerushalmi I* on Lev. 19:18; Augustine, *Sermon on the Mount* 2.22.75; and Ps.-Fabian, *Epistle* 2.2) link the golden rule and Lev. 19:18, and that Matthew thinks of both as being fundamental statements of the Law and the Prophets (7:12; 22:39–40; cf. Rom. 13:8–10; Gal 5:14).

One final point about 7:12. It is not a law that one can obey without reflection. It is rather a general principle that requires imaginative application. Once again, then, and despite the traditional name "golden rule," the text comes to us not with a rule but with an invitation to demonstrate creatively a generosity akin to that of God (see 5:43–48).

For Further Reading

Allison, Dale C., Jr. *The Jesus Tradition in Q.* Harrisburg, Penn.: Trinity Press International, 1997. Pp. 133–67.

Betz, Hans Dieter. *Essays on the Sermon on the Mount.* Philadelphia: Fortress, 1985. Pp. 89–123.

Blomberg, Craig L. "On Wealth and Worry: Matthew 6:19–34." *Criswell Theological Review* 6 (1992): 73–89.

Dillon, R. J. "Ravens, Lilies, and the Kingdom of God (Matthew 6:25–33/Luke 12:22–31)." *Catholic Biblical Quarterly* 53 (1991): 605–27.

Olsthoorn, M. F. *The Jewish Background and the Synoptic Setting of Mt 6,25–33 and Lk 12,22–31.* Jerusalem: Franciscan, 1975.

Ricoeur, Paul. "The Golden Rule: Exegetical and Theological Perplexities." *New Testament Studies* 36 (1900): 49–67.

8

Warnings and Conclusion (7:13-27)

HE SERMON ON THE MOUNT begins with blessings (5:3–12). It winds down with warnings—with the parable of the two ways (7:13–14), the parable of the two trees (7:15–23), and the parable of the two builders (7:24–27). The blessings offer consolation by speaking of rewards in the eschatological kingdom. The warnings gain their force by speaking of eschatological judgment. Behind all this lies an old Jewish tradition. In Deut. 11:26–27 God speaks to Israel through Moses: "I am setting before you today a blessing and a curse: the blessing, if you obey the commandments of the Lord your God that I am commanding you today; and the curse, if you do not obey the commandments of the Lord your God, but turn from the way that I am commanding you today." These words inspired Jer. 21:8 ("Thus says the Lord: See, I am setting before you the way of life and the way of death"), and from Jeremiah on the theme of the two ways became a fixed element of Jewish moral exhortation (1QS 3:13–4:26; 4Q473 frag. 2; *Testament of Asher* 1:3–5; *2 Enoch* 30:15; *Mekhilta* on Exod. 14:28; Babylonian Talmud *Berakhot* 28b; etc.). Matt. 7:13ff. stands in this tradition.

Each one of Matthew's five major discourses (chapters 5–7, 10, 13, 18, 24–25) concludes with eschatological warnings and promises. In this way the text reflects the inevitable flow of history: the present is always being swallowed up by the future, which will someday bring eschatological judgment. Matthew knows that everything falls under the shadow of the conclusion, and that the issue of things determines their meaning. What really matters to the rich man and Lazarus is not their earthly circumstances but how things end up for eternity (Luke 16:19–31). We understand why the Greek philosopher Solon said he could call none blessed before they have died, and why the sentiment reappears in Ecclus. 11:26–28. Stories gain their meaning from their conclusions, and it is the same with our lives.

THE TWO WAYS (7:13–14)

Matthew 7:13–14 has a summarizing character. It looks back over all the demands delivered thus far and says that the "way of righteousness" (21:32), the "way of God" (22:16) propounded therein, is profoundly arduous. Betz is surely wrong to suggest that our text is more generally about "the difficulties of life itself" (*Commentary*, 521).

"Enter through the narrow gate" (cf. Luke 13:23–24) prefaces 7:13, which explains that the road to destruction is easy. The words are directed not to the wayward but to would-be disciples, to those who have heard the Sermon on the Mount, acknowledge its demands, and wish to enter into eternal life. They are being called to flee complacency and to view all except entrance into the kingdom as dangerous divertisement (cf. 6:33). Guided by the words and presence of Jesus (28:20), the faithful reader is to put shoulder to the wheel and forsake every obstacle in the way of obtaining the one true good.

"The narrow gate" has consistently reminded interpreters of the eye of the needle in 19:23. Both passages contain the image of a small opening and have to do with the difficulty of entering into life or the kingdom. Clement of Alexandria mixed the two texts when he wrote of "the camel that passes through a strait and narrow way sooner than the rich man" (*Who Is the Rich Man?* 26.7; cf. Origen, *Against Celsus* 6.16). There is, however, nothing to indicate that Matthew himself linked the two verses.

"The gate is wide and the road is easy that leads to destruction, and there are many who take it" expresses a common theme within the Jewish tradition as well as within the world's religions in general. Everywhere honesty confesses that vice is attractive and easy to succumb to: to sin is natural, to repent unnatural. "The way of evil is broad and well supplied with travellers; would not all people take its easy course if there were nothing to fear?" (Tertullian, *Against*

Marcion 2.13). The story of Noah's flood, which is about the salvation of a single family out of a sea of wickedness, represents the viewpoint of the whole Bible.

Because of its context within the Sermon on the Mount, the gate of 7:13, which is the entrance to life, must be equated with Jesus himself (cf. John 10:9), or more precisely with his demands. No one has expressed this and the attendant difficulties better than Dietrich Bonhoeffer:

> To confess and testify to the truth as it is in Jesus, and at the same time to love the enemies of that truth, his enemies and ours, and to love them with the infinite love of Jesus Christ, is indeed a narrow way. To believe the promise of Jesus that his followers shall possess the earth, and at the same time to face our enemies unarmed and defenseless, preferring to incur injustice rather than to do wrong ourselves, is indeed a narrow way. To see the weakness and wrong in others, and at the same time refrain from judging them . . . . The way is unutterably hard, and at every moment we are in danger of straying from it. (*Cost*, 211)

According to 7:14, "the gate is narrow and the road is hard that leads to life, and there are few who find it." It is not safe to regard this as a dogmatic calculation, a statement that the vast majority of humanity will perish in hell (although such a view would not have been foreign to the first century; see, e.g., 4 Ezra 7:47–51; *2 Bar.* 48:43; Babylonian Talmud *Sanhedrin* 97b.). It is true that in 22:14 Jesus declares that "Many are called, but few are chosen." Matt. 8:11, however, speaks of "many" coming from east and west for salvation, and 20:18 speaks of Jesus' death as a ransom for "many." So in some contexts "many" are saved; in others "many" are lost. This seeming inconsistency is best explained in terms of the Semitic habit of making hyperbolic declarations in hortative material. We read in Mishnah *Qiddushin* 1:10: "If a man performs a single commandment, it shall be well with him and he shall have length of days and shall inherit the land. But if he neglects a single commandment it shall be ill with him and he shall not have length of days and shall not inherit the land." It is impossible to take these words literally. They are exhortation. One is to act as if the fulfillment of one commandment means everything. In a similar fashion, the function of 7:13–14 is to move one to act as if only a very few will enter through the gates of paradise.

Many have sought to discover a coherent image in 7:13–14. Hans Dieter Betz, like many others, imagines travelers on a path who are approaching a city gate: the entrance comes after the journey. One might then compare the gates to the New Jerusalem in Rev. 21:21. But in *Pilgrim's Progress* John Bunyan (who placed the knocking of Matt. 7:7 at the gate of 7:13) depicted a gate at the beginning of a road. This accords with the order of presentation in Matthew. Still others have envisioned a passage or gate on a road. It may be best, however, to abandon such pictures because, as most modern exegetes have supposed, "gate" and "way" seem to function synonymously.

The effect of 7:13–14 in its entirety is to teach that there is a right way and a wrong way. There are those who are perishing and those who are being saved. There are people headed for death and headed for life. All this accords with what we have met before in the Sermon on the Mount. There are those who give and pray and fast rightly and those who do not (6:1–8). There are those with light within and those with darkness within (6:22–23). There are those who serve God and those who serve mammon (6:19–34). All these antitheses do not mean that everything is black or white. Rather, the severe alternatives awake us to the urgent lesson that one must choose clearly and unambiguously—and if necessary at great personal cost—when the issue is the kingdom. There are no options when it comes to God and Jesus' demands in the Sermon on the Mount.

ON FALSE PROPHETS (7:15–23)

This section opens with a general warning to beware of false prophets (7:15). This is then followed by five verses that recount the false prophets' deeds (7:16–20) and three verses that depict their fate before the eschatological judge on the last day (7:21–23). The connection with the two ways of 7:13–14 appears to be this: the false prophets prevent others from entering the narrow gate and from following the difficult path. Some have envisaged false prophets standing before the broad gate, beckoning all to enter in, and standing beside the easy path, spreading their errors (cf. Chrysostom, *Homily on Matthew* 23.7–8).

The major question that modern exegetes occupy themselves with when discussing this passage is, Who are the false prophets? That is, what concrete groups or individuals would first-century readers have thought of? The suggestions are many and include Pharisees, Essenes, anti-Roman Zealots, Judean sign prophets from the 60s, Simon Magus, the Jewish Messiah Bar Kokhba, Gnostics, Paul and his circle of churches, Hellenistic antinomians, Christian enthusiasts, and law-observant Christians. The only thing that can be said with assurance is that the false prophets are Christians of some sort, for they call Jesus "Lord" and perform miracles in his name. Beyond that we do not know their identity or whether Matthew's readers would have thought of particular individuals. This, however, is not such a bad thing, for "the general character of the warning allows concrete applications as they are needed" (Betz, *Commentary*, 528).

Warnings against false prophets are found often in early Christian literature, including the New Testament (Mark 13:21–23; 2 Pet. 2:1–22; 1 John 4:1–3). In most of these texts false prophets belong to the eschatological scenario: they are part of the great apostasy of the end time. The reader of Matthew is also encouraged to think in these terms, for when we meet again with false prophets and warnings about them Jesus is talking about the latter days; see 24:4–5, 10–12, 23–28.

"You will know them by their fruits" (7:15) is the leading theme of 7:15–20 and recurs in 7:20 (cf. 12:33–35, where the application is to the Pharisees). How does one know whether under the artistic veneer there lies true coin or false? The behavior of false prophets will betray their true character. Because like produces like, because evil comes from evil, the outside will inevitably give away what is inside (cf. Ecclus. 27:6; John 15:2–17; Gal. 5:19–23; Jas. 3:10–12; Babylonian Talmud *Berakhot* 48a). False face cannot hide false heart forever. Deeds will ultimately demonstrate nature. Certain actions follow inexorably from certain spiritual causes.

The logic seems plain enough and is consistent with the Sermon on the Mount's emphasis on the importance of right deeds. One may wonder, however, about the usefulness of its application to reveal proponents of false doctrine. Cannot one's theological opponents be good people? And cannot individuals with mistaken beliefs still be virtuous? Even if right doctrine encourages right behavior, must wrong doctrine always encourage bad behavior? Even Matthew must know that rejection of Jesus can coexist with virtue, for he can speak of the righteousness of the scribes and Pharisees (5:20). The truth is that there appears no infallible way of discovering who has and who does not have the truth—which is why our verses have been directed against all heretics, and why all heretics have directed them against the mainstream churches, and why early Christians had to come up with additional criteria for divining false prophets. According to 1 Cor. 12:1–3, the confession "Jesus is Lord" is decisive. (The seeming contradiction between 1 Cor. 12:1–3, where the confession of "Lord" establishes authenticity, and Matt. 7:21, where such confession is rejection, has long exercised interpreters). In 1 John 4:2 the confession is more specific: "every spirit that confesses that Jesus Christ has come in the flesh is from God." In the *Didache* true prophets are authenticated by the harmony between their words and their deeds (11.10) and by their failure to ask others for money (11.5). In the last half of the second century, in *3 Cor.* 3:34–38, disagreement with the apostle to the Gentiles or with the orthodox tradition becomes the mark of the pseudo-prophet. *Pseudo-Clementine Homilies* 2.6–12 records yet one more method: the true prophet utters only prophecies that come to pass.

Matthew 7:15–23 is perhaps not, however, as naive as the criticism of the previous paragraph makes out. For the text is not referring to every proponent of wrong doctrine but to people characterized as "ravenous wolves" (cf. 10:16) in particular. These are individuals who, like the wolf in sheep's clothing in Aesop's fable, are consciously intent on using or even harming others for their own ends. Matthew teaches that their agenda will indeed at some point be exposed by their deeds. Those who come not to serve but to be served will be found out.

Although 7:15–20 is about false prophets, it cannot but also lead the attentive reader to self-inspection. Fruits, grapes, and figs all stand for deeds. Trees, thorns, and thistles all stand for one's character or internal state. And one can evaluate the latter by thinking about the former (cf. 15:18). That is, one can discover the true nature of the self by contemplating one's deeds. The situation is the same as in 6:22–23, which correlates inner light with generosity and inner darkness with selfishness and so teaches that one's internal life can be perceived in one's external deeds.

Matthew 7:18 says that a good tree cannot bear bad fruit, nor a bad tree good fruit. Some early Christian heretics found in this a denial of free will and/or (as with the Gnostics and Manichaeans) an affirmation of the truth of dualism, that there are two very different sorts of human beings. And even today Betz believes that "the strong emphasis on the 'impossible' appears to point to a radical dualism and a kind of predestination" (*Commentary*, 538). But our text says "not this, that for the wicked there is no way to change, or that the good cannot fall away, but that so long as one is living in wickedness, that individual will not be able to bear good fruit. For one who is evil may indeed become virtuous, but while continuing in wickedness one will not bear good fruit" (Chrysostom, *Homily on Matthew* 23.8). Augustine was also correct to observe that "if by these two trees he had meant to represent the two [fixed] natures of the people referred to, he would never [in 12:33] have said, 'make [the tree good],' for what person is there that can make a nature?" (*Sermon on the Mount* 2.24.79).

According to 7:19, which here repeats a word of the Baptist (3:10), the bad tree will be cut down and thrown into the fire. This is obviously an allusion to the unquenchable fire of hell (3:12; 5:22; 13:42, 50; 18:8, 9; 25:41), first encountered in Scripture in Isa. 66:24. How literally Matthew or Jesus thought about this fire is hard to tell. For our Gospel also associates eschatological punishment with darkness (8:12; 22:13; 25:30). One should further observe the tension between the description of Gehenna as eternal (18:18; 25:41) and the threat of annihilation (*apōleia*) in 7:13 (the road to "destruction"). These sorts of incongruities hint that Matthew's language about eschatological punishments is just as figurative as his language about eschatological promises and should not be pressed for details. The Sermon's purpose is to exhort, not to offer a blueprint of future states.

Matthew 7:21-23 builds upon the allusion to eschatological punishment in 7:19 and offers a little picture of self-delusion at the last judgment. The subject shifts from the false prophets' deeds ("fruits") to their words ("many will say") and from recognition by others in the present ("you will know them") to their rejection by Jesus in the future ("I never knew you").

What exactly is the fault of those who say "Lord, Lord" and do not do what the Father wills? The answer is not inactivity. The false prophets are hardly the victims of what Coleridge diagnosed as Hamlet's fatal flaw, namely, the futile ado of thinking and thinking without ever doing. On the contrary, those rejected by Jesus, the eschatological Lord, have performed apparently great things. They have prophesied, cast out demons, and done many mighty deeds. So what is the problem? The answer to this question unfortunately depends on the answer to another, namely, Who are the false prophets?—and the answer to this we do not know. Still, a couple of useful things may be said.

First, our text recognizes that seemingly supernatural phenomena are not sure signs of saving faith. This is in line with the Hebrew Bible, in which the magicians of Egypt do wonders aplenty (Exodus 7-8) as well as with the rest of the New Testament, which foretells that, in the latter days, evil figures will do spectacular works (Matt. 24:23-28; 2 Thess. 2:9-10; Rev. 13:13-15). In 1 Corinthians 12-14 Paul puts tongues and other spectacular manifestations in their place by calling for decency and order in worship and by exalting love above everything else as the more excellent way. Matters are similar with Matthew. Our Gospel knows that the gifts of prophecy, exorcism, and other miracles, while they have an important role to play (witness the ministry of Jesus), are not of utmost import. In particular, they can distract from the one thing needful, which is obedience to the Messiah's words. Jesus calls for obedience to his Torah (5:17–48), sincere practice of the Christian cult (6:1–18), and a right attitude toward the things of this world (6:19–7:12). He has beckoned his followers to travel down a very difficult road (7:13–14), a road without the promise of fame and glory, a road that instead holds forth the prospect of persecution (5:10–12), with reward coming only in the future (6:4, 6, 18, 19–21). Hence, the spectacular things that cannot but promote vanity are far from being unambiguous boons. In no way can they be held up as testimony to faith. They do not make possible entrance into the kingdom of heaven.

Second, the false prophets are not said to have fed the hungry or welcomed strangers or visited the sick, all rather mundane, unspectacular acts. One supposes they have not done so because these acts are, like almsgiving, prayer, and fasting in secret, things for which one may not get much public notice. But Matthew's text demands just such mundane, unspectacular acts. Whereas from one point of view our Gospel, especially the Sermon on the Mount, demands the morally heroic, in another sense "virtue is not far from us, nor is it without ourselves, but it is within us, and is easy if only we are willing" (Anthony in Athanasius, *Life of Anthony* 20). For Jesus does not require supernatural feats but simple charity. The former can be more easily counterfeited than the latter (cf. 24:24). Charity is accordingly the true test of faith. Judgment is rendered not according to spectacular manifestations or verbal confessions but according to the demands of love and the secret matters of the heart.

HEARERS AND DOERS (7:24–27)

The Sermon on the Mount ends with an ominous parable (cf. Luke 6:47–49). It envisages a flooded wadi overcoming a house built on sand while a house founded on rock endures. The import is much the same as 7:13–14. The person who hears Jesus' words and does them, who is like a house on rock, is the same as the one who enters through the narrow gate and takes the hard road to life. The person who hears Jesus' words and does not do them, who is like a house built upon sand, is the same as the one who goes through the wide gate and takes the easy road that leads to destruction.

"Whoever hears these words of mine and acts (*poiei*) on them" takes up the key verb (*poieō*) of our section. It appears nine times and is translated by the NRSV as "bear(s)" in vv. 17–18, as "do(es)" in vv. 21–22, and "acts" in vv. 24–27. The fundamental meaning is "do." Its repetition indicates the goal of the discourse—the Sermon is a call to action—as well as the fact that the goal is easily missed. Throughout this section we are confronted with the problem of all moral and religious discourse: it is only discourse. Instruction and exhortation are not ends in themselves but means to an end, that being proper life in the world (cf. John 13:17; Rom. 2:13; Jas. 1:22). As Luther wrote, "the doctrine is good and a precious thing, but it is not being preached for the sake of being heard but for the sake of action and its application to life" (*Sermon on the Mount*, 281). Sadly, however, it is easy enough, indeed altogether natural, to hear the Sermon on the Mount, to interpret it, and even to memorize it, and still not live it.

The problem is that famously reflected upon by Paul in Romans 7: knowledge of the truth or of right behavior does not in itself bring the strength to live accordingly. Unlike Socrates, who equated sin with ignorance, the Sermon on the Mount knows that the problem is even more fundamental. People are "evil" (7:11), fond of the easy path (7:13), anxious (6:25–34), and beset by temptations (6:13). Given this, our text must do its best to warn, to motivate readers through a terrifying parable (Augustine, *Sermon on the Mount* 2.25.87). "The fear of the Lord is the beginning of wisdom" (Prov. 1:7).

"Like a wise man who built his house upon the rock" refers to basing one's life on the words of Jesus' Sermon, which means, in effect, doing the will of the Father in heaven: it is what 10:32–33 means by "acknowledging" Jesus. Given all the threats and promises of the Sermon on the Mount, "denying" him through one's deeds would be folly. Here Catholic exegesis has something important to contribute to the typical Protestant expositions of our passage, which are so quick to add and insist that what really matters is faith. Our text, on the contrary, says that works truly matter, that authentic discipleship is ethics. One recalls the picture of the last judgment in 25:31–46, where the one criterion at the last judgment is how one has treated others.

"The rain fell, etc." almost certainly does not, against Augustine

(*Sermon on the Mount* 2.24.87), stand for the calamities and afflictions of everyday life. Throughout the Bible the storm often represents God's judgment (Genesis 6–7; Isa. 28:2; etc.). And so probably is it here: the one-time eschatological crisis and judgment—which will fall upon the world as did Noah's flood (24:37–39)—are in view. Only obedience to Jesus will save on the last day. If the church is founded upon the rock, against which the gates of Hades will not prevail (16:18), so in like manner will the individual standing upon the firm words of the Messiah endure the storms of the end times.

The "foolish man who built his house upon the sand" does not build a different sort of house: his only problem is the foundation, which is something other than the Sermon on the Mount. So outwardly the two houses may appear identical.

Interestingly enough, the word translated "foolish man" is the same as that in 5:22, where Jesus condemns the person who calls another a "fool." The tension between the two verses reveals that the call not to insult does not involve blindness to moral differences (cf. the discussion of 7:6).

Later in his Gospel, Matthew offers another parable with wise and foolish. In 25:1–13 wise and foolish maidens await the bridegroom, a transparent symbol of Jesus the Messiah in his second advent. But some are ill-prepared. The oil in their lamps runs out, and while they are gone to get more, they miss the coming of the bridegroom. In this narrative it is quite clear that the foolish virgins are part of the believing community, for they are expecting Jesus to come again. Thus, eschatological judgment does not simply confirm those who identify themselves with the cause of Jesus. Rather it comes upon all without exception (cf. 22:11–14; 1 Pet. 4:17). It is the same in 7:24–27. We are not to identify the wise with those in the church, the foolish with those outside the church. Our parable is rather addressed to those who have heard the Sermon of the Mount, who are aware of Jesus' demands, and who acknowledge their validity. Even these may find themselves rejected (7:21–23). "If you think you are standing, watch out that you do not fall" (1 Cor. 10:13).

FOR FURTHER READING

Hill, David. "False Prophets and Charismatics: Structure and Interpretation in Matthew 7,15–23." *Biblica* 57 (1976): 327–48.

Mattill, A. J., Jr. "The Way of Tribulation." *Journal of Biblical Literature* 98 (1979): 531–46.

Epilogue

I n *Christ and Culture*, H. Richard Niebuhr argued that church history reveals three distinct solutions to the problems of Christian social ethics. One solution he labeled "Christ against culture." Typical of sectarianism, it "uncompromisingly affirms the sole authority of Christ over the Christian and resolutely rejects culture's claims to loyalty" (p. 45). Tertullian, who derided all attempts to wed Athens and Jerusalem, and the early monastics, who literally left the world behind, are representatives.

The second solution to the problem, which Niebuhr discussed under the rubric "Christ of culture," tends to interpret Christian revelation in terms of its own time and place. The Gnostics, who reinterpreted the gospel in accord with the pessimistic dualism of their age, are obvious examples. From the medieval world Niebuhr mentioned Abelard, who thought that Socrates and Plato came "little or nothing short of the Christian religion," and who wrote a book on ethics (*Scito te Ipsum*) that lacks "recognition of the hard demand which the Sermon on the Mount makes on the Christian" (p. 90). Albrecht Ritschl served Niebuhr as an archetype from the modern world. Ritschl sought a harmonization of Christ and (nineteenth-century European) culture through the concept of the kingdom of God, which for him really meant, as the phrase was, "the brotherhood of man."

A third approach to the problem of Christ and culture falls somewhere between the first two and belongs to what Niebuhr calls "the church of the center." It maintains that culture is founded on nature, which God has created, and that culture's demands thus cannot be ignored. At the same time it recognizes the universality of sin and the

172

primacy of God's revelation and so cannot subordinate the claims of Christ to culture. Within this broad agreement Niebuhr discerned three slightly different tendencies, the details of which do not concern us here.

Niebuhr's rough typology of Christian social ethics can help us understand the complex history of the interpretation of the Sermon on the Mount, for most of the commentaries on Matthew 5–7 tend to fall into one of his three categories. Those interpreters who offer more or less literal interpretations—or perhaps it would be better to say who commend more or less literal applications—typically belong with those who think of Christ and culture as being ever discordant ("Christ against culture"). One thinks of the Anabaptist tradition as well as of Tolstoy's influential writings on the Sermon on the Mount, which in so many ways recall sectarian writings. Tolstoy indeed, as we have seen, thought that Christ's teachings were so at odds with his Russian society that he exhorted his fellow citizens to abandon courts, police forces, and military institutions. These things could not for him be made compatible with the truth of the Sermon.

There are also commentators who illustrate the "Christ of culture" position. The once influential *Die Bergpredigt* of Johannes Müller, published in Germany at the beginning of the twentieth century, may serve as an example. Müller, who mocked Tolstoy's exegesis, argued that one must remove from the Sermon on the Mount everything that is historically relative. He included in this its Jewishness and went on to argue that it should be modernized and even, one is sad to report, "Germanized." (Müller was guilty of anti-Semitism.) All this meant contradicting Jesus' imperatives to turn the other cheek, not to store up treasure on the earth, and not to let the left hand know what the right is doing. What mattered for Müller were the humanistic values embedded in the Sermon, values that can be understood only in the living of them.

The third position, that which acknowledges both Christ and culture, is fully on display in Luther's great commentary. This work consistently urges that portions of the Sermon on the Mount have to do with private life alone as opposed to public life. Luther could, for instance, urge that 5:33–37 speaks only against "unauthorized, capricious, or habitual swearing" (*Sermon on the Mount*, 102). The text, for the reformer, said nothing negative about oaths in court. He defended his exegesis with these words:

Similarly, when he forbids you to draw your sword, he does not mean that you should disobey the government if your territorial prince needs you or summons you to go to war. Then you are obliged to slash away with your sword. For your hand and sword are no longer on their own, but have been subordinated to the government. (*Sermon on the Mount*, 102)

How, from an exegetical point of view, do we evaluate the various positions just introduced? Matthew's Christian community was probably a sort of sect within Judaism. Certainly it was alienated from the larger social and political powers of the day. So one might expect the evangelist's view to be akin to the position Niebuhr designated "Christ against culture." In line with this, and as Ulrich Luz has observed,

in the protocols of investigations and disputations with largely quite simple, theologically uneducated Anabaptists, one discovers over and over the basic elements of Matthean theology: the priority of practice before teaching, the will to obedience, the fact that the individual command is taken seriously, that it does not simply dissolve in the commandment to love, the will of the formation of brotherly and sisterly community. (*Matthew 1–7*, 220)

While all this is true, 5:17–20, understood as an affirmation of the Mosaic Torah, demands a significant harmony between the old revelation and the new, which in turn entails significant continuity between Christian practice and the legislation of the Hebrew Bible: the Sermon on the Mount does not undo Moses. This is why, throughout this commentary, an attempt has been made to read Matthew 5–7 as something other than a rebuttal of Jewish law and custom, and why my conclusions are often unlike the conclusions of those who have thought in terms of "Christ against culture." They have been able to maintain their radical views only by urging that Matthew's Jesus does in fact abolish the Hebrew Bible itself, or significant portions of it. But this, in the light of 5:17–20, is not credible.

As for the position designated by the term "Christ of culture," it is problematic for many pious people because at the outset it lays aside authorial intention: what matters is perhaps less what Jesus or Matthew thought than what commends itself to our world. One cannot, however, dismiss this approach without further ado. For it indeed forces us to see that we inevitably interpret the Sermon on the Mount from our own time and place. We are neither ancient Jews nor ancient Christians. We do not live within the first-century world of Jesus or Matthew or share in their culture or participate in their forms of gov-

ernment. We live rather in the age of capitalism, democracy, secularization, and technology—modern realities that largely shape our identity. All this makes it inevitable that we modernize the text. For it was written not with the secularized technocitizens of democratic capitalism in mind but for believers in an almost unimaginably different time and place. But modernizing inevitably means asking in what ways the text may be outdated and insufficient. To this agonizing question, which many are loath to ask, different people will respond differently: the answer depends on the reader, not the author. Honest interpretation nonetheless requires that we ask the question.

Perhaps this requirement will seem more acceptable to some if they turn from the Sermon on the Mount and consider another portion of Matthew, namely, chapter 10. Here Jesus gives missionary orders to the twelve disciples. He tells them, among other things, to take no money and to wear no sandals. Very few Christians have ever applied these words to themselves (although a few have: the literalists we will always have with us). Most have instead been content in this particular to believe that Jesus' words had a one-time application to the Twelve and their missionary work in the pre-Easter period. But both missionary and nonmissionary have very much wanted to apply to themselves much of the rest of chapter 10, such as the demands to confess Christ before others and to take up the cross—even though those demands are also addressed precisely to the Twelve in the context of their one-time mission. Now in thus bringing parts of chapter 10 but not the entirety of it into their own lives according to their own situations, Christian readers have, knowingly or not, been doing something very much like modernizing, that is, construing a text so that portions of it apply to them directly, other portions only indirectly or not at all. The Sermon on the Mount may not so obviously invite similar treatment, but Jesus and Matthew were citizens of another world, and this can hardly be irrelevant for application. Their words must be ever reinterpreted, and that involves not a prosaic response but selection and imagination.

This does not mean, albeit some might protest otherwise, that the authority of the text is thereby vitiated. For one thing, we retain our respect for textual authority when we deny that every interpretation is just as good as any other. We all want the hermeneutical privilege of condemning Müller's anti-Semitic interpretation as well as lesser errors. For another, we cannot deny our own experience, which is this: as we read and hear the Sermon again and again, and as we allow its words and images to become part of us, and as we seek for analogies between its imaginative scenarios and our everyday lives, we do indeed feel ourselves commanded. "But I say to you" haunts us.

What, finally, of the approach of the "church of the center"? This commentary has, on the authority of 5:17–20, tended to keep company with Augustine, Aquinas, Luther, and Calvin. This inevitably implies accommodation to our culture. But the accommodation is seemingly necessary, the attendant rationalizations inevitable. To illustrate: most Christians in contemporary Western Europe and America, unlike many of Jesus' hearers and Matthew's first readers, view their governments as more or less legitimate; and so we find that Romans 13, where Paul declares that the ruling authority is God's servant for the good, has something to say to our situation. We freely recognize that Luther's advice to obey the territorial prince is contingent on the prince's legitimacy, and we know that sometimes (as the book of Revelation so vividly illustrates) the prince is illegitimate. We may, moreover, experience doubt and even guilt when reading Tolstoy as he hurls the rude words of Jesus against our defenseless consciences. But we still, however hesitantly, participate in the courts and are thankful for police officers and serve in the armed forces when called upon to do so. We do not, despite our grumblings against our government and our complaints against our culture, share Kierkegaard's utter disdain for the structures of this world or his radicalism: we cannot be so ungratefully dismissive. The upshot is that we are often nonplussed and even tormented when we sincerely attempt to find guidance in the Sermon on the Mount. For we know that Christ and culture lay conflicting demands upon us, and further that we can ignore neither. So as long as we hold the Bible in our hands we are left with the never-ending task of prayerfully deciding, in fear and trembling, what to give to Caesar and what to give to God.

For that task faith may find that the written word does not suffice. There comes a point at which exegesis can say no more.

Bibliography

Abrahams, I. *Studies in Pharisaism and the Gospels.* First Series. Cambridge: Cambridge University Press, 1917. Second Series. Cambridge: Cambridge University Press, 1924.

Allison, Dale C., Jr. *The Jesus Tradition in Q.* Harrisburg, Penn.: Trinity Press International, 1997.

———. *The New Moses: A Matthean Typology.* Philadelphia: Fortress, 1993.

———. "The Structure of the Sermon on the Mount." *Journal of Biblical Literature* 106 (1987): 423–45.

Andrews, Lancelot. *The Private Devotions.* New York: Meridian, 1961.

Barclay, William. *The Beatitudes and the Lord's Prayer for Everyman.* New York: Harper & Row, 1968.

Barth, Karl. *Church Dogmatics.* 12 volumes. Edinburgh: T & T Clark, 1936–62.

———. *Prayer.* 2nd ed. Philadelphia: Westminster, 1985.

Bauman, Clarence. *The Sermon on the Mount: The Modern Quest for Its Meaning.* Macon: Mercer, 1985.

Bengel, J. A. *Gnomon Novi Testamenti.* London: Williams & Norgate, 1862.

Betz, Hans Dieter. *Essays on the Sermon on the Mount.* Philadelphia: Fortress, 1985.

———. *The Sermon on the Mount: A Commentary on the Sermon on the Mount, including the Sermon on the Plain (Matthew 5:3–7:27 and Luke 6:20–49).* Hermeneia. Minneapolis: Fortress, 1995.

Blomberg, Craig L. "On Wealth and Worry: Matthew 6:19–34." *Criswell Theological Review* 6 (1992): 73–89.

Boff, Leonardo. *Church, Charism and Power: Liberation Theology and the Institutional Church.* London: SCM, 1985.

Bonhoeffer, Dietrich. *The Cost of Discipleship.* London: SCM, 1948.

———. *Ethics.* New York: Simon & Schuster, 1995.

Brown, Raymond E. *New Testament Essays.* Garden City, N.Y.: Doubleday, 1967. Pp. 217–53.

Buber, Martin. *Israel and the World.* New York: Schocken, 1948.

Calvin, John. *Commentary on a Harmony of the Evangelists.* Vol. 1. Grand Rapids: Eerdmans, 1949.

Carter, Warren. *What Are They Saying about Matthew's Sermon on the Mount?* New York: Paulist, 1994.

Collins, R. F. *Divorce in the New Testament.* Collegeville, Minn.: Liturgical Press, 1992.

Davenport, Gene L. *Into the Darkness: Discipleship in the Sermon on the Mount.* Nashville: Abingdon, 1988.

Davies, W. D. *The Setting of the Sermon on the Mount.* Cambridge: Cambridge University Press, 1964.

Deming, W. "Mark 9,42–10,12; Matthew 5,27–32 and b. Nid. 13b: A First Century Discussion of Male Sexuality." *New Testament Studies* 36 (1990): 130–41.

Derrett, J. Duncan M. *The Ascetic Discourse: An Explanation of the Sermon on the Mount.* Eilsbrunn: Ko'amar, 1989.

Dibelius, Martin. *The Sermon on the Mount.* New York: Charles Scribner's Sons, 1940.

Dillon, R. J. "Ravens, Lilies, and the Kingdom of God (Matthew 6:25–33/Luke 12:22–31)." *Catholic Biblical Quarterly* 53 (1991): 605–27.

Dods, Marcus, James Denney, and James Moffatt. *The Literal Interpretation of the Sermon on the Mount.* London: Hodder & Stoughton, 1904.

Dumais, Marcel. *Le Sermon sur la Montagne: État de la recherche Interprétation Bibliographié.* Paris: Letouzey et Ané, 1995.

Eigo, Francis A. *New Perspectives on the Beatitudes.* Villanova: Villanova University Press, 1995.

Farrer, Austin. *St. Matthew and St. Mark.* Westminster: Dacre, 1954.

Friedlander, G. *The Jewish Sources of the Sermon on the Mount.* London: Routledge, 1911.

Galilea, Segundo. *The Beatitudes: To Evangelize As Jesus Did.* Maryknoll, N.Y.: Orbis Books, 1984.

Garland, David E. "A Biblical View of Divorce." *Review and Expositor* 84 (1987): 419–32.

Girard, R. *The Scapegoat.* Baltimore and London, 1989.

Gore, Charles. *The Sermon on the Mount: A Practical Exposition.* London: John Murray, 1897.

Guelich, Robert. "The Matthean Beatitudes: 'Entrance-Requirements' or 'Eschatological Blessing'?" *Journal of Biblical Literature* 95 (1976): 415–34.

———. *The Sermon on the Mount: A Foundation for Understanding.* Waco: Word, 1982.

Gundry, Robert. *Matthew: A Commentary on His Literary and Theological Art.* Grand Rapids: Eerdmans, 1982.

Gutiérrez, Gustavo. *The God of Life.* Maryknoll, N.Y.: Orbis Books, 1991.

Hagner, Donald A. *Matthew 1–13.* Word Biblical Commentary 33A. Dallas: Word, 1993.

Harnack, Adolf. *What Is Christianity?* New York: Harper & Brothers, 1957.

Harner, P. B. *Understanding the Lord's Prayer.* Philadelphia: Fortress, 1975.

Hendrickx, H. *The Sermon on the Mount.* London: Geoffrey Chapman, 1984.

Henry, Matthew. *Matthew Henry's Commentary on the Whole Bible.* Peabody, Mass.: Hendrickson, 1991.

Hermann, Wilhelm. *Die sittlichen Weisungen Jesu.* 2nd ed. Göttingen: Vandenhoeck & Ruprecht, 1907.

Heth, William A., and G. J. Wenham. *Jesus and Divorce: The Problem with the Evangelical Consensus.* London: Hodder & Stoughton, 1984.

Hill, David. "False Prophets and Charismatics: Structure and Interpretation in Matthew 7,15–23." *Biblica* 57 (1976): 327–48.

———. *The Gospel of Matthew.* New Century Bible. London: Oliphants, 1972.

Horsley, R. A. "Ethics and Exegesis: 'Love Your Enemies' and the Doctrine of Non-Violence." *Journal of the American Academy of Religion* 54 (1986): 3–31.

Houk, Cornelius B. "ΠΕΙΡΑΣΜΟΣ, the Lord's Prayer, and the Massah Tradition." *Scottish Journal of Theology* 19 (1966): 216–25.

Kant, Immanuel. *Religion within the Limits of Reason Alone.* New York: Harper & Row, 1960.

Klassen, William. *Love of Enemies: The Way to Peace.* Philadelphia: Fortress, 1984.

Klausner, Joseph. *Jesus of Nazareth.* New York and London: Macmillan, 1925.

Kuhn, Heinz-Wolfgang, "Das Liebesgebot Jesu als Tora und als Evangelium." In *Vom Urchristentum zu Jesus: Für Joachim Gnilka,* edited by Hubert Frankemölle and Karl Kertelge, 194–230. Freiburg: Herder, 1989.

Lambert, J. C. "Lord's Prayer." In *A Dictionary of Christ and the Gospels,* edited by James Hastings, 2:60–63. Edinburgh: T & T Clark, 1908.

Lambrecht, Jan. *The Sermon on the Mount: Proclamation and Exhortation.* Good News Studies 14. Wilmington, Del.: Glazier, 1985.

Lapide, Pinchas. *The Sermon on the Mount.* Maryknoll, N.Y.: Orbis Books, 1986.

Lochman, Jan Milič. *The Lord's Prayer.* Grand Rapids: Eerdmans, 1990.

Lohmeyer, Ernst. *The Lord's Prayer.* London: Collins, 1965.

Luther, Martin. *Luther's Works, Volume 21: The Sermon on the Mount (Sermons) and the Magnificat.* St. Louis: Concordia, 1956.

Luz, Ulrich. *Matthew 1–7.* Minneapolis: Fortress, 1989.

McArthur, Harvey K. *Understanding the Sermon on the Mount.* New York: Harper & Brothers, 1960.

McEleney, Neil J. "The Beatitudes of the Sermon on the Mount/Plain." *Catholic Biblical Quarterly* 43 (1981): 1–13.

Mangan, C. *Can We Still Call God "Father"? A Woman Looks at the Lord's Prayer Today.* Wilmington, Del.: Glazier, 1984.

Manson, T. W. *The Sayings of Jesus.* London: SCM, 1948.

Mattill, A. J., Jr. "The Way of Tribulation." *Journal of Biblical Literature* 98 (1979): 531–46.

Migne, J.-P., ed. *Patrologia Graeca.* Paris, 1857–66.

Minear, Paul S. "Yes or No: The Demand for Honesty in the Early Church." *Novum Testamentum* 13 (1971): 1–13.

Moltmann, Jürgen. *The Way of Jesus Christ: Christology in Messianic Dimensions.* Minneapolis: Fortress, 1993.

Montefiore, Claude G. *Rabbinic Literature and Gospel Teachings.* London: Macmillan, 1930.

––––––. *The Synoptic Gospels.* 2 vols. 2nd ed. London: Macmillan, 1927.

Moule, C. F. D. "Uncomfortable Words I. The Angry Word: Matthew 5,21f." *Expository Times* 81 (1969): 10–13.

Müller, Johannes. *Die Bergpredigt verdeutscht und vergegenwärtigt.* Munich: Oskar Beck, 1906.

Newman, John Henry. *Lectures on the Doctrine of Justification.* Westminster: Christian Classics, 1966.

Newsom, Carol A., and Sharon H. Ringe, eds. *The Women's Bible Commentary.* Louisville: Westminster John Knox, 1992.

Nock, Albert Jay. *On Doing the Right Thing and Other Essays.* New York: Harper & Brothers, 1928.

Nolan, Albert. *Jesus before Christianity.* Rev. ed. Maryknoll, N.Y.: Orbis Books, 1992.

Olsthoorn, M. F. *The Jewish Background and the Synoptic Setting of Mt 6,25–33 and Lk 12,22–31.* Jerusalem: Franciscan, 1975.

Patte, Daniel. *Discipleship according to the Sermon on the Mount: Four Legitimate Readings, Four Plausible Views of Discipleship and their Relative Values.* Valley Forge, Penn.: Trinity Press International, 1996.

Petuchowsky, Jakob J., and Michael Brocke, eds. *The Lord's Prayer and Jewish Liturgy.* New York: Seabury, 1978.

Powell, Mark Allan. "Matthew's Beatitudes: Reversals and Rewards of the Kingdom." *Catholic Biblical Quarterly* 58 (1996): 460–79.

Ricoeur, Paul. "The Golden Rule: Exegetical and Theological Perplexities." *New Testament Studies* 36 (1900): 49–67.

Saldarini, Anthony J. *Matthew's Christian-Jewish Community.* Chicago and London: University of London, 1994.

Schleiermacher, Friedrich. *The Christian Faith.* 2 vols. New York: Harper & Row, 1963.

Schnackenburg, Rudolf. *All Things Are Possible to Believers: Reflections on* the Lord's Prayer and the Sermon on the Mount. Louisville: Westminster John Knox, 1995.

Schottroff, Luise, et al. *Essays on the Love Commandment.* Philadelphia: Fortress, 1978.

Schüssler Fiorenza, Elisabeth, and Mary Shawn Copeland. *Violence against Women.* London: SCM. 1994.

Schwager, Raymund. *Must There Be Scapegoats? Violence and Redemption in the Bible.* San Francisco: Harper & Row, 1987.

Schweitzer, Albert. *The Quest of the Historical Jesus.* London: Macmillan, 1968.

Scott, Bernard Brandon, and Margaret E. Dean. "A Sound Map of the Sermon on the Mount." In *Society of Biblical Literature 1993 Seminar Papers,* edited by Eugene H. Lovering, Jr., 672–725. Atlanta: Scholars Press, 1993.

Scott, E. F. *The Ethical Teaching of Jesus.* New York: Macmillan, 1925.

Stark, Rodney. *The Rise of Christianity: A Sociologist Reconsiders History.* Princeton: Princeton University Press, 1996.

Stendahl, Krister. *The School of St. Matthew and Its Use of the Old Testament.* Rev. ed. Philadelphia: Fortress, 1968.

Strecker, Georg. *The Sermon on the Mount: An Exegetical Commentary.* Nashville: Abingdon, 1988.

Swartley, Willard M., ed. *The Love of Enemy and Nonretaliation in the New Testament.* Philadelphia: Westminster/John Knox, 1992.

Syreeni, Kari. *The Making of the Sermon on the Mount: A Procedural Analysis of Matthew's Redactional Activity, Part I: Methodology and Compositional Analysis.* Helsinki: Suomalainen Tiedeakatemia, 1987.

Thielicke, Helmut. *Our Heavenly Father: Sermons on the Lord's Prayer.* New York: Harper & Row, 1960.

Tholuck, A. *Commentary on the Sermon on the Mount.* Edinburgh: T & T Clark, 1874.

Thurneysen, E. *The Sermon on the Mount.* Richmond: John Knox, 1964.

Tolstoy, Leo. *What I Believe.* London: Elliot Stock, 1885.

Windisch, Hans. *The Meaning of the Sermon on the Mount: A Contribution to the Historical Understanding of the Gospels and to the Problem of Their True Exegesis.* Philadelphia: Westminster, 1950.

Wink, Walter. "Beyond Just War and Pacifism: Jesus' Nonviolent Way." *Review and Expositor* 89 (1992): 197–214.

Index

SELECTED PASSAGES